BEATLES
FOR SALE

BEATLES FOR SALE

HOW EVERYTHING THEY TOUCHED TURNED TO GOLD

John Blaney

BEATLES FOR SALE
HOW EVERYTHING THEY TOUCHED TURNED TO GOLD

John Blaney

A GENUINE JAWBONE BOOK
First edition 2008
Published in the UK and the USA by Jawbone Press
2a Union Court,
20-22 Union Road,
London SW4 6JP,
England
www.jawbonepress.com

ISBN: 978-1-906002-09-1

EDITOR: Thomas Jerome Seabrook
DESIGN: Paul Cooper Design

Origination and print by Colorprint (Hong Kong)

08 09 10 11 12 5 4 3 2 1

Contents

CLOCKWISE FROM TOP CENTRE: Beatles manager Brian Epstein relaxes beside his stereo record console; rock'n'roll manager Larry Parnes, with whom The Beatles were briefly associated early on; a photograph by John Lennon of an early incarnation of the group in front of the Arnheim War Memorial in the Netherlands (left to right: manager Allan Williams; his wife Beryl; his business partner, calypso singer Lord Woodbine; Stuart Sutcliffe; Paul McCartney; George Harrison; and Pete Best).

AME LIVETH
VERMORE

CLOCKWISE FROM LEFT: The Beatles with road manager
and future Apple Corps MD Neil Aspinall (top right);
Lennon and Starr backstage with manager Brian
Epstein (centre); press officer Derek Taylor (left)
receives a set of hand-decorated boomerangs to
commemorate the group's 1964 Australian tour;
Epstein with publisher Dick James (left).

CLOCKWISE FROM TOP LEFT: British fans queue outside the London Pavilion before the premiere of The Beatles' first film, *A Hard Day's Night*; Paul McCartney signs an autograph on a specially commissioned overnight train between the German cities of Essen and Hamburg, while press agent Tony Barrow (top right) looks on; two American fans try out their Beatles wigs in anticipation of the group's arrival in New York City.

CLOCKWISE FROM HERE: Brian Epstein (left) and George Martin (centre) in the Abbey Road control room; The Beatles show off their MBEs; Starr, Harrison, and Lennon react to the news that Epstein has died.

CLOCKWISE FROM HERE: Allen Klein, who took over the running of Apple Corps in 1969; Klein with Apple MD Neil Aspinall (right); fans take advantage of the Apple Boutique 'giveaway'; London policemen inspect a handbag outside the same event.

The Beatles give their final live performance on the roof of the Apple building at 3 Savile Row, London, on January 30th 1969.

Introduction

Q: *"How do you rate yourself musically?"*

A: "Average. We're kidding you, we're kidding ourselves, we're kidding everything. We don't take anything seriously, except the money."

TIME MAGAZINE INTERVIEW, 1964[1]

n 1962 the British music industry was parochial and lacking in ambition. If something didn't happen in London, it didn't happen at all. London wasn't yet the swinging capital it would soon become, but it had the venues, the record companies, the recording studios, and the radio and television stations that the rest of the country lacked.

London might have led the way in terms of other British cities but it lagged far behind America. Uncle Sam had drawn up the blueprint that Britain's managers, publishers, agents, and record companies worked to. In 1955 EMI went so far as to buy Capitol Records on the basis that it would sell more records by American stars than by homegrown talent. There seemed little point in grooming British musicians for international stardom when the USA did it so much better – and little hope for provincial groups such as The Beatles. All Britain had to offer were inferior copies of the American progenitors. Those who didn't fit the American model could forget about making it big in dear old Blighty.

Where America had a range of independent record labels – among them Sun, Chess, Specialty, and Ace – Britain was very different. Four major companies controlled the record market; a handful of publishers controlled what songs their acts could record; one radio station controlled what could be heard; and one musicians' union controlled how many records it could play.

Getting a record made and played was almost impossible. There were only a handful of professional recording studios, and there was no way a singer or group could just walk in and cut a record like Elvis Presley once had. And even if a group did get a record deal, they were highly unlikely to be able to persuade their A&R manager to let them record one of their own songs.

The Beatles were big fish in a small pond. They had acquired a manager and built up a strong local following, but what they really needed was a recording contract. Brian Epstein used his influence to secure an audition for the group with Decca records. Everything hinged on them getting a record deal. John Lennon meant every word when he stepped up to the microphone in Decca's London studio on a cold New Year's Day 1962 and pleaded: "Your lovin' gives me a thrill / But your lovin' don't pay my bills / Now give me money."

Back then The Beatles were a struggling beat group earning £50 per night. A record contract would transform them from local heroes to stars, and so it did: within two years, even after rejection by Decca, The Beatles had become the biggest showbiz attraction the world had ever seen.

How did they do it? Talent had a role to play, but so did luck. The Beatles were the right group in the right place at the right time. They made the right connections with the right people and made all the right moves. When George Martin signed The Beatles to a minor subsidiary of EMI, Parlophone Records, he triggered a series of explosions that rocked the music industry. The recording contract led to a publishing deal, which in turn led to national television exposure, international tours, merchandising rights, worldwide record releases, and a contract with United Artists for three feature-length movies.

The Beatles were much more than just 'Parlophone Recording Artists'. They became an industry. Their records, concerts, movies, merchandising, and songwriting made them rich beyond their wildest dreams. Everything about the group was new: the way they looked, the way they sounded, the way they acted. There had been no group like The Beatles before. They wrote their own songs, owned a share in their publishing company, played in giant football stadiums – earning hundreds of thousands of dollars for the privilege – and sold more merchandising than even Elvis Presley. The scale of their success was unprecedented.

When The Beatles entered EMI's Abbey Road studios in 1962 they would have had no idea of just how much money they would go on to

A note about currency

Much of this book concerns The Beatles' dealings with record labels and other areas of the music industry. As such, there are a lot of figures involved. The following table serves as a rough guide to exchange rates and buying power between English pounds, US dollars, and German marks.

Amount	Worth then	Buying power today
£100 (1962)	$280	£1,480 / $1,860
£100 (1970)	$240	£1,070 / $1,245
$100 (1962)	£35	£520 / $660
$100 (1970)	£40	£440 / $520
DM 100 (1962)	£9 / $25	£130 / $165

Before February 1971, British currency was expressed in pounds, shillings, and pence. One pound (written as £1) consisted of 20 shillings (20s), and one shilling consisted of 12 pence (12d). An amount was usually written down with slashes between the £/s/d, for example £3/2s/6d.

---

earn. That soon changed. Paul McCartney later admitted that a running joke within the group was: "OK! Today, let's write a swimming pool."[2]

Just how much money The Beatles made is anybody's guess. In 1963, the UK's *Daily Mail* newspaper estimated that the group had earned $56 million[3]; a year later, after they hit America, the gross income from Beatles-related products must at least have doubled that figure.

How much of that $100 million The Beatles actually saw is also hard to quantify. They might have been making a lot of money, but holding on to it was not easy.

Record companies made fortunes from Beatles records, but paid the group pennies – literally. Publishers siphoned off 50 per cent of their income from songwriting and 75 per cent for overseas rights. Their manager, Brian Epstein, took another 25 per cent off the top of what was left. Then there was the taxman. In Britain, the Inland Revenue could potentially take up to 98 per cent of a high earner's income. It's no wonder that George Harrison wrote a song bemoaning the situation. Add on touring expenses and accountants' and lawyers' fees and there appeared to be almost as much going out as there was coming in – and yet The Beatles still managed to become millionaires.

Like Midas, The Beatles soon discovered that the thing they had most desired had its disadvantages.

They tried religion, but that didn't work. They tried being businessmen, but that didn't work either. The Beatles were artists, not businessmen, and when they tried to take charge of their empire it crumbled.

Big business made The Beatles and then proceeded to destroy them. The group's attempts to control their business affairs created a financial black-hole that sucked in cash at an alarming rate. Never mind the stories about how Yoko Ono broke up The Beatles. The real villains were the men in suits.

Once the squabbling started, big business took its chance, moved in, and took control of The Beatles' songs – forever. The Beatles found it all too much and folded under pressure. The end had been a long time coming, and when it did come it was every bit as sad as the beginning had been triumphant.

And yet, four decades after their acrimonious break-up, The Beatles are as popular as they ever were. Hardly a year goes by without a new CD or DVD being issued or a new line of merchandising appearing. The Beatles are still big business. The lawyers and accountants are still in control and the whole crazy Apple Corps circus continues on its merry litigious way. Apple isn't the same company it was when The Beatles formed it in 1967, but it continues to make deals and keep the Beatles flame burning. The only difference is that now, instead of losing The Beatles money, it's making it – and lots of it.

Money, That's What I Want

Early gigs, trips to Hamburg, and management contracts

"In another year I'll have me money and I'll be out of here."[1]

JOHN LENNON, 1964

Before high-speed broadband and the world wide web, John Lennon, Paul McCartney, and George Harrison made their music on cheap guitars in tiny coffee bars and seedy dives. The teenage Quarry Men were gifted amateurs at best. The group's original drummer, Colin Hanton, later said they were "probably as good as what was about at the time", but that none of them "would be able to compete with today's groups".[2]

Listening to home recordings made in 1960, it's a wonder the group managed to get any gigs at all. Much of their repertoire consisted of rambling 12-bar improvisations, and not very good ones at that. Without Hanton, who had left the group by this point, their sound lacked even the most basic rock'n'roll element: rhythm. The three Quarry Men might have thought their rhythm was 'in the guitars', but they just sounded feckless. They were further hampered by Stuart Sutcliffe's rudimentary bass-playing, which might at least have given them some much-needed bottom end, but left a lot to be desired from a technical standpoint.

Despite their obvious lack of professionalism the group managed to persuade local entrepreneur Allan Williams to give them a few gigs and become their booking agent. In 1957 Williams had taken out a lease on a former watch-repair shop at 21 Slater Street in Liverpool. He converted it into a coffee bar called the Jacaranda, which opened for business the following September. A year later, Liverpool Art College students Lennon and Sutcliffe began to frequent the coffee bar and get to know its owner, as did McCartney and Harrison, who were both attending the Liverpool Institute.

Williams had tapped into a growing phenomenon. For the first time, young people had money of their own to spend, and coffee bars – a teenage alternative to tea shops and pubs – gave them somewhere to spend it, and somewhere they could listen to music, either on a jukebox or, if they were lucky, performed live. (Coffee bars were popular with musicians, too. The most famous of them was the 2-Is at 59 Old Compton Street in the Soho district of London – *the* place to be seen if you were a wannabe rock'n'roller. Among the stars who got their big break playing there were Cliff Richard, Hank Marvin, Tommy Steele, Joe Brown, Screaming Lord Sutch, The Vipers Skiffle Group, and Ritchie Blackmore.)

Lennon, Sutcliffe, McCartney, and Harrison soon got to know Williams and made it known that they were in a band. To begin with The Quarry Men had booked their gigs themselves, but as their ambitions grew they realised that they needed to become a little more professional. Although Williams initially dismissed them as a bunch of layabouts, he was, like almost everyone who crossed their path, enamoured by their personalities, and decided to offer his services as their booking agent.

They certainly weren't his top priority, however. Williams had more pressing matters to attend to. Having successfully promoted an Arts Ball at St. George's Hall, Liverpool, in 1959, he began to make plans for a larger-scale event at the Liverpool Boxing Stadium on May 3rd 1960 with co-promoter Larry Parnes, a former shopkeeper who was, at the time, Britain's most successful rock'n'roll manager, and whose charges included Tommy Steele and Billy Fury.

The show was set to include performances by Gene Vincent and Eddie Cochran, but on April 17th the American rockers were involved in a car accident in which Cochran was killed. Williams was "shattered"[3] by his death, and assumed that the show would be cancelled. But when he called Parnes a week later he discovered that Vincent hadn't been too badly injured, and was still eager to perform.

As glad as he was that the concert could still go ahead, Williams was concerned that Gene Vincent wasn't a big enough draw on his own. "I thought I'd put on some Liverpool groups to supplement the show," he recalled. These included Rory Storm & The Hurricanes, Bob Evans & The Five Pennies, Cass & The Cassanovas, and Gerry & The Pacemakers, who were suggested to Williams by local DJ Bob Wooler. "I went along to Blair Hall to see them and I was knocked out," Williams said, "and so we went ahead with the first ever merseybeat rock'n'roll show."[4]

The concert was a sell out. Parnes was impressed by the Liverpool groups Williams had booked for it, and suggested that some of them might be suitable to back his growing stable of solo acts. Williams was delighted. Not only had he put on two successful concerts, he'd also impressed the most influential rock'n'roll promoter in the country – and now had the opportunity to supply him with new groups.

A little while later Williams arranged for several local groups to audition for the job of backing one of Parnes's leading stars, Billy Fury. The Silver Beatals, as The Quarry Men were now calling themselves, persuaded Williams that they should get a chance to audition for Parnes and Fury. But there was one small problem. The group had begun the 1960s in a state of flux, forever changing both name and line-up, and still didn't have a drummer. Williams came to the rescue by calling on another of his regulars, Brian Cassar, leader of Cass & The Cassanovas, who recommended 36-year-old Tommy Moore from the Toxteth area of Liverpool. Moore was considerably older than the others but he had his own kit and looked the part. In any case, The Silver Beatals couldn't afford to be choosey.

The auditions were held on May 10th 1960 at the Wyvern Social Club, 108 Seel Street. The Silver Beetles (note the change in spelling) were up against some of Liverpool's top groups, including Derry & The Seniors and Gerry & The Pacemakers, in front of Britain's most powerful rock'n'roll moguls. What The Silver Beetles sounded like has been lost to the mists of time, but photographic evidence remains of Lennon, McCartney, and Harrison throwing shapes and looking every bit like proto-rock stars in black short-sleeve shirts, black jeans, and two-tone shoes.

Only Sutcliffe and Moore looked out of place. Sutcliffe had his back turned to Parnes and Fury for most of the audition and looked uncomfortable in his role as the group's bass player. He'd only bought his Hofner 333 bass in January, and was not a natural musician, as demonstrated by recordings made around the same time. Moore looked like the last-minute stand-in that he was. He was the only member of the group not dressed in black, and seemed distinctly uneasy playing with a group of amateurish musicians 16 years his junior.

In the end Parnes decided against booking any of the groups, and allowed Fury to carry on without a regular backing-band until he acquired The Blue Flames in 1961. (They were replaced a year later by The Tornados.) Parnes did, however, agree to book two of Williams's groups to back other singers from his stable. Cass & The Cassanovas were given the job of backing Duffy Power and, despite Parnes's reservations about Sutcliffe's playing and Moore's age, The Silver Beetles were assigned the job of playing with Johnny Gentle.

Parnes in fact booked The Silver Beetles for a seven-night budget tour of Scotland, for which each bandmember was to be paid between £15 and £18. Parnes was used to sending his bands their wages by post on a Thursday, but on the Monday after the tour began he received a reverse-charge telephone call from John Lennon asking where The Silver Beetles' "bloody money" was. "You haven't even started the week," Parnes replied, but in the end gave in to Lennon's request for "about five pounds each".[5]

The sums involved might have been small, but The Silver Beetles had turned a corner. Being in a band was now more than just a hobby: it was how they made their living. None of them had any other form of income, so from now on they would have to get serious, get an apprenticeship, or get a job. Being a professional musician seemed by far the best option, and it seemed like it might be going somewhere. Despite still not having a regular drummer, The Silver Beetles were offered a residency at the Kaiserkeller in Hamburg, Germany. They got the gig by default: Alan Williams had offered it to several other local groups first, but none were willing or available. The Silver Beetles were his last resort, but he did at least insist that they find a drummer before leaving.

It didn't take them very long to find one. On August 6th the group's regular Saturday night gig at the Grosvenor Ballroom in Liscard was cancelled after complaints had been made to the local council about excessive noise and the loutish behaviour of some of the venue's teenage clientele. The four Silver Beetles headed instead for the Casbah Coffee Club in the West Derby area of Liverpool in the hope that they might be able to play there instead, but discovered when they arrived that another group, The Blackjacks, had beaten them to it.

Later that evening The Silver Beetles approached The Blackjacks' drummer, Pete Best (son of the club's owner, Mona Best), and asked if he would like to join them. The offer of full-time paid employment was too good to resist; an audition was arranged for August 12th at the Wyvern Social Club, which, unsurprisingly, Best passed. Four days later, with hastily arranged passports and visas, the five-piece Beatles (who had now dropped the Silver from their name and changed the spelling of 'Beetles') left for Hamburg with Williams; his wife; and Lord Woodbine, his business partner. The weary band of travellers got their first sighting of Hamburg just as dusk was falling on August 17th. They couldn't have timed it better. Grosse Freiheit was lit up like a Christmas tree and full of the kind of people that only come out at night.

The St. Pauli district of Hamburg was – and still is – notorious. It offered a wealth of experiences that The Beatles could only have dreamed of, and plenty they wouldn't have dreamt up in a million years. This was the start of their German odyssey, during which they learnt how to 'mach schau', take drugs, and play blistering rock'n'roll. It also marked the start of a period of hard graft. The Beatles soon discovered that they had been booked into a former strip club, the Indra, and were expected to sleep in the rear of a cinema, the Bambi-Filmkunsttheater, and play for four-and-a-half hours each night (six at the weekend) – all for the princely sum of DM30 each per day.

As hard as The Beatles were working, the contract they had signed with Bruno Koschmider, the promoter, was not unusual by early-1960s standards. Tony Sheridan and his band The Jets had earned the same amount for playing between five and seven hours per day, Tuesday to Sunday, at the same venue a month earlier. They had Mondays off, and were given the use of two rooms to lodge in and a drum kit, but were required, contractually, to dress cleanly; banned from eating, smoking, or using foul language onstage; and faced a five-mark fine if they were late.

These final clauses are of particular interest, since it is likely that The Beatles would have been bound by the same terms and conditions. If so, could they really have been as debauched onstage as legend has it? The Beatles might have acted like dedicated hedonists offstage, but it doesn't follow that they did so while performing. Few photographs exist of the group smoking onstage in Hamburg, and fewer still of them drinking. While they might well have taken Preludin to get through the long hours, they wouldn't have come back from Hamburg as tight musically as they did had they spent the entire time intoxicated onstage.

The Beatles' residency at the Indra was cut short by two weeks when an elderly lady who lived upstairs complained about the band's excessive volume to Koschmider and the police. The club had only been open for 48 nights. It wasn't all bad, however: The Beatles were transferred to the bigger, plusher Kaiserkeller. To begin with they found the scale of the venue intimidating, and failed to impress the boozy, demanding clientele. Then, ten days into their residency came another telling intervention from Allan Williams, who encouraged them to "Make a show, boys!"

That was, after all, what they were there for. The transformation was remarkable, and instantaneous. Overnight, it seemed, The Beatles developed an energetic stage-act that was so boisterous it eventually destroyed the club's decaying stage. Their entertaining antics and high-energy rock'n'roll quickly attracted a large and dedicated following. They were so successful, in fact, that their contract was extended from October 16th to December 31st, with talk of it being carried over into the New Year.

In late October another new venue, the Top Ten Club, opened at 136 Reeperbahn on the site of a former sex club. Its owner, Peter Eckhorn, set himself up in direct competition with Koschmider's smaller Kaiserkeller, not only luring its customers away but also stealing the Kaiserkeller's head bouncer, Horst Fascher. The Top Ten Club's main attraction was another former Kaiserkeller employee, Tony Sheridan, who had been rapidly making a name for himself on the local club scene. A former guitarist with Vince Taylor and author of the rock'n'roll classic 'Brand New Cadillac', Sheridan had also appeared on Jack Good's *Oh Boy* and toured Britain with Gene Vincent and Eddie Cochran.

The Beatles were fans of Sheridan, too, and began to sit in with him during breaks. "I remember The Beatles were really getting to be popular at the Top Ten," he recalled. "They would sometimes sneak in and join me onstage."[6] Performing with Sheridan at the Top Ten Club contravened The Beatles' contract with Koschmider, which stated that they could not play at any venue within a 25-mile radius of the Kaiserkeller. Koschmider soon found out, of course, and threatened all kinds of retribution before giving the band a month's notice – not that they would last even that long.

On November 21st Harrison was deported for being underage. "The Kontrolle [police] would turn on all the club lights and the band would have to stop playing," he recalled. "Men would go round the tables checking ID. It went on two months before the penny dropped as to what they were actually saying, 'Everybody under 18 get out.'"[7] It didn't take long for them to discover that Harrison himself was only 17.

A couple of weeks later, McCartney and Best were arrested on suspicion of arson after setting fire to a condom while retrieving their possessions from the Bambi-Filmkunsttheater. They were deported on December 5th; Lennon followed them back to England on the 10th, while Sutcliffe stayed on in Hamburg with his German girlfriend, Astrid Kirchherr, and focused his energies on pursuing a career as an artist.

Harrison, McCartney, Best, and Lennon returned to Liverpool in a state of confusion. "After Hamburg it wasn't too good," McCartney recalled. "Everyone needed a rest. I expected everyone to be ringing me to discuss what we were doing, but it was all quiet on the western front. None of us called each other, so I wasn't so much dejected as puzzled, wondering whether it was going to carry on or if that was the last of it."[8]

The four of them did eventually regroup to consider their future. Although they were physically exhausted, they were still keen to carry on gigging, but with Sutcliffe still in Germany they lacked a bassist. Best suggested Chas Newby, the rhythm guitarist in The Blackjacks; Newby agreed, and with a borrowed bass and leather jacket became a temporary Beatle. After 106 nights in Hamburg, The Beatles ended 1960 with four gigs in Liverpool. They played the Casbah Coffee Club on December 17th; the Grosvenor Ballroom on the 24th; the Town Hall Ballroom in Litherland on the 27th; and finally back at the Casbah for a New Year's Eve bash.

If 1960 had ended in disappointment, 1961 could only get better. The Beatles were getting regular gigs and making good money. Their total earnings for 1960 – made up from £90 for the Scottish tour with Johnny Gentle, approximately £1,500 for 15 weeks' work in Hamburg, and around £7 per engagement for 30 local gigs – were in the region of £1,800, which works out to more than £28,000 today. These earnings meant they were each earning a little more than an unskilled worker of the time. Williams's ten per cent commission brought him £180. At this rate neither he nor The Silver Beetles looked like becoming overnight millionaires, but it was a good start – and certainly preferable to 40 hours per week in a factory.

The Beatles success was rooted in the long hours spent onstage in Hamburg, and the hours they continued to rack up back in Liverpool – all of which stood them in good stead for when they made it big in 1963. As 1961 began, Williams continued to work them hard, often booking two or three engagements per day. Before long The Beatles had become the busiest and best band on Merseyside – an early indication of which came in the form of a letter published in the August 17th edition of *Mersey Beat* magazine, which announced, "I saw The Beatles at The Cavern July 21st at the lunchtime session and I think George is the utmost, ginchest, skizzest, craziest cool cat I've ever seen."

But while The Beatles were fast becoming local celebrities (at least among Liverpool's beat fans), the lure of sex, drugs, and rock'n'roll in Hamburg was too strong. Plans were soon afoot for a return visit. With the other Beatles busying themselves in Liverpool, Stuart Sutcliffe was working, with the help of Peter Eckhorn, to clear the way for their return to Hamburg. McCartney and Best could not return without written permission from the German Aliens Police, but Sutcliffe's persistence soon paid off. In January he wrote to Best: "The lifting of the deportation ban is only valid for one year, then you can have it renewed. The thing they made clear, if you have any trouble with the police, no matter how small, then you've had it forever …"[9]

On March 24th, with deportation bans lifted on Best and McCartney (who had by now switched from guitar to bass) and with Harrison having turned 18, The Beatles returned to Hamburg to play a residency at the Top Ten Club for a total of 98 nights. The band's contract with Eckhorn was just as demanding as the one they had signed with Koschmider. They were contracted to perform between 7pm and 2am on weeknights and from 7–3 on Saturdays and 6–1 on Sundays. They were allowed one 15-minute break per hour session, and were paid at an increased rate of DM40 each per day.

The Beatles arrived at the Top Ten Club to find that their old friend Tony Sheridan was still playing there, too. According to Pete Best, "He was really popular in the Hamburg area, and one evening [record producer] Bert Kaempfert came into the club to see what all the commotion was about."[10] Harrison's attitude towards Sheridan, with whom The Beatles alternated onstage each night, was rather more ambivalent. "He was a pretty good singer and guitar player," Harrison recalled, "but at the same time he was such a downer. He'd fled from England, some kind of trouble, and was always getting in fights." In the midst of one such fight, Sheridan severed a tendon on a broken bottle. "When he used his guitar pick after that," said Harrison, "his injured finger stuck right out."[11]

After completing their residency at the Top Ten Club, The Beatles returned to Liverpool a changed group. They must have faced the journey home with some apprehension. During their stay in Germany the group had split with Allan Williams, whom they had refused to pay commission despite his role in helping to arrange their second trip to Hamburg. The Beatles insisted that they'd arranged the booking with Eckhorn themselves, and thus did not owe Williams anything. Williams was incensed, and on April 20th wrote them a stern letter threatening all manner of reprisals.

Unbeknownst to Williams, Pete and Mona Best had started to book gigs for the group, and claimed the Top Ten Club as their own. Quite why – and how – Mona Best took control of the group is unclear. Like many parents she might have wanted to protect her son and oversee his career, particularly if she had heard the group's complaints about Williams's style of management. As the owner of the Casbah Club she probably had at least as many contacts as the diminutive Welshman; perhaps she offered to undercut him. (It's not quite clear whether Mona Best received a cut of her son's group's earnings, but one would assume that The Beatles paid her something.)

Things were certainly looking up for the group and 1961 proved to be a better year financially than had 1960. Assuming that evening shows drew in £7 per performance and lunchtime appearances £5, The Beatles would have earned around £571 between January and March. The residency at the Top Ten Club brought in a total of DM11,760; another DM1,200 came from a deal signed with Bert Kaempfert (as discussed in the next chapter). That's DM12,960 (around £1,150) for three months work, or DM3,240 per man.

Things got even better when the group returned to Liverpool. With evening performances now bringing in £10 per performance, they earned another £1,400 during the remaining six months of the year. In total, then, for 1961 The Beatles earned approximately £3,128. That's £782 per man – a little over the national average wage of the time. Had they taken on apprenticeships rather than dedicate themselves to rock'n'roll they would have been earning considerably less. Lennon's Aunt Mimi's lament that a guitar is "all right for a hobby … but you'll never make a living from it" seemed no longer to ring true.

The Beatles weren't the only Liverpool group doing well. Rory Storm & The Hurricanes, featuring a certain Ringo Starr, were also making a good living from rock'n'roll. As Johnny 'Guitar' Byrne later recalled, "We had a car each in 1960! The Beatles had a battered old van."[12]

On November 9th 1961 Brian Epstein went to the Cavern to see The Beatles. Like Larry Parnes, Epstein had a background in retail. At the age of 16 he had taken a job at the family furniture store, NEMS (North End Music Stores) on Walton Road, Liverpool, to which he returned after National Service as a director. Later in the 1950s, Epstein grew tired of selling furniture and enrolled at the Royal Academy For Dramatic Art in London, where his classmates included Susannah York, Albert Finney, and Peter O'Toole, but he dropped out after the third term and returned to Liverpool.

Epstein's time at RADA might have been short but it informed his entire approach to management. It was there that he learnt the importance of glamour and fantasy, and honed a sense of style that he then applied to everything from record shops to The Beatles. When his father opened a new NEMS store on Great Charlotte Street, Epstein was put in charge of the ground floor, where he stocked gramophone records. His fastidiousness made the record department a runaway success, to the extent that a new NEMS branch was opened at 12–14 Whitechapel, with Epstein in charge. A profile of him in the May 9th 1963 edition of *Record Retailer* described him as a "strong believer (and in this he might be copied by others) in a record store being a glamorous place conveying the feeling of show business", and noted the importance Epstein placed on "giving the public what it wants".

Epstein was certainly a high flyer, but soon he grew bored of the retailer's life. Perhaps it was a need for more challenging pursuits that led him to the Cavern. Whatever it was, he was immediately smitten with the group he saw playing there, and began making plans to manage them. One of the first things he did was ask Allan Williams about them. Unsurprisingly, Williams warned Epstein not to "touch 'em with a fucking bargepole". Undeterred, Epstein invited The Beatles to a meeting at NEMS on December 3rd, a little over three weeks after watching them play at the Cavern. Lennon, Harrison, and Best all arrived on time; McCartney, who had a reputation for tardiness, was late, much to Epstein's annoyance. A second meeting was arranged for three days later at a local milk bar.

Epstein clearly took his potential management role seriously, even going so far as to consult his solicitor, E. Rex Makin, about the legal and financial ramifications. He gave the impression to The Beatles that he wanted to manage them because he liked them, but his main concern, from the outset, was money. He was, first and foremost, a businessman. Although Makin was not impressed by what he viewed as Epstein's latest folly, Epstein himself was convinced: managing a beat group, which he knew nothing about, was the right thing to do.

Epstein outlined the terms of his proposed contract with The Beatles at their meeting on December 6th. As both manager and booking agent, he would take a 25 per cent commission from their earnings. This was, to some extent, quite reasonable, particularly in light of the fact that singers such as Tommy Steele and Marty Wilde were paying their management teams up to 40 per cent. But Epstein was a shrewd businessman, and his 25 per cent commission would be taken from the group's overall earnings, not just from concerts and records, and would also leave The Beatles having to pay the majority of expenses incurred in managing the group.

It was also considerably more than the ten per cent taken by Allan Williams, but still seemed like a good deal, particularly as Epstein promised to find The Beatles gigs outside Liverpool; improve the way their bookings were organised; and increase their fee to a minimum of £15 per engagement (except for lunchtime shows at the Cavern, which doubled to £10).

The group was suitably impressed. "Right then, Brian," said Lennon. "Manage us. Now where's the contract?"[13] Therein lay one small problem: there was no contract, at least not yet. Epstein had acquired one from a friend in the music business, but was so disgusted with its borderline fraudulent appropriation of funds and enslavement of the artist that he refused to use it – although it did form the basis of the new contract he drew up himself.

The Beatles met Epstein again on December 10th at the Casbah Club, where all four members agreed in principle to his terms. Epstein formed a new company, NEMS Enterprises, with his brother Clive to handle this new business of artist management and concert promotion. "I felt this could be a useful way of diversifying," Clive recalled. Epstein Sr. wasn't involved in this latest venture, having decided, according to Clive, that "entertainment activities weren't for him".[14]

Lennon, McCartney, Harrison, and Best eventually signed the contract at Epstein's office on January 24th 1962 in the presence of a witness, Alistair Taylor (Epstein's assistant, and later general manager of NEMS). One signature was conspicuous by its absence: Epstein's own. Why he chose not to sign remains a mystery. One theory is that he didn't want to tie the group to a contract that they might one day wish to terminate; another suggests that Epstein himself was wary of committing himself, and didn't sign so that he could drop them swiftly if things didn't go to plan. Both seem unlikely given that the updated contract he signed with the group on October 1st contained a clause that allowed either party to end the agreement as long as three months written notice was given.

It seems possible that Epstein was inspired to add this clause after reading the contract The Beatles signed with Bert Kaempfert (as discussed in the next chapter). Perhaps the most likely reason for Epstein not signing the original contract is that he felt bound more tightly to a gentleman's agreement with the group. "I never signed a contract with The Beatles," he said. "I had given my word about what I intended to do, and that was enough. I abided by the terms and no one ever worried about me not signing it."[15] Epstein took this attitude with him to the grave. Only weeks before his untimely death in

1967, Epstein noted, "The principal value of a contract between us is really for the benefit of the lawyers, accountants, and all the scene, because those people always think these things should be proved on paper."[16]

Epstein might have been a gentleman, but any contract, even a verbal agreement, is legally binding – except for when any party involved is under the age of 21, as McCartney and Harrison were. For Epstein's contract to be truly binding, McCartney and Harrison's legal guardians should have signed it for them.

It was in Epstein's best interests, of course, to get as much money as he could for the group. His rate of commission increased in relation to how much money the group was making, so the more they earned, the more he earned. According to the October 1st 1962 contract, Epstein received 15 per cent of earnings up to £100 per week, and 20 per cent of anything from £100–200. He only received the top rate of 25 per cent when the group's weekly earnings hit £200 or more. (He later claimed that The Beatles were earning so little that he didn't take any commission for the first four months.)

Once Epstein had The Beatles' signatures, he began to take control of every aspect of their professional lives. He first asked local DJ Bob Wooler – who knew the Liverpool beat scene inside out – for advice on concert promotion, and then began to look further afield and increase The Beatles' fees. Getting the group known outside Liverpool was an important part of his plan – partly, perhaps, as a means of avoiding having to deal with local promoters in what was a very busy and competitive market. Although his new charges were big fish in a small pond, Epstein still had to be aware of rivals such as Joe Flannery, who would often book his small stable of local acts (which included Lee Curtis & The All Stars and, later, Pete Best) in direct competition with The Beatles.

The Beatles were already well established on Merseyside; it was up to Epstein to develop their potential elsewhere. In the early 1960s, as now, groups stood to make more money from performing than from record sales. In order to develop their earning potential, Epstein had to create a demand for The Beatles outside Liverpool.

Within weeks Epstein had transformed the group. The October 1st contract states that he would "advise on all matters concerning clothes, make-up and the presentation and construction of the artists' acts". His detailed itineraries helped with McCartney's tardiness, and his eye for detail and theatrical background helped improve the way they presented themselves onstage. The Beatles might have liked dressing in leather but it made them look like hooligans. While The Beatles looked like Gene Vincent clones, a large part of their audience wore suits and ties. Cilla Black later recalled how the pre-fame Lennon's hair "was much longer then than Brian Epstein would ever let him wear it later on. It was brushed forward instead of back and he had an enormous pink leather hat over it. He had black leather pants on, lined with red satin, black t-shirt, black leather jacket, and high black boots with Cuban heels. I took one look and thought, 'Oh my God!'"[17]

Epstein knew that The Beatles needed to clean up their act if they were to play anywhere other than dance halls and the Cavern. The band knew it too, but were distinctly reticent to change. When they ventured south for their one and only gig in Aldershot, The Beatles' leather suits and pink caps shocked the promoter. "Outside of Liverpool ... the dance-hall promoters didn't like us," recalled Lennon. "They thought we were a gang of thugs."[18] As Harrison put it, "People thought we looked undesirable, I suppose. Even nowadays kids with leather jackets and long hair are seen as apprentice hooligans, but they are just kids; that's the fashion they like. And it was like that with us."[19] In Aldershot, The Beatles looked so alien that the local police ordered them out of town and told them never to darken its streets again.

Epstein's solution was simple: put them in suits like every other band. Unable to see beyond the stereotype established by the likes of Cliff Richard and The Shadows, he made The Beatles fit his image of how a beat group should look. Most Merseyside groups of the time were already conformed to the dress code of the day – Gerry & The Pacemakers wore blazers and slacks long before Epstein became their manager, too. The Beatles were an exception, but their visual style was an important part of their appeal. Epstein was risking a lot by putting them in suits, but as much as leather made them stand out it also made them look like delinquents. Lennon later recalled that Epstein had told the group that, if they were serious about stepping up to bigger, more prestigious venues, they'd have to "stop eating on stage, stop swearing, stop smoking". [20]

Epstein put a stop to drinking onstage, too. As Johnny Hutchinson later recalled of the night his group The Big Three supported The Beatles at the Tower Ballroom, "Lennon was so stoned [that] we took the strings off his guitar. He went on stage to play and he didn't even notice that they were missing." [21] It's unlikely that this kind of thing happened all the time, but it was clear that The Beatles would have to adopt a more professional attitude if they were to move on from local dancehalls. Epstein made sure of it.

On March 24th 1962 The Beatles ditched their leather look and wore matching lounge suits (purchased from Beno Dorm in Birkenhead) for the first time. Now, at last, they looked like respectable young men. Epstein even managed to convince them to trim the ends off their guitar strings to stop them from looking untidy.

The move to bigger and better venues was slow but steady. The Beatles continued to play at the Cavern and Casbah Club during the first few months of 1962, but were also booked into more impressive venues such as the Kingsway Club in Southport. And with 'My Bonnie' having been issued by Polydor on January 5th, Epstein started to bill the group as great recording stars, too.

The Beatles' first steps outside Liverpool were fairly tentative. On February 2nd, Epstein booked them into the Oasis Club in Manchester, 30 miles east of Liverpool. An even bigger gig followed three weeks later when they played with Gerry & The Pacemakers, Rory Storm & The Hurricanes, and The Chris Hamilton Jazzmen at Floral Hall, Southport, 20 miles north. The gig was billed, by Epstein, as a Rock'n'Trad Spectacular.

The combination might seem odd now, but it's worth remembering that music wasn't so rigorously categorised then as it is today. (It was still possible, much later in the 1960s, to see The Walker Brothers, Cat Stevens, Engelbert Humperdinck, and The Jimi Hendrix Experience on the same bill.) Epstein was simply exploiting a popular trend to generate as much interest in The Beatles as he could. In 1962, trad jazz was incredibly popular and would only fade away after The Beatles' emergence as the new kings of pop. Hamilton's Jazzmen would have been as strong a draw as any of the other groups on the bill. Richard Lester, who would later direct *A Hard Day's Night* and *Help!*, had just completed *It's Trad, Dad!*, which was released with a tagline that trumpeted "The newest, most frantic fad".

After booking The Beatles into their biggest theatre yet, Epstein's next move was to get them on the radio. On January 10th he visited BBC Manchester and proposed an audition. A month later the group performed for producer Peter Pilbeam. They played the same four songs they'd played for Decca a few weeks earlier: 'Like Dreamers Do', 'Till There Was You', 'Memphis Tennessee', and 'Hello Little Girl'. Pilbeam didn't think much of McCartney, but he did like Lennon, and was impressed by the group's musicality. "An unusual group," he wrote on the audition application form, "not as rocky as most, more c&w with a tendency to play music."[22]

The Beatles returned to Manchester on March 7th to record three songs – 'Dream Baby (How Much Must I Dream)', 'Memphis Tennessee', and 'Please Mister Postman' – for *Teenagers' Turn – Here We Go*. Getting on the BBC was a major achievement for Epstein, who had yet to find a recording contract for his charges. In 1962, hardly any pop music was played on the BBC. Most of the Beeb's Light Programme station was aimed at adults: *Housewives' Choice*, *Music While You Work*, *Your Date With Val: Val Doonican And His Guitar*, and so on were dominated by easy-listening music for mums and dads.

The BBC made little attempt to address teenage listeners and their cravings for pop. The amount that could be aired was limited to a certain number of hours per day, with this 'needle time' regulated by a company called Phonographic Performance Ltd (PPL). The PPL represented record companies, which had an agreement with the Musicians' Union, which in turn had the ultimate say over how many hours of needle time should be allowed. Even when Radio 1 was launched in 1967, it was allocated only seven hours of needle time per day.[23]

In order to have enough music to fill its broadcast schedule and satisfy its agreement with the PPL, the BBC recorded groups in its own studios, as playing back these recordings would not eat into needle-time allowances. As such, the producers of BBC shows such as *Teenagers' Turn, Parade Of The Pops*, and *Pop To Bed: While David Gell Spins The Pops* were keen to book The Beatles and their peers for studio sessions.

This was a mutually beneficial arrangement, as it also provided The Beatles with important national radio exposure and extra income. They were paid £37/18s for their first radio session in London, on November 11th 1962, and by the following year were earning up to £52 (plus a £10 travelling allowance) per show. The group's total earnings for BBC radio sessions for the year 1963 came to just over £1,200 – which today would be around £17,500, or more than $35,000.

The general pattern of these sessions was for The Beatles to play two contemporary hits and an oldie. They stuck exclusively to material by American rhythm & blues acts, whom British pop fans still considered to be superior to their homegrown counterparts, despite the popularity of The Shadows and Cliff Richard. Gerry Marsden of The Pacemakers later recalled going into Brian Epstein's shop and asking for "records from America, not British ones, because Cliff was in the charts, and Adam Faith ... great lads, but we didn't play their type of music. We wanted stuff from America by Fats Domino, Jerry Lee Lewis, Ray Charles."[24]

When the British music press first started writing about The Beatles, the group were praised for their ability to interpret American popular music. Less than a year after their appearance on *Teenagers' Turn*, Norman Jopling of the *New Record Mirror* pointed out the key difference between The Beatles and contemporaries such as Adam Faith and Cliff Richard. "The Beatles sing the bluesy stuff well," he said, "whereas Adam and Cliff don't. Which is probably why it never really caught on in this country."[25]

The Beatles continued to appear regularly at the Cavern and the Casbah Club before returning to Hamburg, this time to the Star-Club, on April 13th 1962 for a seven-week residency. The Beatles' first trip to Hamburg under Epstein's management was better paid and at a bigger venue. The previous December, just weeks after The Beatles had verbally agreed for Epstein to take them on, Peter Eckhorn, owner of the Top Ten Club, had come to Liverpool on a scouting mission with Tony Sheridan.

In the past, Eckhorn had booked The Beatles through the Bests; now he would have to strike a deal with their new manager. Eckhorn offered DM450 per man per week, but Epstein asked for more: DM2,000 per week total, which was too much for Eckhorn. It looked for a while as though Epstein had let a good opportunity slip by. But then, three weeks later, he was visited by Horst Fascher, whom The Beatles remembered as a bouncer at the Kaiserkeller and the Top Ten Club but who now managed the 2,000-capacity Star-Club, and wanted The Beatles as his opening act. Fascher was more than happy to pay DM2,000 per week for the privilege, and signed a contract with Epstein to that effect on January 22nd 1962.

No sooner had Epstein acquired his beloved boys than he had to let them go. Having only just formed a relationship with the group, sending them to Hamburg might seem like an odd move. Epstein wanted to turn the rough-and-tumble Beatles into all-round entertainers, but such a transformation was unlikely to occur in the red light district of a rough seaport. And while there was plenty of work available on Merseyside, where Epstein could keep a closer eye on the group, it didn't pay as well, or as steadily, as a residency in Hamburg. It was a sound business decision, even if it meant that Epstein had little control over the group while they were away.

Three of The Beatles flew in to Hamburg from Manchester Airport on April 11th; Harrison, who was ill, followed a day later. They arrived to bad news from a distressed Astrid Kirchherr, who informed them that Stuart Sutcliffe had died a day earlier of a brain haemorrhage. The Beatles were naturally distraught at the loss of their friend. Sutcliffe hadn't been a great bassist, but was a gifted artist with a promising career ahead of him. Even Brian Epstein, who never met Sutcliffe, was shocked. The news made The Beatles' first night at the Star-Club all the more emotional. They were on the verge of making it big, but unable to share their success with the one friend who had been with them from the start. On the day of the group's first Star-Club performance, Millie Sutcliffe arrived in Hamburg to identify her dead son and make arrangements to have his body flown home.

The Beatles trip to Hamburg grossed DM14,000, a considerable improvement on the DM11,760 they received after enduring 15 weeks there in 1960. Moreover, they were now the opening act at an impressive new club, not just another beat combo at the sweaty Cavern club. This was a big step up the showbiz ladder.

A week after returning from Hamburg, The Beatles made their second appearance on *Teenagers' Turn*. Their three songs – 'Ask Me Why', 'Besame Mucho', and 'A Picture Of You' – were taped at Manchester's Playhouse Theatre on June 11th before an invited audience and broadcast four days later. Ten days after that they appeared on a bill in New Brighton (just across the river from Liverpool) with Bruce Channel, who had just had a hit with one of Lennon's favourite songs of the time, 'Hey Baby'. The concert was promoted by NEMS Enterprises and held at the 3,500-capacity Tower Ballroom, which in 1921 had boasted the world's largest stage and was still one of the largest venues in Britain – much larger than most beat groups were used to playing.

Concert promotion was a major undertaking for Epstein, who had to hire and pay for the venue, book the acts and guarantee payments, promote the event, sell tickets, and more. He already had a small staff to call upon, but this in itself was still a considerable investment given that the group at the centre of it had yet to issue its first proper record. But while there was an element of risk and a lot of expense involved with promoting these concerts, they did have their rewards. As well as taking 25 per cent from The Beatles, Epstein also received any overall profits, and by booking the venues and bands himself he was able to cut out the middlemen, reduce his overheads, and increase his income.

By the summer of 1962 Epstein's NEMS Enterprises was fast becoming the busiest concert promoter on Merseyside. Epstein had started booking acts such as Bruce Channel, Little Richard, and Joe Brown, and picked support acts from the cream of the Liverpool beat groups. His concert promotions allowed The Beatles to move out of dingy clubs and into the plush ballrooms of success. Booking the group for his own blockbuster events at the biggest and most impressive venues around allowed Epstein to shamelessly promote them – often at the expense of the headline acts. An advertisement in *Mersey Beat* billed them as "The North's Number 1 Group".[26] These sorts of pronouncements paid dividends when The Beatles began to break nationally. Writing in the October 26th edition of the *New Musical Express*, Alan Smith was able to associate The Beatles with Little Richard, Bruce Channel, Gene Vincent, and Joe Brown. As far as the reader was concerned, any group that had appeared with stars of this calibre must be good.

Concert promotion generated additional income for NEMS Enterprises and gave Epstein control over where, when, and with whom The Beatles appeared. He put himself in charge of everything from poster design to show times. The level of detail to which he worked was confirmed by his assistant, Alistair Taylor, who later described how all NEMS acts were given "gig sheets" that included information on everything from the contact at the venue to the number of power outlets. Epstein, said Taylor, "created a whole new form of management".[27]

This isn't too exaggerated a claim. Epstein devised a blueprint for band management that is still used today by taking his knowledge of running a busy record department and his understanding of theatre management and applying it to The Beatles. It wasn't the only way to go about managing a group, but it was certainly the best. Epstein was beginning to develop The Beatles as a brand. The more successful he could make them look, the more recognisable their name and likeness would be. And as their popularity grew more people would want to know more about the group, see them in concert, and buy their records. Eventually, he'd be able to further exploit The Beatles with all sorts of merchandising schemes (more on this later).

So far Epstein had got The Beatles on the radio, moved them to larger venues, improved their earning potential, and changed their image. The only obstacle in the group's path was their lack of recording contract. Although beat groups generally earned considerably more from performing than from recording, The Beatles needed to sign a deal with a major record company if they were to move on to national and international success.

As luck would have it, just such a deal was right around the corner. On June 4th 1962, The Beatles were signed by George Martin to Parlophone Records. From here on things began to escalate. With The Beatles now signed to Parlophone, Epstein could start to book them into bigger venues for a lot more money. Before he could launch the group into the big-time, however, he had a more unpleasant task to perform.

On August 15th he called Pete Best to his NEMS office. Although The Beatles had passed their audition at EMI, their new Recording Manager had a few issues with the drummer. "I learnt later that I wasn't the only one who had reservations about him," George Martin recalled. "On that first recording I was aware that I needed a stronger and more steady and more powerful drumbeat that I was getting."[28]

It has since been suggested that Best's lacklustre drumming was just the excuse The Beatles had been looking for to sack him. He might not have been the world's greatest musician, but he was certainly popular with the fans – perhaps too popular. He was well liked, but had never really fitted in. While the rest of the group bonded over a few beers, he would be off on his own somewhere. Worse still, he refused to adopt the regulation mop top.

Even if it was jealousy that led to Best's sacking, it's obvious from the recordings The Beatles made with him that they could do better. If they were to progress further they needed a rock-solid drummer, and Best wasn't one. Best seemed to take the sacking well – or as well as can be expected – at first, and even agreed to play a few more gigs with the group until they found a replacement. An official statement published in *Mersey Beat* stated that he left "by mutual agreement" and that the decision had been "entirely amicable".[29] In reality, the split was far from amicable, and created a hostility between the two parties that lasted for decades. Best's final performance with The Beatles was at the Cavern just hours after he was sacked. He had originally agreed to play the following night's gig at the Riverpark Ballroom in Chester, but decided against it. Johnny Hutchinson from The Big Three took his place, but only for that one concert. Two days later, Ringo Starr was installed and made his debut at Hume Hall in Port Sunlight.

The Beatles had known Starr for some time, having first met him in the basement of the Jacaranda. ("We didn't know his name at the time," George Harrison confessed.[30]) He had first played the drums in The Eddie Miles Band, who later evolved into Eddie Clayton & The Clayton Squares. Then in 1959 he joined The Raving Texans, who subsequently mutated into Rory Storm & The Hurricanes and got a gig in Hamburg in October 1960. It was there that Starr really got to know The Beatles. He would sit in occasionally for Pete Best, and show himself clearly to be everything Best wasn't. He was sociable, outgoing, and, most importantly, rock-solid.

Starr was playing at a Butlins holiday camp with Rory Storm & The Hurricanes when he got the call to join The Beatles. He'd had his eye on the job for some time. "I was dropping hints to them about it and hoping to talk my way in," he said in 1964.[31] He had in fact already decided to leave Rory Storm and join Kingsize Taylor & The Dominoes, but then The Beatles came along with a better offer.

With a new drummer on board and a debut Parlophone single on the way, Epstein began to increase The Beatles' live-performance fee. He was surprisingly cautious. Four days after 'Love Me Do' was released he arranged for The Beatles to play a five-night tour of Scotland. The very fact that 'Love Me Do' had been issued meant he could command much larger fees, but Epstein settled for £42 per night – just £12 more than they were being paid before the record came out.

The fact that The Beatles were now on the cusp of success posed several problems when it came to booking gigs in advance. Bands without a hit record were paid a lot less than those with. If Epstein charged too much The Beatles could find themselves priced out of the market; too low and the only person to make anything out of the gig would be the promoter. Epstein's plan was to accept moderate fees and work hard, with the group, to generate maximum exposure. Once The Beatles had paid their dues, he reasoned, he could mine the success and fortune that would surely follow.

Paul McCartney has since noted that the group was happy to honour contracts even if it meant losing money. "After we started making records, we wouldn't say, 'Hey, you've got to pay us £500,'" he recalled in *The Brian Epstein Story*. "We'd say, 'No, no, no, the deal was for £50. We'll do it for £50.' Brian was keen that we do that ... he was an honourable businessman."

Whether The Beatles were really quite so happy to accept such significantly reduced payment is open to question. It's hard to believe that the money-minded George Harrison would have been content to play for £50 rather than £300 or more, which is what The Beatles should have been earning. In any case they weren't the only group whose earnings suffered because of Epstein's decision to book gigs months in advance, and not all of them were as accepting of it as McCartney claimed to be. "Brian had lifted our money by about five pounds a night, but we had quite a few months of work at 'old money' to honour when we arrived," recalled Gerry Marsden. "Even when we had a hit with 'How Do You Do It?', we had to play the Cavern cheaply because we'd signed the contract to appear six weeks before we'd hit the chart!"[32]

Epstein gave the impression of being the ultimate 'gentleman' manager, but his attitude to contracts could be ambivalent. He was happy to honour some, but wasn't beyond reneging on others, particularly if he thought he could get more money elsewhere. On August 29th 1962 Epstein signed a contract with Joe Flannery for The Beatles to play at the Royal Lido in Prestatyn, North Wales, on November 24th. In the intervening period, 'Love Me Do' hit the charts. "Brian wanted to cancel the arrangement," Flannery recalled, "as they could now command larger venues, but I insisted against it. We managed a lot of popular Liverpool artists, such as Cilla Black and Gerry & The Pacemakers, and I feared the Royal Lido would cancel their dates if we denied them The Beatles."[33]

In the end, Epstein honoured the contract simply as a way of safeguarding future bookings – an act of good business sense more than anything. Had he angered promoters by cancelling engagements simply because he could get more money elsewhere, he risked his reputation and future bookings for The Beatles and the other acts he represented.

By the autumn of 1962, The Beatles were still earning less than £50 per night, but Epstein clearly knew it was time to take his management responsibilities seriously. Three days prior to the release of 'Love Me Do' he finally put his signature on a contract with the group.

The October 1st 1962 contract put Epstein in charge of negotiating all contracts on The Beatles behalf, and entitled him to 25 per cent of all monies earned from a wide range of entertainment activities, including vaudeville and revue; motion pictures; balls and dances, whether of a public or private nature; radio and television broadcasting; concerts, private parties, and cabarets; phonographic and tape recording; and sponsorship products. As manager he would advise on stage presentation and the music they performed. But while The Beatles did change the way they dressed at his request, they paid little attention to his musical advice, and with good reason, particularly after a frustrating audition for Decca, at which Epstein had the group play a string of lightweight contemporary hits that were hardly representative of their rocking sound and emerging songwriting talent. Epstein might have had an ear for picking hits, but he much preferred jazz and classical to 'beat' music. Although he took an interest in what The Beatles recorded, the group soon made it clear that he should concentrate on the business side of things and leave them to look after the music.

The contract also stated that Epstein could, with the group's written permission (and at their expense), delegate his managerial duties and obligations to sub-agents – something that would prove particularly disastrous later on, when he allowed a third party to manage the group's merchandising. Although it was Epstein's duty as manager to find them employment, The Beatles were responsible for all travelling expenses, including those of their road managers, unless the promoter covered them.

This wasn't a problem at first, but meant that the group's costs would skyrocket once they started booking expensive suites or whole floors in five-star hotels. (In fairness to Epstein, he did at least pay his own expenses when travelling with the group.) They would also be responsible for paying for all publicity photographs, and for any necessary musical arrangements and rehearsal sessions. Epstein would organise publicity and advertising, but The Beatles would pay for it, and for the running of their fan club.

Given that it made The Beatles responsible for meeting most of the costs involved in running the group, the contract certainly favoured Epstein. In return for being given 25 per cent of the group's earnings, he gave the four of them a ten per cent share in NEMS Enterprises, but since this amounted to two-and-a-half per cent each it was hardly generous.

Rock'n'roll managers are notoriously tight-fisted. One of Larry Parnes's acts, Joe Brown, later recalled having to travel to gigs by public-transport bus. "It got really embarrassing in the end," he said, "because I was supposed to be a bit of star ... and there I was scrambling about on the bus with me guitars over one shoulder and me stage suit over the other."[34] At least The Beatles never suffered that indignity.

Epstein's 25 per cent commission would probably have sounded fine when The Beatles were earning £50 a night, from which the manager's cut would have been £12/10s. But when The Beatles hit the big time and started earning $160,000 per night, Epstein would rake in a cool $40,000. The Beatles' second US tour grossed a million dollars (which works out to over $18 million in today's money), from which Epstein earned $250,000, even though he – unlike the band – hadn't had to break a sweat to make it.

One thing missing from the October 1962 contract was any mention of money earned through songwriting. Epstein had given this side of the business so little thought prior to the release of 'Love Me Do' that he had to make hasty arrangements with Ardmore & Beechwood Ltd, to publish both sides of the single, and draw up another contract between himself, Lennon, and McCartney that related to them specifically as songwriters.

Epstein didn't just stop at The Beatles. With an overabundance of local talent to choose from, he set his eyes on several other Merseyside groups. Why only make 25 per cent from one group when he could take the same commission from several? Shane Fenton, a contemporary of The Beatles, saw firsthand how Epstein managed his acts. "Brian was very sensitive and put his heart into things he believed in," he said. "But he wasn't interested in anything unless he was convinced that it would be a financial success."[35]

"The reason I decided to handle other people too," Epstein told *The Beatles Book*, "was not because I was having second thoughts about The Beatles' future destiny but because I saw the advantages of running a busy office. I am keen to run a successful business, which means that NEMS Enterprises should make profits, increasing profits as we expand ..."[36]

NEMS did generate huge profits, but it also cost a lot to run. "Our outlay is vastly greater but the range of things we do for our clients is greater too,"

Epstein explained, noting that the company brought in "our own experts ... to direct and guide and shape careers". NEMS had its own public-relations division, too, which operated, according to Epstein, "on a worldwide scale". "These things cost a fortune if you are going to see that they are doing it the right way," he said.[37]

Epstein drew particular attention to the "tremendously expensive" phone bills he ran up as manager of The Beatles, but if that was his biggest worry then NEMS Enterprises must have been doing very well indeed. There were other overheads to consider, as well as the fact that not all of the groups he signed would be anywhere near as successful as The Beatles. But they all generated income, and Epstein took 25 per cent off the top of each of them.

The pattern was the same for every group he managed. He cleaned them up, bought them suits, made them presentable, and increased their booking fees. Berry Gordy did exactly the same thing with the stars he groomed for Tamla Motown. Motown took artist development very seriously, grooming, dressing, and choreographing its acts not just for professional reasons, but also to ensure that they became positive ambassadors for other African-American artists trying to break into the white mainstream. Many of the Motown acts were, like Epstein's working class kids, short on the kind of social skills and dress sense required to be successful in the entertainment industry. Like Gordy, Epstein had set about creating a presentation style that would become a key part of the NEMS brand. But while it worked for The Beatles and Gerry & The Pacemakers, it didn't work for all of Epstein's groups.

The Big Three were one such example. Although they were pleased to have their fee bumped up straightaway from £6 to £9 per performance, their enthusiasm for Epstein's methods soon dwindled. "His ideas were based on, I suppose, his background and his style of dress and everything else," recalled bassist Johnny Gustafson. "He wanted us to be suited up in the best finery money could buy, but we didn't really think very much of that idea."[38] Drummer Johnny Hutchinson was particularly baffled by Epstein's decision to send the group to Germany. "I've no idea why he did it," he said. "He wanted to make us conform, and yet he sent us to the Star-Club where nearly everyone became a head case."[39]

Epstein was an inventive manager in some respects, but in others he was no more imaginative than Larry Parnes. Good luck helped him steer The Beatles onto bigger things, but the same couldn't be said for some of his other groups. Epstein often just went with what he and the other Merseyside managers knew. There was a huge market for rock'n'roll in Hamburg, for example, and The Big Three were one of the best rock'n'roll groups on Merseyside. Why not send them to the Star-Club?

Part of the problem was that Epstein was collecting groups like most people collect records. His roster of acts grew rapidly, but he didn't have the time, resources, or inspiration to give them all the same level of attention The Beatles received. Sending groups to Hamburg often seemed like the best option as it got them out of the way. It's no wonder, then, that quite a few of them quickly grew dissatisfied with Epstein and his methods and fell by the wayside.

Another sign of Epstein's naivety arose when he brokered a deal for new amplifiers with Jennings Musical Instruments. The Beatles desperately needed new amps, having been told by George Martin that their equipment was defective. So in the early summer of 1962, on the advice of Bernard Michaelson, manager of Hessy's music shop, Epstein approached Jennings with the intention of acquiring a set of Vox amplifiers for The Beatles. His plan was to offer the group's endorsement in return for free equipment. Once again, his terms were generous: Vox could use The Beatles to promote its equipment for as long as he remained their manager.

Sponsorship deals weren't new, but Epstein obviously wasn't clear on how they worked. They tend, generally, to be for specific periods or events – a particular tour, for example. The Beatles might still have been relative unknowns when Epstein approached Jennings, but he should have added options to the contract, whereby Vox got The Beatles' services free for the first year, for example, but would have to negotiate a fee for the next.

After The Beatles exploded onto the music scene in 1963 Jennings would have paid handsomely for their endorsement. The beat-group boom was all-embracing; it saturated every section of the music business and beyond. Companies as diverse as Timex and Kellogg's wanted a piece of the action, and were falling over themselves to sign up musical acts to sell their products. If The Rolling Stones could sell Rice Krispies then surely The Beatles could get more out of their deal with Jennings than a few free amplifiers. This might seem a little harsh until you consider that, when The Beatles broke America in 1964, they created such a demand for Vox amplifiers that Jennings Musical Instruments simply couldn't keep up. As was so often the case, The Beatles were making someone else a lot of money. To be fair to Jennings, they did provide The Beatles with a considerable amount of equipment and support, but one can't help thinking that Epstein had given away a cash cow for a handful of beans.

Epstein's desire to book the group months in advance continued to have a negative impact, too. At a time when they should have been promoting 'Love Me Do', The Beatles were forced to return to Hamburg to play at the Star-Club to fulfil two two-week engagements, from November 1st–14th and December 18th–31st. (They received DM600 per man per week for the first visit, and DM750 for the second.) Had Epstein coordinated the release of the single with a series of concert appearances in Britain he could have maximised the impact of both and improved the chances of 'Love Me Do' being a hit.

It's tempting to assume that Epstein hadn't yet formulated a long-term plan for the group, but as he'd put so much time and effort into securing a recording contract for them, one might have expected him to have given some consideration to the fact that any records The Beatles issued would need to be promoted. He knew from past experience how important in-store appearances could be for attracting customers to shops. If he'd applied the same logic to 'Love Me Do' – instead of taking any bookings that fell into his lap – it might have fared better.

Under Epstein's management The Beatles' earnings from live engagements doubled in 1962 to approximately £6,780. But although he had increased the group's earnings, Epstein claimed, surprisingly, to have made a net loss on them during the first year.[40] His earnings for that year would in theory have been £1,700. Although he claimed not to have taken a commission for the first few months, he had initially run his business from his parents' shop, where he would probably have got free office-space and used shop staff to do his administration. Apart from buying them suits, he didn't have to spend much on The Beatles because they were contractually responsible for their own expenses. With this in mind, one might have expected him to make some sort of profit, even if it wasn't very big. He would, in any case, do much better in 1963.

With 'Love Me Do' in the charts, Epstein began planning The Beatles itinerary for the start of the following year. This time his marketing plan was better conceived. On Saturday October 28th he called Arthur Howes, the king of British package tours, at his Peterborough home and turned on his salesman's charm. By the end of the conversation, Howes had provisionally booked The Beatles to appear with teen sensation Helen Shapiro on their first nationwide tour – subject to an audition, to be held at the Embassy Cinema, Peterborough. The Beatles didn't go down particularly well, but Howes agreed to book them anyway. Epstein was so grateful that he accepted a modest fee – £30 per night – and gave Howes the first option on all of the group's future tours.

Although the tour didn't pay well, it did provide considerable publicity and exposure at a time when The Beatles needed it most. Package tours were at the cutting edge of popular entertainment in the early 1960s, and, despite having a lot in common with the kind of variety show one might see at the end of a seaside pier, remained largely unchanged until the end of the decade. The tour gave The Beatles the chance to play some of the largest venues in Britain. It also provided, as George Harrison recalled, a turning point in their popularity. "We were quite happy that Helen Shapiro was established, she'd been around and had a bunch of hits," he said. "But when 'Please Please Me' got to Number 1, all the people coming to the show were just waiting for The Beatles. It was embarrassing, because she was a very nice person."[41]

On January 19th the group made their first national TV appearance on *Thank Your Lucky Stars* to promote their new single, which might not have fared any better than 'Love Me Do' without such a promotional push. One contemporary report, later reprinted in *The Beatles Book*, noted how, to begin with, 'Please Please Me' languished at Number 39 on the *Melody Maker* singles chart, but that, after The Beatles' appearances on *Thank Your Lucky Stars* and BBC Radio's *Saturday Club*, "sales ... have been fantastic, and EMI are confidently expecting the single to zoom up the charts next week".[42]

'Please Please Me' did indeed begin to make its way up the charts. *Melody Maker*'s review of the tour suggested that Helen Shapiro's set was under-rehearsed, but praised Kenny Lynch and The Beatles as "the pick of the supporting acts".[43] Gordon Samson of the *New Musical Express* noted that the "colourfully dressed" Beatles "almost stole the show, for the audience repeatedly called for them while other artists were performing!"[44] A month later, Shapiro was still struggling to win over audiences and critics. "She had a lukewarm reception," reported *Melody Maker*'s Ray Coleman, "and her stage presence was not exactly stunning."[45] By the time the tour ended, 'Please Please Me' was Number 1 and The Beatles were stars in the making, but Shapiro's popularity was on the wane.

With The Beatles riding high in the charts, Gerry & The Pacemakers preparing to release their debut single, 'How Do You Do It', and several other NEMS-managed acts on the cusp of success, Epstein took another step towards world domination by organising a series of Mersey Beat Showcase events, which featured The Beatles, Gerry & The Pacemakers, The Big Three, and Billy J. Kramer & The Dakotas. The music press was already using the term merseybeat to describe the types of groups that Epstein managed; all he had to do was reinforce the brand and expose it to as many people as possible.

Whether by accident or design, the Mersey Beat Showcase took a similar form to Tamla Motown's Motortown Revue, which showcased established acts and gave new artists a chance to hone their performance skills and gain much-needed exposure. Epstein adapted the format of earlier concerts such as Operation Big Beat and The Bruce Channel Show and took them on the road. This was one of the first examples of Epstein developing a brand that would benefit all of the acts he represented, but not everybody was keen on the idea: The Beatles were among the first to suggest that merseybeat was little more than a generic term invented by the press to pigeonhole groups, and wanted to distance themselves from the phenomenon.

The first Mersey Beat Showcase took place on March 7th at the Elizabethan Ballroom, Nottingham, for which 80 Beatles fans travelled down from Liverpool in a coach booked by The Beatles Fan Club. This became a regular and mutually beneficial feature of the group's out-of-town concerts. It gave fans another chance to see and support them, and made The Beatles look good in the eyes of local promoters and press – which in turn made Epstein's job of securing a return engagement that little bit easier.

On April 6th *Melody Maker* reported on a remarkable 'Hat-trick for Epstein' when The Big Three's 'Some Other Guy' joined 'Please Please Me' and Gerry & The Pacemakers' 'How Do You Do It' in the newspaper's Pop 50 chart. Shortly thereafter Epstein added a fourth star to his expanding universe when Billy J. Kramer hit big with his reading of Lennon/McCartney's 'Do You Want To Know A Secret'.

Interest in The Beatles was beginning to hot up. Frankie Vaughan's manager, Paul Cave, wanted to book the group, as did Harold Fielding, one of Britain's most prominent theatrical producers. But Epstein stood by his agreement with Howes and continued to use his agency to book the group onto package tours. The original plan for The Beatles' second package tour was for The Beatles to play beneath a pair of American headliners, Tommy Roe and Chris Montez. But while each had a couple of hits to his name, neither was a huge star; they were at least American – which still counted for something – but the tide was beginning to turn. After lukewarm reviews of Roe and Montez's appearance on *Thank Your Lucky Stars*, The Beatles were moved up to the headline spot in time for the first night of the tour, on March 9th.

According to the March 15th edition of the *New Musical Express*, "The Beatles stole top honours for entertainment and audience reaction. This all-action quartet from Liverpool has everything: exciting new sound, terrific instrumental attack, exhilarating solo and group vocal effects, and a fresh energy that leaves them (they told me later) limp at the end of each act." As the tour progressed The Beatles continued to grow in popularity. One report suggested that it was only their presence on the bill that prevented the tour from being a financial disaster.

Tour costs were kept to a minimum by the acquisition of a new van fitted with a hi-fi system and bunk beds, which made better sense than spending hard-earned cash on hotel rooms. Under the terms of their contract with Epstein, this expensive item was paid for by the group. Without knowing it, The Beatles had invented the modern-day tour bus, which allowed them to travel overnight and thereby save time and money.

After the tour finished Epstein kept the group busy with radio and concert appearances. These still included a stop at the Cavern, but in general the venues were getting bigger and more prestigious. With 'From Me To You' on sale and about to begin a 21-week run on the charts, The Beatles performed at the Royal Albert Hall, London, as part of a BBC radio broadcast, *Swinging Sound '63*, that also featured The Springfields, Del Shannon, Shane Fenton & The Fentones, and jazz stalwart George Melly. The Beatles played four songs, of which two were broadcast: 'Twist And Shout' and 'From Me To You'.

Three days later The Beatles appeared at the *New Musical Express*'s annual Poll-Winners concert at the 10,000-capacity Empire Pool in Wembley, London. Such was their popularity that, although they hadn't won any of the categories, the *NME* added them to the bill at the last minute. The group was featured towards the end of the show, right before the headliners, Cliff Richard & The Shadows, and played four songs: 'Please Please Me', 'From Me To You', 'Twist And Shout', and 'Long Tall Sally'. Later the same day they performed at a charity showcase at the Pigalle Club in front of London's top booking agents and television producers, whom Epstein was keen to book the group. He also believed that the group's clean-cut image would be enhanced by playing charity events (which is why he booked his charges to perform at similar events at the Grafton Rooms, Liverpool, on June 12th, and at the Grosvenor House Hotel on December 2nd).

The Beatles still had a few £50 engagements to honour, but overall their performing fees had risen considerably to around £250–300 per night. In May the group began their third national tour with Roy Orbison, Gerry & The Pacemakers, and six other acts. Unlike the two previous tours, this one was promoted by Kennedy St. Enterprises, and would have starred Duane Eddy but for a management mix-up. Once again the initial headliner,

Orbison, was relegated to the role of supporting The Beatles. Ever the professional, he took it on the chin, and was gracious enough to tell the *New Musical Express* that The Beatles had what it takes to make it in America. (Capitol Records lacked Orbison's foresight, and didn't get around to releasing any Beatles records until the very end of 1963.)

Although The Beatles topped the bill and were paid well for their appearance on the tour, Epstein's ability to secure good money for his other acts was still lacking. Gerry & The Pacemakers, whose 'How Do You Do It' had topped the charts a month before the tour was booked, were on the verge of making it big, but Epstein asked for only £25 per night. Fortunately for Epstein – and the group – his willingness to honour bookings without demanding bigger fees sometimes paid off. On this occasion, Kennedy St. Enterprises upped the group's pay to £250 per week without any intervention from Epstein – who nonetheless took his £62/10s cut. (According to Gerry Marsden, the promoter still considered £250 to be a bargain.)

NEMS Enterprises rode the crest of a beat boom that spread across the country like a sonic wave. Most of the country's beat groups owed their success to The Beatles, who were the first and most successful of these groups and were ultimately responsible for the acres of press coverage that appeared everywhere about the beat phenomenon. Even if they weren't recording songs by Lennon/McCartney, being produced by George Martin, or managed by Epstein, it was enough for beat groups and solo artists just to be able to say that they came from Liverpool.

The Beatles themselves were averaging £300 per night and clocking up tours of the Channel Islands (£1,000 for five dates) and Sweden (£2,000 for eight shows in five days). They also played weeklong residencies in Margate, Weston-super-Mare, Llandudno, Bournemouth, and Southport, which cut travelling expenses and could be promoted in a more cost-effective fashion than a tour of one-nighters. During their Margate residency The Beatles played to 20,000 people over six nights and enjoyed, according to the *New Musical Express*, "packed audiences at each show".[46]

Epstein had decided by then never to book The Beatles into anything smaller than a theatre. This gave the group added prestige, but was primarily based on a need for greater capacity and security. Safety had become a problem as early as January 1963, when the police had to be called to stop ticketless fans from breaking into the Majestic Ballroom in Birkenhead, where The Beatles played on the 17th. Demand to see the group grew to the extent that all future concerts there were double-headers, with matinee and evening shows.

Epstein was interviewed by the *New Musical Express* in October. Part of the article explored his rise to fame, but most of it was about money. "Some highly inaccurate figures have been reported," he said, when asked how much The Beatles were earning. "I'd say between £1,000 and £1,500 between them each week, exclusive of record royalties." Asked how much he earned as their manager, Epstein claimed not to know. "I'm not that interested in the money side," he said. "I know it sounds phoney and all that, but I enjoy it. Really and truly. I love the music."[47]

Epstein also admitted that he was "not the world's best businessman" – a claim that few would argue with. It's surprising, however, that he was prepared to admit such a thing publicly, even if it was true. While he put a lot of effort into managing The Beatles' creative output, he neglected their business dealings. Delegating the group's financial affairs to a fudge of accountants who knew no more about the music business than he did might not have been a particularly good idea, but it was within the terms of the contract. And if Epstein really had no interest in business, it probably made no difference anyway.

By November The Beatles were on their fourth national package tour in nine months, with support provided by The Brook Brothers Rhythm & Blues Quartet, The Vernon Girls, Peter Jay & The Jaywalkers, and The Kestrels. The tour visited 34 towns, with matinee and evening performances given to meet demand. The three main American television networks – ABC, NBC, and CBS – all sent crews to capture the mass hysteria of Beatlemania in full swing.

According to the American journalist Walter Cronkite, it was a clip of The Beatles' November 16th concert at the Winter Gardens in Bournemouth, aired on *CBS Evening News*, that first alerted Ed Sullivan to the group. "Ed Sullivan was on the phone to me before I was away from the anchor desk,"

Cronkite recalled. "He said, 'Tell me about these bugs or whatever they call themselves ... how do I get in touch with them?'"

Sullivan himself remembers things rather differently. He claims to have first become aware of the group on a trip to London with his wife, whereupon he saw "hundreds of youngsters ... waiting to greet The Beatles on their return from Sweden. Always on the lookout for talent, I decided that The Beatles would be a great attraction for our TV show".[48]

On November 5th 1963, Brain Epstein flew to New York with Billy J. Kramer. The reason for the trip was ostensibly to promote Kramer, but Epstein was more concerned with his plans to launch The Beatles in America. He met with Ed Sullivan to arrange for the group to appear on his show, insisting that they receive top billing – a rather audacious demand, given that The Beatles were still relatively unknown in America. Epstein's ploy was to offer Sullivan the group at a knockdown price of $10,000 plus airfare and accommodation; in return The Beatles would record three appearances for *The Ed Sullivan Show*.

It was an old trick, but it worked. Epstein also met with promoter Sid Bernstein, who booked The Beatles into Carnegie Hall, New York City, and made arrangements for the group to perform at the Washington Coliseum, which would be filmed and shown in cinemas across America.

Back in Britain, the music press was as intoxicated by The Beatles as the group's fans were. What started as a fad became a trend and then a habit. Liverpool might have started it all, but other cities were soon haemorrhaging beat groups like there was no tomorrow. The British music scene was changing fast. The Beatles swept away all that had gone before, and by the end of the year had revolutionised almost every aspect of the music industry. Groups with guitars were no longer on the way out, but were very much the in thing.

At the end of the year Epstein reworked the Mersey Beat Showcase into The Beatles Christmas Show, for which he hired the Astoria Theatre in London for 16 nights over the Christmas and New Year period. The show combined two existing formats, the pantomime and the package tour, into one festive extravaganza.

Pantomime was – and is – a big tradition in Britain. During the 1950s and early '60s it had provided seasonal employment to stars such as Lonnie Donegan, Cliff Richard, and Freddie & The Dreamers. Epstein's plan was to dress Britain's most original pop group in silly costumes and have them perform hackneyed sketches before an audience of screaming, hysterical girls.

A manager would be laughed at for suggesting such a thing today, but Epstein didn't have much else to work with. He had become well versed in theatrical razzle dazzle during his time at RADA, while in the early 1960s pop stars were expected to be all-round entertainers as much as musicians. The Beatles were in show business, and if that meant appearing in comedy sketches with Morecambe & Wise then that is what they would have to do. Even their appearances on 'serious' music programmes such as *Ready Steady Go!* tended to involve wearing bizarre costumes and performing faux-Shakespearian skits. Pantomime it was.

Putting on The Beatles Christmas Show was an expensive undertaking. In an interview in *Play And Player* magazine, the actor Michael Billington said that the cost of staging *Man In The Moon*, which ran at the London Palladium over the same Christmas season, was between £80,000 and £90,000 – "and that is not much above average".[49] The Beatles Christmas Show might have cost a little less because Epstein used his own artists, but he was still faced with the expense of hiring the theatre, staging the production, and advertising the show.

He needn't have worried too much, however. All 100,000 tickets, which cost between five and 15 shillings, sold out in 25 days. Epstein planned to transfer the show to the West End and then maybe even take it out on tour. (Fortunately for The Beatles, they made it big in America before Epstein could make good on this scheme.) Although The Beatles Christmas Show was a commercial success, it was not an artistic success. It was under-rehearsed and plagued by minor accidents, while the fans' screaming was so loud that you couldn't hear any of the dialogue.

It wasn't a particularly happy time for The Beatles, either. Colin Manley of The Remo Four, who backed Tommy Quickly during the show, recalled, "I don't think they had any interest in what they were doing. No one could hear what they were playing. It was like being in the birdhouse of a zoo, greatly amplified. They threw their guitars on the floor when they'd finished ... [and] fled as fast as they could."[50]

The Beatles Christmas Show brought an end to another incredibly busy year for the group that had taken in three package tours, two trips to Hamburg, and a string of one-nighters, plus their first national television and radio appearances. The group's earnings soared accordingly. It's difficult to arrive at exact figures without access to the actual contracts, but most indications suggests that Epstein's off-the-cuff calculation that The Beatles were earning somewhere between £1,000 and £1,500 per week wasn't far off the mark.

At the start of 1963 The Beatles were still playing for £30 per night. Their first £100 booking didn't come until March 4th, at the Plaza Ballroom in St. Helens. Three months later they were able to command £300 for a night's work. It's likely therefore that The Beatles earned somewhere in the region of £42,600 from concert appearances. They picked up an average of £55 per session for their 40 BBC radio appearances (£2,200 total), and brought in another £2,774 from BBC television shows and repeat fees. On top of this there were record royalties and fees from independent radio and television companies, while Lennon and McCartney also received revenue from songwriting. All in all, The Beatles' earnings for 1963 could easily have topped £75,000, which works out to over one million pounds today.

NEMS Enterprises performed so well in 1963 that it had to be restructured. On April 27th 1964 the company's share value was increased from £100 to £10,000. Epstein held £5,000, his brother Clive £4,000, and the rest was split between Lennon, McCartney, Harrison, and Starr. Although a two-and-a-half per cent share was hardly generous, Epstein didn't have to make such a concession, since it was standard practice at the time for manager and group to keep their business interests separate. But while this reveals a certain benevolence on Epstein's part, it also led to a conflict of interest, as Epstein shared his lawyers and advisers with the group – not that they knew at the time. In the end, this would lead them to lose more than just money.

Epstein faced another problem. In just over a year he had gone from shopkeeper to empire builder. For all his creative flair, he knew little about the music business. He was an innovator in many respects, but had little interest in broader financial matters. And while he brought in a pool of advisers, most of them had no more of an idea than he did. What The Beatles needed was a strong business manager to complement Epstein's creative and marketing skills because, like everyone else at the time, he was making it up as he went along.

Nevertheless, if he and The Beatles thought they'd done well out of 1963, it was nothing compared to what they would achieve in 1964, which would be another year of progress and success, but also of further missed opportunities. Global Beatlemania beckoned, but although The Beatles would make even more money in 1964, it was nowhere near as much as they could have made, had Epstein been more interested in business.

Mean To Me

Record deals and battles with EMI

"For years EMI were giving us one old penny between us
for every single and two shillings for every album."

GEORGE HARRISON[1]

P arlophone issued The Beatles' debut single, 'Love Me Do', on Friday October 5th 1962, ten months after Epstein first approached EMI. It was the first of many milestones in the group's career, and allowed them to escape Merseyside and crash into the national psyche. Within a year The Beatles were the biggest band in Britain, and six months after that the biggest band in the world. Up until that point, however, their road to stardom had been long and rocky. It wasn't as if 'Love Me Do' was their first record – they already had a Top Ten hit in Germany with Tony Sheridan – but it was the one that set them on the road to fame and fortune.

Although they entered EMI Studios with some trepidation, The Beatles were no strangers to the recording process. Their first, self-financed experience of it came in 1958 when The Quarry Men (Lennon, McCartney, and Harrison plus John Lowe and Colin Hanton) paid 17s/6d to record a double-sided acetate at Phillips Sound Recording Service in Kensington, Liverpool. The ten-inch record featured two songs, both sung by Lennon: Buddy Holly's 'That'll Be The Day' and 'In Spite Of All The Danger', a McCartney/Harrison composition. Only one disc was cut, which the group shared – each member kept it for a week before passing it on.

Like Elvis Presley and countless teenagers before them, The Quarry Men had made a record simply for the sheer pleasure of hearing themselves blast out of a Dansette record player. "It was just done for a giggle," John Lowe recalled. "Anyone who was a friend could borrow it for a couple of days."[2] The record was only intended for family and friends, so wasn't going to do much to further The Quarry Men's career, but it did at least give them some experience of recording – even if the 'studio' was situated in a terraced house in suburban Liverpool.

Two years passed before Lennon, McCartney, and Harrison entered another recording studio. On Saturday October 15th 1960, midway through their first stint in Hamburg, they made their second self-financed record with the help of Ringo Starr and Walter Eymond of Rory Storm & The Hurricanes. Crammed into Akustik, a small studio located at 57 Kirchenallee, they cut a version of 'Summertime'. This was, again, little more than a vanity project, paid for by Eymond. The song was cut onto nine 78-rpm discs that featured a message from a leather salesman on the B-side.

Four months later, during their second visit to Hamburg, The Beatles were spotted at the Top Ten Club by Tommy Kent, a popular German recording artist of the time. "One of Germany's biggest rock'n'roll stars came into the club," McCartney wrote in a letter home dated May 4th 1961, "and said we were the best group he ever heard. Hope he means it."[3]

Kent did mean it. He returned to the Top Ten Club the following night with his producer, Bert Kaempfert, an orchestra leader and songwriter who had made his name writing and recording easy listening and jazz-orientated records. Kent joined the group and Tony Sheridan onstage for a few songs, including 'Be-Bop-A-Lula', before introducing them to Kaempfert, who was impressed enough that he returned to the club a few nights later with his business partner, Alfred Schacht. "It was obvious to me that they were enormously talented," Kaempfert said in 1964, "but nobody – including the boys themselves – knew how to use that talent, or where it would lead them."[4]

Kaempfert returned to the Top Ten Club for a third time in June with his engineer, Karl Hinze, to discuss details of an upcoming recording session with the group. "The decision was made to make a demo record," Hinze recalled, "and that they should just play what they had in their repertoire."[5]

The contract that Lennon, McCartney, Harrison, and Best signed with Bert Kaempfert Produktion was for one year, from July 1st 1961 until June 30th 1962, but would be renewed automatically for another year unless terminated by either party in writing three months before expiration. It stipulated that Kaempfert would record at least four titles with the group or individual members, with at least two of them being recorded by the group as a whole.

The Beatles and Tony Sheridan's first session for Bert Kaempfert Produktion took place on June 22nd and 23rd at Friedrich-Ebert-Halle, a concert hall on Alter Postweg in Harburg, south of Hamburg. Karl Hinze set up a two-track Telefunken tape machine in a dressing room and placed two microphones on the stage. All he had to do was wait for the group to arrive, set up, and play, and record them live onto two-track stereo. No overdubs were recorded, although in some instances the tapes were edited.

The night before they were due to record, The Beatles and Sheridan played their regular weekday session at the Top Ten Club until 2am. Kaempfert went to collect them, and later recalled having to "tramp up these narrow stairs to a small attic-like room", where the group were "still in their bunks. ... The only other furniture in the room was a chair – with their clothes piled high on it".[6]

Once they'd arrived and set up at Friedrich-Ebert-Halle, The Beatles and Sheridan recorded 'My Bonnie' (in English and German), 'Why', 'The Saints', 'Nobody's Child', 'Cry For A Shadow' (a Harrison/Lennon instrumental), and 'Ain't She Sweet' (with Lennon on vocals). They were paid a flat fee of DM300 each for the sessions. This was a standard arrangement for the time. Lonnie Donegan, for example, was paid £3/10s for recording 'Rock Island Line'. "There were no royalties then," he recalled. "The big companies made their own recordings, employed their own staff, and hired musicians and singers on a musicians union fee basis."[7] (According to Hans Olof Gottfridsson's *Beatles Bop – Hamburg Days*, however, The Beatles received a five per cent royalty for records sold in German stores and two per cent on those sold through record clubs. The rate was lower for records sold outside Germany.)

While The Beatles were in Hamburg, an art-school friend of Lennon's, Bill Harry, had started up a local music paper, *Mersey Beat*. The first issue, published on July 6th 1961, featured an article by Lennon entitled 'Being A Short Diversion On The Origins Of Beatles'. The second issue had on its front page an article about the group's recent session with Kaempfert. As excited as The Beatles were about having made a record, they would have to wait a while until they heard it. 'My Bonnie' (German Intro) / 'The Saints' is listed as having been released in Germany on October 23rd, but it seems that at least a few advance copies crept out some time earlier than that. In August, Harrison wrote to Sutcliffe to ask if it was true that the single was being played on Hamburg jukeboxes. Apparently it was, but there is nothing in Polydor's archives to suggest an August release.

What happened next had a profound impact not just on The Beatles but also on pop music in general. In late October 1961, a young man by the name of Raymond Jones walked into the record department of North End Music Stores and asked for a copy of 'My Bonnie' by a local group, The Beatles. For years it was assumed that 'Raymond Jones' was really Brian Epstein's assistant,

Alistair Taylor, who at one point claimed to have made up the name simply because Epstein wouldn't stock a record unless he had a confirmed order. That was until music historian Spencer Leigh tracked down the real Raymond Jones to a small farm in Spain. Jones, it transpired, had heard about 'My Bonnie' through his then brother in law, Kenny Johnson, who played with Mark Peters & The Cyclones, and went to NEMS to order it. "Brian Epstein said to me, 'Who are they?'," he recalled, "and I said, 'They are the most fantastic group you will ever hear.'"[8]

It seems odd that Epstein would have claimed to have never heard of The Beatles as they were already big news on the local music scene. Moreover, NEMS stocked *Mersey Beat*, which they had appeared on the cover of twice, and sold tickets for the Operation Big Beat concert, tickets for which featured the group's name prominently. The Beatles themselves were frequent visitors to Epstein's shop – not that he would necessarily have known who they were – and played regularly at the nearby Cavern. As the manager of a busy record department, one might have expected Epstein to have kept abreast of the music scene, but neither he nor Taylor were particularly interested in pop music.

Whether he had heard of The Beatles or not, however, Epstein was a businessman, so when Jones asked for The Beatles' single he made it his business to track down them and the record. Shortly after Jones placed the order, Epstein and Taylor caught a lunchtime performance by the group at the Cavern. After the gig Epstein spoke to Harrison, who informed him that the record had only been issued in Germany. Taylor ordered 25 copies, which arrived in late November and reportedly sold out in a single day, leading him to order another 50.[9] In *A Cellarful Of Noise*, Epstein claimed to have sold over 100 copies of the single, but other sources have put the figure at 200 or more, which would be more in line with the popularity of a group that regularly packed out the Cavern and was promoted through Merseyside by Bob Wooler.

The simple act of Epstein ordering an obscure record issued only in Germany led to him managing The Beatles. One of his first duties was to try to secure a recording contract for the group with one of the four major British record companies, and at the same time try to extricate them from their arrangement with Bert Kaempfert Produktion.

Liberating The Beatles from Kaempfert was hardly difficult, as it required nothing more than a letter from the group stating their wish to terminate the agreement. Finding a major record company to sign them would prove to be considerably less straightforward. Although there were a lot of record labels to choose from, each of them was controlled by one of four companies: Decca, Pye, Philips, and EMI. At the time British record companies were only interested in acts willing to record cover versions of recent American hits. Britain was still looking to the USA for inspiration at this point, and getting a homegrown act to record a song that had already been a hit across the pond was seen as a sure-fire way of guaranteeing chart success in the UK – which is why Epstein had The Beatles perform so many cover versions during auditions. Lennon and McCartney might have wanted to record their own songs, but few A&R men of the time were interested in recording unproven songwriters. They wanted hits, and there was no guarantee that The Beatles could deliver.

While The Beatles were big in Liverpool, they meant little elsewhere. This was clearly something that Epstein needed to rectify, but his initial attempts at doing so appear somewhat clueless. All the major record companies were based in London, but rather than approach some of them with a good-quality demo tape – or even a copy of 'My Bonnie' – Epstein decided first of all to get in touch with Disker, the author of the *Liverpool Echo*'s record-review column.

Disker, aka Tony Barrow, was a London-based Liverpudlian who worked as a freelance journalist and wrote liner notes for Decca. He and Epstein met in London, where Epstein handed over an acetate of The Beatles recorded at the Cavern. Barrow was unimpressed by what he heard, and in any case wouldn't have reviewed it because it hadn't – and wouldn't ever be – released. He was, however, intrigued by the group. After meeting Epstein he called Decca's sales department and explained that one of their best customers had approached him about securing a record contract for a group he was managing. The sales department duly called the A&R department and suggested that it might be a good idea, for reasons of diplomacy, to offer The Beatles an audition.

This came as good news to Epstein who had, in the meantime, sent 'My Bonnie' and a copy of the Kaempfert contract to Ron White, General Marketing Manager of EMI Records. White replied on December 7th with a translation of the contract and informed Epstein that in order to terminate the agreement he must do so in writing three months before the end of the following June. He wrote again on December 18th after passing 'My Bonnie' on to a pair of EMI producers, Walley Ridley and Norman Newell, who were less than impressed with what they heard. As a result, White told Epstein, EMI was not interested in signing The Beatles.

Decca on the other hand had just established a new A&R department with its finger firmly on the pop pulse. The December 23rd edition of *Cash Box* magazine enthused about the appointment of a new A&R team headed led by Dick Rowe and also featuring Tony Meehan, formerly of The Shadows, both of whom were "more than capable of producing the kind of sound that makes for chart success". In reality, however, Rowe and his colleagues were no more aware of the sweeping changes that The Beatles were about to bring than anyone else. Rowe offered The Beatles an audition, but did so mostly just to keep Epstein happy. It certainly wasn't a priority, and in fact he left it to his assistant, Mike Smith, to go to see the group play at the Cavern on December 13th. "I was impressed by what I saw," Smith recalled, "and on the strength of their stage show and the reaction from their local fans, I had no hesitation in telling Brian that we'd fix an audition as soon as possible."[10]

The audition was set for January 1st 1962 (which at the time was not a public holiday in the UK). Having packed all of their gear into a battered old van, The Beatles drove the 200 miles from Liverpool to London through freezing snow on New Year's Eve. When they arrived at Decca's studio in Broadhurst Gardens, West Hampstead, The Beatles found that they needn't have brought their amplifiers and drum kit, as Decca insisted they work with in-house equipment. Dick Rowe was still on his Christmas break so Mike Smith took on production duties as The Beatles ran through 15 songs live in the studio. The session seemed to go well, and led Tony Barrow to report in the *Liverpool Echo* that Smith "thinks The Beatles are great" and "is convinced that his label will be able to put [them] to good use".[11] In fact, as Smith later admitted, "they were not good, and their personalities didn't come across".[12]

Nine days after the audition, Epstein decided to call Rowe's bluff by writing to tell him that "the Group have received an offer of a Recording Contract from another Company".[13] This seems rather unlikely, given the reaction he had from EMI, but perhaps Epstein was referring to the imminent British release, by Polydor, of 'My Bonnie'. In any case his bluff failed. Smith had his eye on another pop band, Brian Poole & The Tremeloes, and after careful consideration decided to sign them instead. While Rowe became known as The Man Who Turned Down The Beatles, the decision was actually Smith's, but as head of department Rowe shouldered the blame.

It's difficult to say whether or not Smith was right to reject The Beatles without now being able to hear The Tremeloes' audition tape. Most of The Beatles' Decca audition has since been issued, and while it's interesting to listen to it's no better than the recordings made with Bert Kaempfert or the test session the group would subsequently record for EMI. But then George Martin didn't sign The Beatles because he thought they were good musicians, but because of their personalities. And as Smith noted, the group's charisma wasn't apparent during the Decca audition. Perhaps, had they been less nervous, or had Smith shared Martin's sense of humour, The Beatles might have ended up signing to Decca instead.

At the same time as calling Rowe's bluff, Epstein also turned down the production services of Tony Meehan. Meehan had begun working for Decca as a trainee producer in October 1961, and was present when The Beatles auditioned for Decca. At one point Epstein considered asking Meehan to produce a Beatles single, but the former Shadows drummer turned up late for a meeting with him and showed little interest in the group, leading Epstein to look elsewhere. (He also made plans for the group to record an album with Bert Kaempfert. Sessions were booked for May 28th and 29th but these too came to nothing.)

Epstein's next move was to take a copy of the Decca audition tape to the HMV shop in Oxford Street, London, to have an acetate cut. The store was part of the EMI family of companies with a small disc-cutting suite on the third floor. The disc cutter that day was Jim Foy, and he liked what he heard. When he learnt that several of the songs had been written by the group, he suggested that Epstein visit the offices of Ardmore & Beechwood Ltd, a music-publishing subsidiary of EMI Records. Their offices just happened to be located on the top floor of the shop. General Manager Syd Coleman liked the group too, and offered to buy the rights to the Lennon/McCartney songs he'd just heard. Epstein must have been pleased that at last someone was interested, but nonetheless explained that what he really wanted was a recording contract. His luck was in. Coleman called the head of A&R at Parlophone Records (another EMI subsidiary), George Martin.

Martin wasn't available when Coleman called, but did agree to see Epstein on February 13th to discuss the group. Martin has since suggested that he wasn't overly impressed by what Epstein played him – the Decca audition tape – but was intrigued enough that he wanted to see the group.

Three months passed before Epstein heard again from Martin, and even then the producer needed to be pressed into action by Syd Coleman. Martin arranged to meet Epstein at EMI Studios, Abbey Road, London, on May 9th, and to Epstein's great delight offered The Beatles a recording contract, subject to an audition. This was good enough for Epstein, who immediately called his parents to tell them the news and sent telegrams to The Beatles (who were still in Hamburg) and Bill Harry of *Mersey Beat*.

On May 18th Martin applied to EMI's administration department for an 'Application For Artiste Contract'. A typed contract, post-dated to June 4th, was returned to Martin for his approval before being dispatched to Epstein. Then on Wednesday June 6th John Lennon, Paul McCartney, George Harrison, and Pete Best arrived at EMI Studios to attend what was both an audition and their first proper recording session. As was typical of the time, the session lasted for three hours, from 7–10pm. Martin initially left the job of overseeing the session to producer Ron Richards and engineer Norman Smith. The Beatles played a number of songs from their current repertoire before recording four of them: 'Besame Mucho', 'Love Me Do', 'PS I Love You', and 'Ask Me Why'. Neither Richards nor Smith was particularly impressed by the group or its equipment, but Smith knew a good song when he heard one. After hearing 'Love Me Do' he sent tape operator Chris Neal to find George Martin.

Martin stayed on for the rest of the session but was far from convinced. "I wasn't at all impressed with their music," he told *Mojo* magazine in March 2007. "They were crap. What made me sign them was their charisma. They had this wonderful quality that when you were there with them you felt enriched by their presence, and when they left you, you felt diminished."[14] Like many before him, Martin was captivated by The Beatles' personalities, and realised that, if he could capture their essence on record, he could turn them into stars. With the contract already drawn up and ready to sign, he seized the opportunity to sign The Beatles to Parlophone Records.

The contract The Beatles signed was the standard EMI deal of the time. It wasn't, as Martin later recalled, particularly fair, but "I had nothing to lose and Brian needed this record deal".[15] The contract lasted for one year, beginning June 4th 1962, and required the group to record eight songs per year. It included three one-year options and expired on June 5th 1966.

At the time a seven-inch vinyl single cost 6s/3d and an LP 30s/11d, but The Beatles would only receive one old penny per double-sided single. According to the contract, this would rise to a maximum royalty rate of one-and-a-half pence during the second and third option years, but Martin decided to increase it to two pence in June 1963 in response to The Beatles' incredible success. He put the idea to his boss, Len Wood, who suggested it would be all right as long as Martin could negotiate a new five-year option. "I said, 'No, you don't understand,'" Martin recalled. "'I don't want to ask for anything; I want to give it to them.' From that moment on I was considered a traitor within EMI."[16]

The stance EMI took says a lot about how record companies viewed their artists. They wanted to keep their artists hungry so that they would record more songs and therefore make more money for the company. If he'd had his way, Wood would have insisted on further options, which wasn't what Martin wanted. He made his objections known to Martin in no uncertain terms, declaring that, without further options, "all we have done is give away a fair chuck of company money".[17]

Regardless of Wood's concerns, EMI made a lot of money from The Beatles. The company's pre-tax profits during 1960–3 were five million pounds, and showed no sign of growth. But when The Beatles broke in America, profits soared. In 1964, EMI's profits rose by a massive 80 per cent to nine million pounds (£126 million today), and by 1966 were over £11 million. Most of this was directly attributable to the success of The Beatles and other NEMS-managed acts. In 1963 a run of Martin-produced hits held on to the Number 1 position on Britain's singles charts for 37 weeks. This came at a time when EMI's music division was one of the company's only subsidiaries to make a profit. (Other EMI subsidiaries, such as the domestic electrical appliances manufacturer Morphy Richards, were struggling.)

One penny – even one old penny – for every single sold doesn't sound bad when you consider that The Beatles sold hundreds of millions of records around the world. They did however have to sell 240 singles to generate one pound, which would be split five ways: NEMS took 25 per cent, leaving each Beatle with 18.75 per cent of one penny for each single sold. In the first quarter of their EMI contract, The Beatles earned just £130 in mechanical royalties from 'Love Me Do' on top of the standard Musicians' Union fee of £7.10s that EMI paid each musician for the recording session. Even a million-selling single such as 'She Loves You' brought in only £833 per Beatle – and there was tax to pay on that. And even after year-on-year increases, by 1967 they were still only earning £1,666 each for a million-seller.

The Beatles' contract with EMI might not sound particularly good, but it was all that was on offer. As Larry Page, who faced a similar struggle to find a deal for The Kinks, notes, "If you knock on every door and nobody's interested, when somebody actually opens the door, it's a good deal."[18] Epstein, like Page, had tried every record company in the country, and there was little else he could do beyond that. There were no independent labels back then, and even if Epstein had started one of his own there were no independent distributors to support him. He had no choice but to take the deal Martin offered him.

The only alternative to signing a standard EMI contract, which Epstein briefly considered, would have been to record The Beatles independently and then lease the recordings to any company that showed an interest. Epstein had previously approached Bert Kaempfert and Tony Meehan about the possibility of making independent records, but the idea seemed too costly. In the long term, however, it would have been more profitable and given The Beatles a lot more control over their music. It would have meant that the group (and NEMS) owned the masters, and would have put them in a better position to renegotiate their contract as their popularity grew. Lots of artists today –

including Paul McCartney – do exactly this. It might not have been standard practice during the early 1960s, but it wasn't unheard of. Joe Meek and Dave Clark both licensed their self-made recordings to record companies – in Clark's case, to EMI subsidiary Columbia.

Now that The Beatles had a recording contract with one of the four major British record companies – albeit a subsidiary label with little experience of pop music – it ought to have been relatively easy to have their records released in other countries. Epstein set his sights straightaway on America. If his Beatles were to be bigger than Elvis Presley, that was the market to crack. In January 1955, EMI had acquired a 95 per cent interest in Capitol Records for the sum of $8.5 million. The deal not only allowed EMI to issue Capitol recordings – by artists including Frank Sinatra and Nat 'King' Cole – outside America, but also gave Capitol first refusal on any recording made by EMI. But Capitol was under no obligation to sign artists it felt there was no market for – as was the case, much to the frustration of both Epstein and George Martin, with The Beatles.

Although EMI had purchased Capitol in part as an outlet for British recording artists, most of the trade was one-way. EMI enjoyed considerable success with Capitol artists, but few British records – with the exception of the independently produced 'Telstar' by The Tornados – had bothered the American charts. There was simply little demand for British records in the USA at that time. Until The Beatles emerged, British pop was seen as a pale imitation of its American counterpart.

'Love Me Do' was moderately successful in Britain, and 'Please Please Me' a Number 1 hit, but Capitol showed no interest in releasing either. Martin began to apply pressure within EMI, but was told that Capitol was an autonomous entity and that nothing could be done about it, despite the close links between the two companies. Fortunately, Martin had another avenue open to him. In August 1961 EMI had entered into a partnership with another American company, Transglobal. EMI did not officially own Transglobal, but did subsidise it, and was the company's only foreign client. Transglobal was formed to "assist record manufacturers and music publishers in the placement and acquisition of masters and copyrights in the USA, Europe, and throughout the world".[19]

Consequently, EMI transferred the rights of The Beatles' recordings to Transglobal in the hope that it could place them with another label. Atlantic Records rejected 'Please Please Me' as "inauthentic", but Vee-Jay Records, having recently achieved success with Frank Ifield's 'I Remember You', agreed to license it. Transglobal licensed 'Please Please Me' and 'Ask Me Why' to Vee-Jay for five years as of January 10th 1963, and gave the label first refusal on all subsequent Beatles recordings.

Vee-Jay issued 'Please Please Me' / 'Ask Me Why' on February 20th. It was not a huge success, perhaps justifying Capitol's decision to reject it. It did get some airplay on Chicago's WLS, and spent two weeks on the station's Top 40, but did little elsewhere, to the extent that fewer than 7,000 copies of the single were pressed. On May 6th Vee-Jay issued 'From Me To You' / 'Thank You Girl', which again failed to dent the national charts, but did perform slightly better than its predecessor, selling 22,125 copies over a ten-month period. It also achieved considerable airplay in the Los Angeles area. Things seemed to be looking up, but it wasn't to last.

Vee-Jay had begun to fall into financial difficulties, leading to the delay of its planned release of the *Please Please Me* LP, which was to be retitled *Introducing The Beatles*. Calvin Carter, head of A&R, told *Goldmine* magazine, "We had too many items in our catalogue already, and the distributors were complaining. So we eliminated some of these albums we were set to release, and The Beatles' album was one of them, because The Beatles just did not sell very well the first time around".[20]

Because of cash-flow problems, Vee-Jay hadn't sent Transglobal a royalty statement for several months. On July 24th, Transglobal wrote to Vee-Jay requesting an immediate statement and payment by return. The label failed to respond, although it was later revealed that it owed just $859 on sales of Beatles records. On August 8th Transglobal sent a telegram demanding Vee-Jay "immediately cease manufacture and distribution of any and all records containing performances of Frank Ifield and The Beatles".[21]

Transglobal considered this a termination of its agreement with Vee-Jay, but that didn't stop the label from issuing *Introducing The Beatles*. Vee-Jay no longer had the right to issue any recordings by Ifield or The Beatles, but carried on regardless, issuing no fewer than five albums using previously acquired masters. These included two Beatles albums, *Introducing The Beatles* and *Songs, Pictures And Stories Of The Fabulous Beatles*; two compilations of material by The Beatles and Frank Ifield, *Jolly What! The Beatles & Frank Ifield On Stage* and *The Beatles & Frank Ifield On Stage*; and a similar set called *The Beatles vs. The Four Seasons*. The situation became even more despicable when these sought-after albums were subsequently counterfeited, thereby cheating The Beatles out of further royalties.

Even before The Beatles had stepped on American soil, certain sections of the US music industry seemed to be prepared to cheat them out of royalties, break contracts, and risk litigation. Vee-Jay closed down its Chicago offices in an effort to avoid the bailiffs, but the situation didn't end there. A newly interested Capitol Records filed papers at the Circuit Court of Cook County, Illinois, on January 13th 1964. Two days later Transglobal joined in the action, followed by Beechwood Music Corporation and Ardmore & Beechwood Ltd. As the licensees of 'Love Me Do' and 'PS I Love You', they wanted to prohibit Vee-Jay from manufacturing records containing these titles.

All of this amounted to a ploy by Capitol to block Vee-Jay from selling Beatles records – and it worked. On January 16th Vee-Jay was ordered to stop manufacturing and distributing copies of *Introducing The Beatles*, which featured the songs administered by Beechwood Music Corporation and Ardmore & Beechwood Ltd. But the battle was not over yet. Vee-Jay appealed the ruling, and on February 5th was granted permission to restart manufacturing and distributing Beatles records providing they did not feature 'Love Me Do' and 'PS I Love You' – at least until March 19th, when Vee-Jay was again prohibited from selling Beatles records. Then on April 1st Vee-Jay signed a new agreement with Capitol that allowed the label to carry on selling the Beatles and Frank Ifield records it had previously issued under the Transglobal arrangement at a new royalty rate of nine cents per single, 11 cents per EP, 32 cents per mono LP, and 41 cents per stereo LP.

Vee-Jay paid Capitol a $300,000 advance against future royalties, and a further $60,000 licensing fee. Vee-Jay's total royalty payments to Capitol ended up at almost one million dollars, but this was set against gross profits of around five million dollars on the sale of Beatles albums and singles. And in a bizarre twist, Capitol had to pay Conrad Publishing Co, a Vee-Jay subsidiary, in order to use 'Thank You Girl' on *The Beatles' Second Album* because Conrad had already acquired the rights to license the song in America. Further legal action followed when Vee-Jay put out its 16 licensed Beatles songs with new album titles and cover artwork. Capitol considered this to be an infringement of its settlement agreement, and claimed that Vee-Jay was allowed only to issue records in the same form as had preceded the April 1st agreement. This time Vee-Jay won.

By then Capitol was beginning to reap the rewards of The Beatles' success. But in the meantime The Beatles' third US single, 'She Loves You' / 'I'll Get You', had been issued on September 16th 1963 by the much smaller Swan label, which was based in Philadelphia and best known for releasing Freddy Cannon's 'Palisades Park'. Like its predecessors, 'She Loves You' was (at least to begin with) an unmitigated flop, despite having been a massive hit in Britain. Neither Martin not Epstein could understand why The Beatles records weren't achieving the same success in America. "For God's sake, do something about this," Martin told Capitol. "These boys are breaking it, and they're going to be fantastic throughout the world."[22]

Capitol did eventually relent, but not without further internal resistance. The label's president, Alan Livingston, gave the job of listening to and deciding on the merits of EMI's new records to producer David Dexter. Dexter was Capitol's Dick Rowe – he heard nothing of merit in The Beatles and rejected them time and time again. But after the termination of Transglobal's initial agreement with Vee-Jay, Livingston, aware of The Beatles' success in the UK, began to reconsider Capitol's position.

Dexter was still sceptical. "They're a bunch of long-haired kids," he told Livingston. "They're nothing. Forget it."[23] Livingston didn't force the issue. He trusted Dexter's opinion and, as he later recalled, had "no interest in British product at that point" anyway.[24] In fairness, he had no real reason to. Several British acts, including Cliff Richard, had tried and failed to crack America, while between 1939 and 1962 only four British records – by Vera Lynn, Laurie London, Mr Acker Bilk, and The Tornadoes – had managed to reach the top of the US singles charts. America dominated popular culture and pop music, and there was no reason yet to suggest that The Beatles would break the mould, even if they had begun to achieve success in other parts of the world ('From Me To You' reached Number 2 in Israel, Number 3 in Ireland, Number 6 in Australia, and Number 10 in both Norway and Austria).

Even after Martin and Epstein convinced Capitol of The Beatles' worth, David Dexter vetoed the release of their fourth single, 'I Want To Hold Your Hand'. It took a personal call from Epstein to Alan Livingston to reverse the decision. When Livingston eventually took the trouble to listen to The Beatles, he liked them, and called Epstein back to tell him so. That in itself wasn't enough for Epstein, who, as Livingston recalled, said, "I'm not gonna let you have them unless you spend $40,000 to promote their first single." Such an outlay was "unheard of", according to Livingston, but "for whatever reason I said, 'OK, we'll do it,' and the deal was made".[25]

He was right to, as 'I Want To Hold Your Hand' became the group's first American Number 1 hit in early 1964. Swept along on a wave of Beatlemania, 'She Loves You' at last started to sell, too. It entered the US charts on January 25th, and by March 21st had reached the top spot, marking an incredible turnaround in The Beatles' fortunes. In less than a year, the group had gone from being virtually unknown to becoming America's biggest pop sensation.

A lot changed in the four years between the signing of The Beatles' contract with EMI in 1962 and its expiry in June 1966. Exactly how many millions of records the group sold globally during that time is difficult to calculate. By August 1965, The Beatles were reported to have sold 100 million singles and 25 million albums worldwide. Two years later, EMI announced that if world sales were converted into singles (one album being equal to six singles) then they would total 200 million. By 1972, The Beatles' total international sales stood, according to *Billboard*, at a world-record 545 million.

Whatever the figure, The Beatles sold a lot of records. Their reward for shifting this mountain of vinyl was somewhere between one and two pence per single record sold. By the end of 1963, The Beatles' British record retail sales amounted to £6.25 million,[26] yet royalties paid to the group for the first quarter of 1964 were only £104,550. In *Northern Songs*, Brian Southall claims that, from 1962–6, The Beatles were paid a total of £419,743 in royalties by EMI for worldwide sales. Anything sold outside of the UK was calculated at half of the UK royalty rate. Had EMI paid the full royalty rate on all American and overseas sales it would have cost them an extra £227,475. It's no wonder, then, that The Beatles and Epstein were unhappy with the terms of the contract. The Beatles were making a lot of money for EMI, which put their manager in a strong position when it came to renegotiating their contract. It was simple, really: all he had to do was suggest that The Beatles would stop writing and recording until EMI gave in to his demands. EMI wouldn't have wanted to stop the goose laying its golden eggs – but then nor would Epstein, who continued to take his 25 per cent share. For him, it was better to keep what they had than risk losing everything. As George Martin later noted, Epstein would have struggled to negotiate a new contract any earlier "without jeopardising the success that was going on".[27]

At the time, nobody – even Epstein – knew how long The Beatles might last. No one could have foreseen that the group's success would stretch into the 21st century. They might just as easily have been a flash in the pan. But by 1966 Epstein knew he was in a good position to renegotiate. EMI had already doubled The Beatles' royalty rate after a year, which alerted Epstein to the influence he and the group had. EMI was obviously keen to keep the group on its books. The income they were generating for the company, even early on, was substantial. Just two years after issuing The Beatles' first single, EMI announced a 12 per cent rise in sales, while during the same period Capitol's sales rose 17 per cent – again largely due to The Beatles' success. According to a report in *Time* magazine, EMI's total sales for 1963–4 totalled $265 million, which the company's chairman, Sir Joseph Lockwood, put down to "the outstanding success everywhere of The Beatles".[28]

Epstein might have been in a fantastic position but, as Peter Brown, later Executive Director of Apple Corps, noted, this was entirely new territory. "It's standard procedure now in the music business that you have a contract and the moment you have a big hit you go back and renegotiate," Brown said. "But we were doing things for the first time, so what [Epstein] did was he waited till the end of the contract and then renegotiated for infinitely better terms and made them retrospective."[29]

By June 1966, The Beatles were the greatest entertainment sensation the world had ever seen. Everything they touched turned to gold. Epstein could in theory have started a bidding war and signed The Beatles to whoever offered the best deal. It wouldn't have been the first time an act had changed labels for more money: in 1958 The Everly Brothers moved from Cadence Records to Warner Bros in a reported million-dollar deal, while Allen Klein had managed to squeeze a cool $1.25 million out of Decca when it came to renegotiating The Rolling Stones' deal with the label. By now the tables had turned, and Epstein had the upper hand.

Contract negotiations would normally be conducted with the label manager, but George Martin was sidetracked, and was perhaps too close to the group to broker a new deal with them. "EMI negotiated directly with Brian," he recalled. "They did renegotiate and they did get a much better deal but [Epstein] was negotiating with one arm tied behind his back."[30]

Epstein had a phalanx of solicitors and senior managers at his disposal, but took with him only Geoffrey Ellis, the Chief Executive of NEMS Enterprises, to his first meeting with EMI. Ellis later recalled that he and Epstein were up against "six or eight company officials" as well as the chairman, Sir Joseph Lockwood.[31] Epstein was better prepared for the second meeting, for which he brought along his accountant, Jim Isherwood, and solicitor, David Jacobs. Epstein's demands were simple: an improved royalty rate and fewer deductions for packaging. Even so, the negotiations took months. EMI weren't about to give anything away. A new deal wasn't agreed until January 1967, by which time The Beatles had been working without a contract for six months.

The Beatles knew all along that their initial deal with EMI only lasted a few years. As early as August 22nd 1964, at a press conference in Vancouver, Canada, they had taken to giving typically ambivalent responses to queries about their contract. "Is it a long-term contract?" a reporter asked. "I think it expires next year or something like that," Lennon replied. "Will you remain with [EMI]?" the reporter continued. "Depends what they say," Lennon said, to which Harrison added, "Who knows?"

The group's ambivalent attitude appears to have stayed with them. Incredibly, The Beatles provided EMI with new material even while not technically under contract. As the negotiations progressed, The Beatles issued *Revolver*, the Capitol LP *Yesterday ... And Today*, and the 'Eleanor Rigby' / 'Yellow Submarine' single, all of which seems extraordinary. What was Epstein thinking? What was EMI thinking? What were The Beatles thinking? Either side could have walked away from the negotiating table at any point. EMI had the most to lose. Had their contract not been renewed, The Beatles could have signed for whomever they liked – and for more money. And even if they'd moved labels they could have taken George Martin with them, since by then he had become a freelance record producer.

Everybody knew *Revolver* was something special. It could have been a fantastic bargaining chip, but Epstein simply gave it away. Unbelievably, The Beatles gave it to EMI while not under contract and with no idea of what they might receive in return. Why didn't Epstein simply refuse to hand over the album until the contract negotiations were resolved? The Beatles were certainly unhappy with the way EMI treated them, so giving the label a new album at this point – and such an important one at that – makes little sense.

Perhaps Epstein and The Beatles felt an obligation to meet the insatiable appetite for Beatles records. Unlike today's bands, 1960s groups were expected to issue two albums and four singles each year. "It was important to keep it out there in the market place," notes Larry Page, who managed The Kinks and The Troggs. "In those days you were putting out two or three albums a year, and as many singles, because you had to keep that market going."[32]

There was an even greater demand for new product in America, where Capitol issued 11 albums between 1964 and '66. Epstein and Martin knew it was important to keep The Beatles in the charts. "Brian Epstein and I worked out a plan in which we tried – not always successfully – to release a new Beatles single every three months," Martin recalled. "I was always saying to The Beatles, 'I want another hit, come on, give me another hit' and they always responded. ... Right from the earliest days they never failed."[33]

Nobody knew how long The Beatles were going to last. As well as being asked continually about how much money they had made, The Beatles were forever being probed on how long they could sustain their popularity. "Do you have any fears that your public will eventually get tired of you and move onto a new favourite?" asked CBS reporter Josh Darsa in 1963. "Depends on how long it takes them to get tired, don't it," Lennon replied. "It's stupid to worry about things like that," McCartney added. "It could happen tomorrow ... [or] we could have quite a run."[34]

Epstein knew that by maintaining the album/tour/album cycle he could keep the group in the limelight and maintain their popularity. The press was always on the lookout for stories about The Beatles, and as ever found it easier to file negative reports than positive ones. The Beatles had broken every record in the book. Surely the only way for them to go now was down? To counter these sorts of suggestions, the group had to keep their momentum going. Issuing a new album, even without a written contract, ensured that the gap between records was kept as small as possible. It didn't matter who they were – The Beatles or Herman's Hermits – they had to keep churning out hits.

Epstein didn't have to play by the rules. Had he applied the same maverick approach to his management of The Beatles as they did to their songwriting and recording he might have struck better deals. He was a gentleman businessman, but that didn't mean that he couldn't be difficult to deal with. EMI referred to retail prices when discussing royalty rates – the price it charged its dealers. Epstein, however, referred to the wholesale price, which for EMI was about 20 per cent lower. Len Wood, who was part of the EMI negotiating team, struggled to make Epstein understand the difference. Ten per cent of the retail price would have been a good deal, but ten per cent of the wholesale price was no more than average. Wood suggested that they both refer to the dealer price, but Epstein was adamant that the contract employed the word 'wholesale'.

Was Epstein being awkward or just plain stupid? As an ex-manager of a record shop he would have known the difference between wholesale, dealer, and retail prices. He also had a reputation for accuracy and detail. Had he simply made a mistake, but found himself unable to admit it? What he wanted, and got, was a percentage of what EMI charged its dealers – a percentage of what EMI knew to be the retail price. "I knew what he meant," Wood recalled, "but he would call it wholesale and he couldn't be shifted."[35]

The Beatles' new nine-year contract stipulated that they should record seventy songs – the equivalent of five LPs – over a five-year period. For the remaining four years The Beatles, either as a group or as individuals, were not tied to a minimum number of songs. Furthermore, they were not allowed to re-record any of the songs they recorded for EMI (unless the re-recording was for EMI) for ten years following the end of the contract. In return, they would receive ten per cent of the British wholesale price of their records, or 15 per cent on sales of more than 100,000 singles, 10,000 EPs, or 30,000 LPs. For Record Club and low-price sales the royalty was lowered to five per cent. In the USA, Canada, and Mexico, The Beatles received ten per cent of the wholesale price of their records, which increased to 17.5 per cent on sales of more than 100,000 singles and 30,000 albums. They were also given the right to approve the producer of their recordings and control artwork and tracklistings, and would receive quarterly statements showing sales figures and royalties due.

EMI, meanwhile, reserved the right to delete records from its catalogue, but could not reissue them without permission during the nine-year term. The label also deducted 15 per cent to cover returned or damaged records or demonstration copies, less a 15 per cent allowance for packaging of LPs, which was taken off the dealer price of the first 30,000 albums. Finally, although The Beatles still owed United Artists one further soundtrack LP for the American market under the terms of a deal agreed in late 1963 (discussed elsewhere), EMI requested that the group's management seek to obtain a release from this commitment if possible.

The January 1967 contract came as a considerable improvement on what preceded it, and better rewarded The Beatles for their work – and their value to EMI. The first record issued after it was agreed was 'Penny Lane' / 'Strawberry Fields Forever' (which also bore the distinction of being the first Beatles single not to reach Number 1 in the UK). It was followed by the landmark release of *Sgt Pepper's Lonely Hearts Club Band*.

Whatever changes the contract made had little impact on Brian Epstein, however, as he died eight months after signing it, on August 27th 1967. The Beatles were devastated. And although they didn't realise it at the time,

Epstein's death would have significant consequences on their business dealings. "We didn't know what to do," Harrison later admitted. "We suddenly had to find out how to be responsible for ourselves."[36]

Rather than drift aimlessly without a manager, The Beatles decided to manage their own affairs. They had in fact already taken a first step towards this when, on April 19th 1967, they signed a deed of partnership to become The Beatles & co, in order to restructure their finances for tax purposes. In the months following Epstein's death they made plans to establish their own company, independent of NEMS. The new venture would be called Apple, but as Lennon explained it had its roots in another of Epstein's business plans. "Apple was conceived by the Epsteins and NEMS before we took over," he recalled. "They were going to set it up, sell 80 per cent to the public, and we were going to be the 20 per cent minority shareholders, with five per cent each, and God knows who else running it. And that was the idea for Apple. But I dunno, it got screwed up somehow."[37]

Apple Corps was meant to simplify things, but like so many of The Beatles' business dealings it got complicated. Although the group had formed a partnership, they weren't all bound to the same management. By 1968 the group had appointed John Eastman – brother of McCartney's soon-to-be-wife, Linda – to negotiate contracts on their behalf. Lennon, Harrison, and Starr understandably saw this as favouring McCartney.

It was at around the same time that Lennon discovered that Apple Corps was losing vast amounts of money at an alarming rate. "This accountant, Stephen Maltz, sent me a letter one day," he recalled, "saying 'You're in chaos. You're losing money. There is so much a week going out of Apple.'"[38] On January 13th 1969 Lennon revealed to *Disc & Music Echo* that The Beatles were having financial difficulties. The interview was read with interest by a certain Allen Klein.

Klein had longed to manage The Beatles since first hearing 'I Want To Hold Your Hand' in 1964, and saw this as the perfect opportunity to get a piece of the action. A 1956 graduate of Upsala College, East Orange, New Jersey, Klein had started out as a bookkeeper. He worked for several show business figures, and developed a knack for auditing record companies for his clients, often to their advantage. In 1967 he bought Cameo Records, a Philadelphia label that specialised in teen-orientated pop. With the label came the rights to music by The Animals, Herman's Hermits, Bobby Rydell, and Chubby Checker.

Klein then turned his attention to The Rolling Stones, who had been having problems with their manager, Andrew Loog Oldham. Mick Jagger was impressed by Klein (at least to begin with) and recommended his services to The Beatles.

Lennon and Klein first met on December 11th 1968 during the filming of The Rolling Stones' *Rock'n'Roll Circus*. "I didn't know what to make of him," Lennon recalled. "We just shook hands."[39] Klein had tried to contact Lennon after reading the *Disc & Music Echo* interview, but found it difficult to get to him. In the end he used his network of contacts to put the word out that he wanted to speak to Lennon, and could solve his financial problems. Tony Calder, cofounder of Immediate Records, told Derek Taylor, Apple's press officer, who in turn informed Apple Corps Executive Director Peter Brown.

On January 27th 1969 Klein flew to London and met with Lennon at the Dorchester Hotel. "John had made a public statement about the financial problems that Apple had and, from the statement, I was aware of what I had been already aware of," Klein explained. "So I called him and asked if I could help."[40] Lennon was impressed by Klein's sharp-talking, streetwise attitude and knowledge of the music industry, and asked him to manage his personal affairs. He sent EMI's Sir Joseph Lockwood a note to say, "Dear Sir Joe, I've asked Allen Klein to look after my things"[41] – and with that, The Beatles began to split. The Eastmans represented McCartney; Klein took on the interests of Lennon, Harrison, and Starr.

On February 3rd, after several meetings, Klein's Cameo-Parkway company was appointed to investigate the financial affairs of The Beatles and their businesses. Unlike Epstein, who took 25 per cent of everything, Klein offered his services for 20 per cent of their increased business only. While McCartney had appeared content with the 25 per cent cut taken by Epstein, he was less happy with Klein's demands. "I remember being at Olympic Studios one evening when I think we were supposed to be doing something on *Abbey Road*," McCartney recalled. "We all showed up, ready to record, and Allen Klein showed up too." His bandmates asked him to sign the deal with Klein, but McCartney wasn't keen. "We're a big act," he told them, "The Beatles. He'll take 15 per cent." But for "some strange reason", as McCartney put it, the others insisted that Klein should get 20 per cent. "You've got to sign, now or never," they told him. Not wanting to be pushed into a corner, McCartney said, "Right, that's it, I'm not signing now."[42]

On March 12th 1969, the day after McCartney announced that he was to marry Linda Eastman, Klein instructed Goodman Myers & co "to investigate and analyse the expenditure of The Beatles and co, Apple, Apple Electronics Limited, and Apple Publishing Limited on entertainment, travelling, insurance, legal and professional charges and other expenditure".[43]

After purging Apple Corps of unnecessary management and staff, Klein turned his attention to acquiring NEMS and renegotiating The Beatles' contract with EMI. Ownership of NEMS had passed to Epstein's mother, Queenie, with his brother Clive appointed as manager. Although it no longer provided any essential services for The Beatles, NEMS still siphoned off 25 per cent of their gross income.

John Eastman had already been appointed as a business adviser to the group and had begun negotiations with NEMS over a proposed buyout. "You can't get the money out of the company to pay estate taxes," he told Clive Epstein, "so why don't we buy NEMS and you'll get the money as a capital gain?"[44] Eastman offered Epstein a million pounds for the company. Even The Beatles didn't have that sort of money available, so they approached EMI for an advance. EMI agreed to the loan, but Allen Klein objected to it, reasoning that in order to pay back the advance The Beatles would need to earn at least twice the amount, thus doubling the cost of purchasing NEMS.

Although the Epsteins were keen to maintain control of NEMS, they were also required to pay £500,000 in death duties. In late 1967 Clive Epstein received an offer from the Triumph Investment Trust to buy NEMS. He didn't want to sell the company – which had been renamed Nemperor – as he had plans to expand its operations and, like his brother, felt an obligation to the artists it represented. But by the end of 1968 he was rumoured to have entered takeover talks with the British Lion Film Company. "I never really felt that NEMS could continue as it was, once Brian died," Clive explained, "because we had nobody with Brian's imagination, expect possibly [Robert] Stigwood, and between Stigwood and The Beatles there was quite a clash. ... I was little more than a caretaker."[45] (Stigwood, a booking agent, had bought into NEMS in January 1967.)

Clive Epstein received a second offer from Triumph Investment Trust chairman Leonard Richenberg in late 1968, but initially rejected it because he'd already been made a similar offer by The Beatles, whom he believed had a moral right to the company. He gave the group three weeks to close the deal, but, after they failed to meet the deadline, reopened talks with Triumph, to whom he eventually sold NEMS on February 17th 1969 for a reported £750,000 (paid in a mixture of cash and stock).

According to John Eastman, The Beatles' failure to secure NEMS was the fault of Allen Klein. "Klein was the fly in the ointment," he said. "True, I wanted NEMS to assume complete liability for taxes, but that wasn't important. Klein showed up in the meantime and said, 'Forget it, I'll get you NEMS for nothing because the Epsteins owe you money.'"[46] Clive Epstein however has suggested that Eastman was to blame. The two men spent a week negotiating but, according to Epstein, Eastman insisted on so many conditions, warranties, and clauses that the deal fell through.[47]

With NEMS now in the hands of Triumph, it fell to Klein to begin negotiations. He told Triumph's Richenberg that NEMS owed The Beatles a considerable sum of money from concert tours dating back to 1966, but that they would be prepared to write it off if Triumph agreed to forego the 25 per cent cut of the group's earnings it had acquired from NEMS. Perhaps unsurprisingly, this tactic also failed.

Klein's next move was to send a note signed by all four Beatles to Sir Joseph Lockwood, informing him that the group's royalties should now be paid directly to Apple (not to NEMS). Klein's ploy was well timed, as EMI was about to release £1.4 million in royalties, but it too failed. Rather than risk upsetting either The Beatles or NEMS-Triumph, Lockwood decided to defer payment to either party until the situation was resolved. Triumph responded by applying to the British High Courts to have the money frozen. On April 2nd, Mr Justice Buckley decided that, since EMI had already refused to release the money, it should be deposited with Lloyd's Bank until the matter could be settled. The time had come for some serious negotiating.

Klein, The Beatles, and Richenberg arranged to meet at Apple's Savile Row offices to hammer out an agreement in late 1968. Triumph agreed to surrender all contractual rights concerning The Beatles plus its entitlement to 25 per cent of their mechanical royalties for the remainder of their contract, for £750,000 and 25 per cent of the £1.4 million royalty payment being held by EMI. Triumph also received £50,000 for its 23 per cent of The Beatles' Subafilms company, and five per cent of the group's gross record royalties from 1972–6. They also received an option on the four-and-a-half per cent of Northern Songs shares owned by NEMS, which were valued at £355,000. Triumph also bought The Beatles' ten per cent share in NEMS for £266,000 in Triumph Investment Trust stock, which was then valued (pre tax) at £420,000.

Although Klein hadn't been able to buy NEMS, he had freed the group from its clutches – but at a cost. According to John Eastman the deal with Triumph had cost more than £1.5 million, which was a lot more than The Beatles could originally have bought NEMS for. Eastman also suggested that Klein's intimations that NEMS had acted improperly were unfounded, and that his mishandling of the situation forced The Beatles into accepting a deal with Triumph. If the five per cent of The Beatles' gross record royalties from 1972–6 is taken into account, Eastman's assertion that the deal cost the group more than £1.5 million is probably right. What is clear too, however, is that The Beatles might have acquired NEMS for a fraction of the final cost to them had they not been split over management issues.

As negotiations with NEMS-Triumph continued, Klein also decided to try to increase The Beatles' record royalties. The group's financial situation was, he told them, potentially hazardous. The best way to alleviate this situation, he said, was "to negotiate a new recording arrangement with EMI".[48] A meeting on May 7th with The Beatles (minus Ringo Starr, who was busy on the set of *The Magic Christian*), Yoko Ono, Sir Joseph Lockwood, Len Wood, and Ken East (another EMI executive) came to nothing, as the label was not prepared to discuss the issue for as long as the NEMS claim was outstanding. But once that situation was resolved, negotiations began in earnest.

Since re-signing to EMI, The Beatles had worked hard to fulfil their contractual obligations. They had issued a string of hit singles; a double EP, *Magical Mystery Tour*; the *Yellow Submarine* soundtrack album; and two LPs – one of which was a double set containing 30 songs, almost half the number they were required to record under the terms of their current contract. The release of *The Beatles* in November 1968 was so successful that it pushed EMI's overall share of the record market up from 28 per cent to around 40 per cent, and accounted for £900,000 in retail sales. (Decca and Pye each held 12 per cent of the market; Polydor ten per cent; and Philips and CBS five per cent.)

Like Epstein before him, Klein had the upper hand in negotiations with EMI, even if he was unlike Epstein in character. He was certainly out to cut the best possible deal, for which he had a very good incentive: he only collected his 20 per cent commission if he was able to generate an increase in the group's income. Furthermore, he needed to prove to Lennon, Harrison, and Starr that he really was as good as he said he was, as they were not yet convinced.

Since The Beatles were close to meeting their commitment to EMI, Klein demanded the company increase the group's royalties. Otherwise, he said, there would be no new Beatles records. Klein maintained this position through months of negotiations with EMI in London and Capitol in Los Angeles. His persistence paid off. When the new deal was concluded in September it improved considerably on the contract Epstein had agreed in 1966. Under the new terms, The Beatles would supply EMI with two albums per year (whether as a group or as individuals) until 1976. In return, EMI increased the group's royalty to 25 per cent of the wholesale US price. Providing the group delivered two albums per year, all new albums would earn 58 cents until 1972, which would increase to 72 cents thereafter. Reissues of old material would earn 50 cents to begin with, but would also rise to 72 cents in 1972.

Klein also secured Apple the right to manufacture and sell Beatles records in America. Although EMI retained ownership of The Beatles' recordings, Capitol would now manufacture records on Apple's behalf. Apple's profit came from the difference between the price it paid Capitol to manufacture the records and the amount the label charged retailers to buy them. For the first time The Beatles had control over the way their records were manufactured and sold, not just the way they looked (as had been the case under their old contract with EMI).

By 1971 The Beatles entire back catalogue was available on Apple Records. The reissue campaign, masterminded by Allan Steckler, not only ensured that all of the group's singles and albums were available, but reinforced the connection between Apple and The Beatles.

Klein had achieved a major success. Not only had he increased The Beatles' royalty rate to unprecedented levels, he had also secured a regular income for Apple until at least 1976. He had also dramatically improved The Beatles' income. When McCartney took Lennon, Harrison, Starr, and Apple Corps to court in 1971, it was revealed that the group's earnings had increased from £850,000 for the year ending March 31st 1969 to £1.7 million for the nine-month period ending December 31st 1971. In 1970, meanwhile, the group made £4.4 million – not bad considering that, in the 28 months before Klein became their manager, The Beatles brought in a combined net profit of just £122,000.

The Beatles might have split in 1970, but that didn't stop EMI from issuing new compilation albums – or stop The Beatles from finessing their contract by demanding further royalty increases. Once the group's contract with EMI ended in January 1976, the label was free to exploit The Beatles' catalogue to its heart's content.

In March 1976, EMI reissued all 22 of The Beatles' British singles, plus a new pairing of 'Yesterday' and 'I Should Have Known Better'. The reissue campaign was a huge success. At one point all 22 were in the UK Top 100 at the same time, while 'Yesterday' peaked at Number 8. In the USA, Capitol took a slightly different approach by issuing a 'new' single, 'Got To Get You Into My Life' / 'Helter Skelter', which hit Number 7. The release was intended to promote Capitol's new Beatles compilation album, *Rock'n'Roll Music*, which was the first of several compilation volumes of the late 1970s and early 1980s. It too was a success, peaking at Number 2 in the USA and Number 11 in the UK.

The desire to keep pumping out Beatles product was as strong as ever, particularly as it kept on selling. The group's back catalogue was so valuable a commodity that EMI established a Beatles Committee to oversee its marketing. Although EMI had some of the world's most popular groups on its books – including Pink Floyd and Queen – these artists weren't producing albums at the rate The Beatles once had. Several years could pass between new releases by major acts. EMI needed to fill its release schedule with albums by big names, and The Beatles fitted the bill perfectly.

An important member of the Beatles Committee was Bob Mercer, who was brought in by EMI to give new impetus to its marketing strategies. Mercer was assisted by the advertising agency Collet Dickenson Pierce, with whom he worked to create new product to boost EMI's revenue. Collet Dickenson Pierce suggested that EMI develop a line of television-advertised compilations similar to those being issued by K-Tel. This was a first for EMI – as, one assumes, was employing an advertising agency to develop its catalogue. EMI launched its line of television-advertised albums with The Beach Boys' *20 Golden Greats*, which topped the British charts for ten weeks. Buoyed by its success, and that of *Rock'n'roll Music*, Capitol decided to reactivate an old scheme: a Beatles live album. *The Beatles At The Hollywood Bowl* had been scheduled for release by Capitol during the mid 1960s, but the group vetoed it. Now that their contract had expired, however, Capitol was able to dig out the old tapes, pay George Martin to remix them, and issue the results as a 'new' Beatles album.

At about the same time, Lingasong Records made plans to issue a record of The Beatles performing at the Star-Club, taped in 1962. The group sought to prevent its release but failed. It might well have been the case that Capitol took note of this dispute – and Apple's unsuccessful attempts at preventing the release – when deciding to put out *The Beatles At The Hollywood Bowl*. The label certainly brought the album's release date forward, but claimed this was because certain radio stations in America were playing unauthorised bootleg recordings of The Beatles in advance of the official release. Like *Rock'n'Roll Music*, *The Beatles At The Hollywood Bowl* sold well and reached Number 2 in the charts. In Britain, it was the first Beatles album to be included in EMI's new television-advertised campaign, and reached Number 1.

Capitol continued to exploit The Beatles' catalogue in much the same way as it had during the 1960s. There was only so much material to recycle, however, and sales diminished as the compilations became increasingly tacky. The October 1977 release of a two-disc *Love Songs* album reached Number 24 in the USA and Number 7 in the UK. Capitol followed it with a *Rarities* collection, which peaked at Number 21 in 1980. In the UK, EMI had included its own *Rarities* set in a 1977 boxed-set of all of The Beatles' British albums before later issuing it separately. The UK-only album *Beatles Ballads* reached Number 17 in 1980, but 1982's Capitol-conceived *Reel Music* failed to chart at all. (It did, however, make it to Number 19 in America.)

Apple and The Beatles still had the right to veto anything they didn't like, which makes one wonder why they sanctioned these increasingly tawdry releases. Having previously been so protective of their image, the group appeared to have lost interest in the way they were being presented. The greatest band in the world was, all of a sudden, allowing its back catalogue to be endlessly repackaged in a string of poorly conceived and executed albums.

Perhaps The Beatles had grown complacent and assumed that EMI was maintaining the same high standards they'd set in the 1960s. Speaking to Denis Elsas in 1974, Lennon complained about the use of fake stereo for the 'red' and 'blue' compilations, *The Beatles 1962–1966* and *The Beatles 1967–1970*. "I just thought, or rather presumed, they'd just copy them off the masters and put them out," he said. "I didn't even listen to it until it was out and I took it back and listened to it and I played it and it was embarrassing! Some fool had tried to make it stereo and it didn't work!"

The days when The Beatles would agonise over every detail of an album had long since passed. These albums looked like they'd been put together over a very liquid lunch. But it was no good presuming that somebody else would get it right. If The Beatles wanted to maintain their own high standards they had to take control of what was being issued in their name, which was one reason why they'd started Apple Corps in the first place. But whether The Beatles had become complacent of not, the compilations just kept on coming.

The next, *20 Greatest Hits* (1983), peaked at Number 10 in Britain but stalled at Number 50 in America. The tracklistings varied in an effort to best represent the singles issued in each territory. One might have expected the album to have been more successful in the USA because it was a bigger market, but *20 Greatest Hits* just didn't connect with the American record-buying public.

Despite having split up ten years earlier, The Beatles were still capable of selling a lot of records. But as far as the group was concerned, they weren't being properly reimbursed for them. Allen Klein's trick of auditing record company accounts to uncover often-unintentional mistakes had turned into a major business over the years. In 1979 The Beatles took EMI to court claiming that they'd been cheated of millions of pounds in royalties. Apple's claim, filed on April 30th and May 1st in state courts in Los Angeles and New York, addressed inconsistencies in the auditing of royalties. The Beatles initially claimed they were owed $2.3 million plus interest, but this amount was drastically reduced on the first day of the hearing.

This wasn't the first time the group had complained about being underpaid. In 1975 their accountants, Prager and Fenton, established that Capitol owed the group $3.2 million in royalties for the period 1969–73. The dispute centred on a clause that Klein had inserted into the Beatles contract that gave the group a 25 per cent royalty increase as long as the last two Beatles albums – or solo albums by group members – issued before August 31st 1972 sold a minimum of half a million copies by the time their contract with EMI expired (January 26th 1976). The trouble was that Lennon's 1972 album *Some Time In New York City* had sold only 200,000 copies. It was left to The Beatles' lawyers to argue that *Some Time* wasn't a Beatles album because it featured Yoko Ono.

Litigation dragged on until 1982, at which point The Beatles installed new lawyers, who claimed that Capitol's underpayment amounted to fraud. They also filed a similar suit against EMI in Britain over royalties owed to them outside America. Although the High Court could find no evidence of fraud, Mr Justice Gibson decreed that "many matters need investigating", and that EMI should have paid royalties on at least 85 per cent of net sales. No money was awarded, but a complete court-supervised audit was ordered. Unsatisfied with the court-supervised audit, Apple attempted to initiate one of its own, but Mr Justice Gibson dismissed it in the London High Courts on March 26th 1986. As EMI had already agreed to pay Apple $2.8 million in 1984 for past royalties and interest, Gibson ruled that Apple only be allowed to audit overseas accounts.

The Beatles were split on how to proceed. They had two options: accept EMI/Capitol's offer of eight million dollars and an increased royalty of $1.20 per album, or confront the company in court. McCartney was keen to accept EMI's offer but Harrison, Starr, and Ono wanted their day in court. The situation was further complicated by the fact that The Beatles had since fallen out with Allen Klein, which meant that there was every possibility he might testify against them. (Klein had in fact tried to delay the release of *Some Time In New York City* because he knew it wouldn't hit the sales target of half a million copies.)

Moreover, by taking EMI to court The Beatles also faced negative publicity. EMI could easily turn around and reveal that the men who had preached peace, love, and global harmony during the 1960s were now unwilling to accept an offer of $8 million and an increased royalty rate (which, contractually, they were never entitled to). Litigation also cost the group a great deal of money – up to $75,000 per month in legal fees, according to John Eastman. Suing EMI cost Apple as much as its annual income, and led the company, in 1985, to report a loss for the first time.

The case took a slightly odd turn when an audit uncovered the fact that McCartney had accepted a higher royalty rate on Beatles records when he re-signed with Capitol/EMI (after a brief stint with Columbia) in 1985, which he hadn't told the rest of the group about. It wasn't the first time that he had acted in his own interests without informing the others. In 1969 he had managed to acquire some extra shares in Northern Songs at a time when The Beatles as a whole were trying, unsuccessfully, to buy the company – much to Lennon's annoyance.

McCartney's latest deal didn't go down well with Harrison, Starr, and Ono, who promptly filed a lawsuit against him in the New York State Supreme Court. Quite how and why this deal ever reached the courts is a mystery. McCartney's lawyers freely admitted that he had taken a higher cut as an incentive to re-sign. But as the agreement had no effect on royalty payments to the other three Beatles, what was there to sue over? Harrison, Starr, and Ono claimed that the increased royalty rate should have been paid to Apple and not directly to McCartney.

This dispute with Harrison, Starr, and Ono is probably what led McCartney to drop out of the case against EMI/Capitol. Apple (Harrison, Starr, and Ono) fought on. They claimed that Capitol had designated a large number of albums as promotional copies, for which The Beatles received no payment, but which had then somehow found their way to wholesalers. Apple claimed $30 million in compensation and a further $50 million in punitive damages, and also requested the rights to all of The Beatles' master tapes and records.

The battle then moved to the New York district court. On April 8th 1986 Judge Dontzin dismissed seven of the long-standing claims brought by Apple against EMI/Capitol, but allowed all other outstanding charges to proceed. In August, he ruled that Apple was entitled to backdate their claim for unpaid royalties to 1969, and raise their claim for compensatory and punitive damages ($80 million clearly not being enough).

The lawsuit dragged on into 1987. In September Apple instigated two further actions: a $40 million lawsuit that alleged that, because a previous action had yet to be settled, EMI/Capitol had deliberately delayed the release of Beatles albums on compact disc. (EMI put the delay down to its unhappiness over having to pay a royalty on each CD sold to Sony and Philips, the inventors of the new format.) Apple also claimed that it was being charged too much for the packaging of CDs. The second lawsuit concerned "improper exploitation of The Beatles' image and goodwill" by Nike, which had used 'Revolution' in a television advert. Little headway was made over the next year, although on May 17th 1988 a four-judge Appellate Division of the New York State Supreme Court ruled that Apple could resume its $80 million case against EMI/Capitol for "fraud and illegal conversion".

Not everything went Apple's way. The same four judges also ruled that a previous ruling by Judge Dontzin, in which he had dismissed claims by Apple that EMI should declare escalated royalty payments under agreements dated 1969 and 1973, should stand. Four days later Apple's claim for $40 million in compensation and punitive damages for EMI's delaying until 1987 of the release of Beatles CDs and underpayment of CD royalties was dismissed. If Harrison, Starr, and Ono wished to pursue this claim they would have to do so through the English courts.

After a decade of litigation, delays, allegations, and legal arguments, EMI formally settled the case on both sides of the Atlantic. EMI Music issued a press release that gave little away except for the fact that both parties had kissed and made up. "The parties have agreed," it read, "as a specific term of the settlement, that neither they nor their representatives or advisors will be permitted to make any comment or statement regarding the settlement other than appears in this announcement."[49] Although there was no official confirmation, the resulting payout was rumoured to be an "eight-figure sum" – the $80 million The Beatles had sued for. The group had spent more than five million pounds in legal fees but got a pretty good return. The terms of the contract meant that The Beatles' CDs all sold for premium prices, which meant that retailers would have to charge £29.99 in 1994 for double CDs such as *The Beatles*. An EMI spokesman confirmed that Apple had stipulated that EMI "must charge retailers the maximum possible amount for Beatles albums".[50]

One might have assumed that, after a decade of battling their way through the courts on both sides of the Atlantic, Apple might have had enough. On the contrary, Apple went to court over EMI's plans to release the 'red' and 'blue' compilation albums, *The Beatles 1962–1966* and *The Beatles 1967–1970*, on CD without permission. Since The Beatles' 1967 contract gave them the right to approve and control artwork and tracklistings, EMI was on shaky ground. Apple won the case when a High Court judge ruled that they had artistic control of their output – which it soon took full advantage of.

In 1994 EMI/Capitol issued *Live At The BBC*, the first new Apple album for almost 20 years. It was a smash hit on both sides of the Atlantic, selling 350,000 copies in the UK and 750,000 in the USA on its first week of release. It topped the British albums chart and peaked at Number 3 on *Billboard*, clearing the way for perhaps the biggest and most successful campaign of The Beatles' post-break-up career.

The Beatles' *Anthology* project had been in and out of production since the early 1970s. It was originally intended as a visual history of the group entitled *The Long And Winding Road* and an album of outtakes entitled *Sessions*, but in its final form amounted to three triple-albums, two hit singles, multi-part VHS and DVD boxed sets, and a lavish book by Weidenfeld & Nicolson.

The film element of the *Anthology* project went through several revisions before it eventually emerged as a television series and video/DVD boxed set. Apple formed a new Apple Productions division to oversee it and to record new interviews with the surviving Beatles. It also commissioned promo videos for the two 'new' Beatles songs, 'Free As A Bird' and 'Real Love', the opening tracks on the first and second volumes of the *Anthology* series, for which George Martin and Geoff Emerick compiled six CDs of previously unheard material.

The *Anthology* albums were tremendously successful. American sales of the first volume were reportedly worth between $60–70 million, while the television rights also brought in a lot of cash. ABC Television paid $20 million and the UK's ITV network a further five million pounds for the broadcast rights. By July 1995, the series had been sold to 110 channels around the world, and was eventually screened in 94 countries.

Anthology 1 was issued in Britain on November 20th 1995 and more than matched the success of the previous year's *Live At The BBC* by selling a record 450,000 copies on its first day of release. In the USA it sold 855,797 copies in its first week on sale and was the first Beatles album to officially debut at Number 1 on the *Billboard* 200. Within six weeks, it had sold three million copies in the USA alone. Released in March 1996, *Anthology 2* wasn't quite as successful as its predecessor, but it did still enter the *Billboard* 200 at Number 1 and spent a total of 22 consecutive weeks on the chart. Its total US sales to date are in the region of 1.7 million copies. The album hit Number 1 in Britain, too, but sold a more modest 78,000 copies in its first week.

Anthology 3 completed a seven-month hat trick of Number 1 debuts on *Billboard*. Not only had the series put The Beatles back at the top of the charts for the first time in years, it had also broken all of the group's previous sales-records. The Beatles sold more albums in 1996 than they had during any single year in the 1960s. By December 1996, the first two *Anthology* albums had achieved total combined sales of 13 million. Sales of *Anthology 3* – which stalled at Number 4 in the UK after selling 52,000 copies in its first week – were slower, and meant that the series as a whole didn't quite reach Apple's target of 20 million sales. Overall, however, global sales of Beatles records in the year 1996 were said to have brought in £490 million.

Despite the phenomenal success of the project, Apple found itself back in the High Courts. The *Anthology* albums include early recordings featuring Pete Best, Stuart Sutcliffe, and others. Apple might have been awash with cash following its recent victory over EMI but appeared to have been less than generous when it came to paying former bandmembers for their performances. Colin Hanton, who played drums on both of the Quarry Men recordings used on *Anthology 1*, was allegedly offered only £500 to begin with. Apple increased the offer to £800, but Hanton sued for a bigger slice of the pie. So too did Pauline Sutcliffe, Stuart Sutcliffe's sister, who felt Apple's original offer of £800,000 for her brother's performances to be insufficient.

In December 2000 The Beatles issued *1*, which proved to be even more successful than the *Anthology* series. Its title was perfect. Not only did it include all of The Beatles' US and UK Number 1 hit singles but it also topped the charts itself in 35 countries. It sold more than 3.6 million copies in its first week on sale, and after three weeks had amassed worldwide sales of 12 million, making it the fastest-selling album of all time and the biggest-selling album of the 21st century to date. This vast success came despite the fact that the album itself was little more than an amalgamation of the US and UK versions of *20 Greatest Hits*, released by Capitol in 1982.

In Britain, *1* was The Beatles' 15th chart-topping album. It sold 319,000 copies in its first week, and by July 2003 had been certified as eight-times platinum for sales of more than 2.4 million copies in the UK. In the USA it held onto the Number 1 spot for eight weeks and spent a total of 197 weeks on the *Billboard* 200. By April 2005 it had been given the Diamond Award by the RIAA in recognition of sales of 10 million copies.

One might have expected all concerned to be happy with such incredible commercial success, but they weren't. Further litigation between The Beatles and EMI commenced in 2003. Two years earlier, Apple had begun new negotiations with EMI over royalties and payments, but these had reached an impasse. According to Neil Aspinall, who was Apple's Chief Executive at the time, "We have tried to reach a settlement through good faith negotiations and regret that our efforts have been in vain. Despite very clear provisions in our contracts, EMI persist in ignoring their obligations and duty to account fairly and with transparency."[51] So in December 2005 Apple took EMI to court in a replay of their 1979 lawsuit, claiming that The Beatles were owed £30 million in unpaid royalties. EMI tried to bring a halt to proceedings, but on August 23rd 2005 New York State Supreme Court Justice Moskowitz withheld the company's request that the fraud and breach of contract suit be dismissed.

Apple claimed once again that EMI/Capitol had incorrectly classified copies of The Beatles' records as destroyed, damaged, or promotional but sold them anyway. (A similar allegation had previously been levelled at Allen Klein, who was indicted on charges of evading $125,000 in federal income taxes gained from selling promotional records.) Apple also alleged that EMI/Capitol underreported the number of units sold, and, as in 1979, claimed an unspecified amount in punitive damages (to be determined at the trial) and sought the rights to the group's recordings.

EMI claimed in its defence to have "no problem" with the suit, a spokesman said on *BBC News* in December 2005, as "we like to have full financial transparency with our artists. Sometimes there are differences of opinion, not least when record contracts are complex. Sometimes artists resort to the courts or mediation, and 99 times out of 100 the problems are resolved amicably for a small proportion of the claim. EMI has offered to go to mediation but, sadly, Apple rejected that offer."

On April 11th 2007, Neil Aspinall resigned as chief executive of Apple. He was replaced by Jeff Jones, a former executive vice president at Sony BMG. EMI settled its royalties dispute with Apple two days after Aspinall resigned, clearing the way for negotiations over a new royalties deal to cover online downloads. Rumours that The Beatles' back catalogue would soon become available for download were all over the media in 2007. By the end of the year, solo works by all four Beatles were available to buy online. The only recordings not available for download were those made by The Beatles for EMI between 1962–70. But in November 2007 Paul McCartney suggested that Apple's lawyers were working on the small print, which implies that 2008 should see the release of The Beatles' back catalogue in a digital format for the first time.

Only A Northern Song

Publishing, royalties, and the value of a song

Playboy: "There's been some dispute among your fans and critics, about whether you're primarily entertainers or musicians... or perhaps neither. What's your own opinion?"
John: "We're money-makers first; then we're entertainers."[1]

f Brian Epstein had put as much effort into securing Lennon and McCartney a decent publishing deal as he did in getting them a standard recording contract, they would all have made a lot more money. But Epstein had no more of an idea about publishing than he did about any other aspect of pop management. It hadn't occurred to him that music publishers were just as important as – if not more important than – A&R managers. Without songs, there were no hit records; without hit records, no stars; no stars, no business. Music publishers were, in fact, the kings of the music business.

If Epstein knew anything about publishing it was that it had something to do with the sheet music he sold in his shop. Lennon and McCartney were no wiser. "John and I didn't know you could own songs," McCartney later told Beatles biographer Miles. "We thought they just existed in the air. ... A song not being a physical object, we couldn't see how it was possible to have a copyright in it. And therefore, with great glee, publishers saw us coming."[2]

If Lennon and McCartney had no concept of copyright, they couldn't possibly understand its value, much less work out whether or not they were being taken for a ride. And not only were they naive to the concept of copyrights, they were probably baffled by the percentages they were offered in return for their work, too. Receiving a 50 per cent cut of something might sound pretty good, but could, if taken at the wrong stage in proceedings, end up losing a lot of money.

Neither Lennon and McCartney nor Epstein had even considered the possibility that they might need someone to publish the songs they were so eager to record. Most pop stars of the day wouldn't have encountered this problem, as they tended to rely on professional songwriters for their material, so had little contact with the world of music publishing. It was the A&R manager's responsibility to work with publishers and source new songs for their acts to record. So when Lennon and McCartney insisted on recording their own songs, rather than those offered by George Martin, they became the exception to the rule.

When The Beatles recorded 'Love Me Do' and 'PS I Love You', Epstein was faced with a problem: the songs had to be published. Fortunately George

Martin was on hand to offer advice and alerted Epstein to the fact that EMI had its own publishing company – the very same company, in fact, that had put Epstein into contact with him in the first place: Ardmore & Beechwood Ltd. Epstein offered 'Love Me Do' and 'PS I Love You' to Ardmore & Beechwood partly in return for them having put him in contact with Martin and partly because he knew that he had to act quickly or risk delaying the release of The Beatles' first single.

Epstein already had a relationship with Ardmore & Beechwood Ltd through Syd Coleman, who had been impressed enough by what he heard of the group's Decca audition tape to suggest he meet with Martin. Coleman was keen to publish the two new Lennon/McCartney songs Epstein offered him. The two men met at Coleman's Oxford Street office in London and agreed terms on September 7th 1962, with Epstein signing the contract on Lennon and McCartney's behalf.

At the time Epstein hadn't even signed a contract with The Beatles himself, so had no authority to strike a deal with Coleman. It's also unlikely that he did much more than inform them of his actions or that Lennon and McCartney were shown the contract or given legal advice before Epstein signed.

In return for an advance of one shilling, Ardmore & Beechwood Ltd received full, worldwide copyright of 'Love Me Do' and 'PS I Love You'. In return, the songwriters received 50 per cent of all royalties from the sale of records in Britain and overseas, plus 50 per cent of money brought in by the Performing Right Society (PRS), which collects royalties for its members whenever their music is performed in public, broadcast, or transmitted. (The PRS divides the income it collects equally between publisher and artist, as long as they are members of the PRS. There are two similar societies in the USA – the American Society Of Composers, Authors, And Publishers [ASCAP] and Broadcast Music Inc [BMI] – that provide the same service.)

The contract Epstein signed with Ardmore & Beechwood Ltd was standard for the time. An established songwriter such as McCartney would today expect a much higher royalty – perhaps even an 80/20 split in his favour – or might own the publishing outright but pay a publisher to administer it. But in the 1960s, a 50/50 split was the norm. Publishers did more than collect money from the record company and the Performing Right Society. They were also responsible for issuing licences for songs used in films and television, the publication of sheet music, and most importantly for promoting and marketing the song. This last point was of utmost importance. Without adequate publicity and promotion there was little chance of 'Love Me Do' becoming a hit.

Although EMI placed advertisements for 'Love Me Do' in the music papers, the company wasn't prepared to spend a lot of time or money on a relatively unknown group. This wasn't helped by the fact that EMI's press department was run by Arthur Muxlow, a traditionalist who could see no potential in a group of long-haired kids from Liverpool. At the time, EMI placed greater emphases on getting records heard than on paying for advertisements in the print media. "It has long been EMI Records Limited's contention that records must be heard by the largest possible audience to compete successfully with vigorous competition," read a statement in the August 10th 1963 edition of *Cash Box*.

Getting records played on the radio was paramount – and it meant a lot to The Beatles, too. "First hearing 'Love Me Do' on the radio sent me shivery all over," George Harrison later recalled. "It was the best buzz of all time."[3] The song was also played on both Radio Luxembourg and on the BBC, as well as featuring in a session The Beatles recorded for the Corporation. The group also performed 'Love Me Do' twice on Granada Television's *People And Places* show, on October 17th and 29th 1962.

Ardmore & Beechwood Ltd did little to promote the record. This was partly because EMI just wasn't very interested in music publishing, which it saw as little more than a sideline that happened to generate a little extra income without much effort. Had they worked harder, Ardmore & Beechwood might have secured further Lennon/McCartney copyrights, and what followed might have been very different. But EMI didn't start to recognise the value of publishing until the 1970s (when it acquired a number of publishers, including Columbia Pictures' SBK Entertainment and Filmtrax divisions).

Although he wasn't getting much help from either EMI or Ardmore & Beechwood Ltd, there were things Epstein could do on his own to help the record. As the manager of a chain of chart-return shops, he would have known how the charts were complied – and how to influence them. It wasn't unheard of for managers and record companies to manipulate the charts to benefit their artists. The payola scandal that rocked America in the 1950s showed just how far record companies were prepared to go to get their records played on the radio, and it took a while for things to change. According to Larry Page, it was common for managers to buy up copies of their artist's records. "I used to have bloody teams of people all over the country," he later revealed. "You load the shops up and then you empty the shops. And I think everybody was doing it in those days."[4]

Whether or not Epstein helped 'Love Me Do' into the charts has never been proved. Rumour has it that he ordered 10,000 copies of 'Love Me Do' for NEMS. According to John Lennon, however, he didn't: "Everybody down south thought, 'Ah-ha, he's buying them himself or he's just fiddling the charts.' But he wasn't."[5]

Lennon might have been right. Had Epstein ordered 10,000 copies of 'Love Me Do', Liverpool would probably still be flooded with mint copies of the single. Perhaps he returned the unsold stock to EMI: once The Beatles became famous the company was hardly likely to say no. But then Epstein didn't actually need to sell any records to hype 'Love Me Do' into the charts. In those days, the charts were complied by telephoning a small sample of chart-return shops and asking for sales figures. All Epstein had to do was claim to have sold more copies of the single than he had. Ultimately, without access to NEMS's accounts or EMI's order books, there is no way of knowing if Epstein bought 10,000 copies of the single or not.

'Love Me Do' had an erratic journey through the UK charts before it eventually landed at Number 17. Unhappy with the way Ardmore & Beechwood had handled the record, Epstein asked George Martin for advice on finding a new publisher for the forthcoming 'Please Please Me'. "He said he thought he'd go to Hill & Range," Martin recalled. "I said, 'don't do that, that's silly ... you'll be just another little fish in a big pond."[6] Instead, Martin suggested three names, one of whom was Dick James.

James wasn't Epstein's first port of call, but he had decided against working with Francis, Day & Hunter on principal after being kept waiting during a meeting. James had only recently started his own business, having previously been a singer and then a songwriter. But he was primed to impress Epstein, having heard all about The Beatles from Martin, and been told by his son, Stephen, that it would be a good idea to sign them.

James's enthusiasm about 'Please Please Me' had a positive effect on Epstein, who told the publisher that, if the record reached Number 1, he could expect a long-term agreement. James immediately began working his contacts. His first call was to Philip Jones, the producer of ABC TV's new light-entertainment show *Thank Your Lucky Stars*. "I played him 'Please Please Me' over the phone," he recalled. Epstein was "a bit taken aback by this very direct sort of approach", but it worked: Jones booked The Beatles for the show.[7]

Dick James Music published both sides of The Beatles' second single, 'Please Please Me' / 'Ask Me Why'. He offered the standard ten per cent royalty on the A-side, with a 15/85 split on the mechanical copyright for the B-side. All royalties were to be paid directly to Epstein, care of NEMS Enterprises.

October 1st 1962 was a busy day for both Epstein and The Beatles. Besides signing the group to a five-year management contract, Epstein also agreed a three-year songwriting deal with Lennon and McCartney. With the Ardmore & Beechwood deal in the bag, he'd been rushed into drawing up a new contract to cover their income from songwriting – something he'd completely failed to consider beforehand. Under this three-year deal, royalties from songwriting would be split 50/50 with any publisher – except for Ardmore & Beechwood – that he signed them to. Lennon and McCartney would supply 18 songs, either together or as individuals, during the three-year period from February 28th 1963, and, of course, Epstein would take his 25 per cent off the top.

The Beatles were booked to appear on the January 19th edition of *Thank Your Lucky Stars,* during which they performed their new single for the first time on national television. The performance did in Britain what their spot on *The Ed Sullivan Show* would do a year later in America, turning them into overnight stars and sending their single to the top of the charts – or at least to the top of the *New Musical Express* chart. The single only reached Number 2 in the *Record*

Retailer chart, but did top the magazine's most-played songs listing, which suggests it to have been as popular with broadcasters as it was with the public. Every time a DJ played 'Please Please Me', Lennon and McCartney received a royalty. A turntable hit like that could be as lucrative as physical sales.

James's role in taking 'Please Please Me' to Number 1 was integral to The Beatles' success. Without his contacts they would have found it very difficult – if not impossible – to get on national television. His reward for what took little more than a telephone call was an exclusive contract to publish Lennon and McCartney's songs: a contract that would make him a multi-millionaire.

Lennon and McCartney came along at just the right time. James had published a few copyrights, including songs by George Martin, but was struggling to establish himself. Unlike Epstein, James knew the value of copyrights, and realised that a hit song would earn him money year after year. What he didn't know, however, was whether he would be able to keep hold of Lennon and McCartney and their future copyrights. As such, he devised an arrangement that he thought they might find more attractive to them than the standard publishing deal – and a revolutionary one at that.

"I suggested to them that what I would like to do is set up a company in which they, John, Paul, and Brian, would make 50 per cent, and my company would make 50 per cent," James recalled. Lennon and McCartney would be signed exclusively to the new company, and would split their 50 per cent share of the equity as they saw fit. James also had another important suggestion. "I said that, considering you're all from the north, perhaps it should be called Northern Songs."[8]

James's decision to form a new company was driven less by generosity than by a desire to hold on to valuable copyrights. He was just as keen to keep Epstein, Lennon, and McCartney happy as he was to hang on to his 50 per cent of the copyrights. According to Larry Page, James "would have lost Lennon and McCartney there and then" had he tried to maintain a standard agreement. Forming Northern Songs, says Page, allowed James to "keep them happy – and keep a piece of it".[9]

What was also true, however, was that James had Epstein under his control from the moment The Beatles' manager walked into his office. Epstein knew nothing about publishing, or about the value of the copyrights he, Lennon, and McCartney were about to sign over. By offering the songwriters and their manager shares in the company, James could exert even greater control over them. From the moment they signed the contract they were obliged to supply him with a set number of songs. But James did more than just control their songwriting output: he took charge of where their songs were issued, who could record them, how much money they made, and, most importantly, who owned them.

That's not to suggest that James was The Beatles' puppet master. In fact, according to Larry Page, he wasn't even in overall control himself. James's partner in Dick James Music and Northern Songs was his lawyer, Charles Silver. "He was a little city man," says Page. "And he really was the man controlling everything. Dick James would open the post in the morning, and read it over to Charles Silver in the city, and Charles would tell him exactly how to answer every letter and what to do throughout the day."[10]

Forming Northern Songs was a bold move, since neither James nor his adviser could be sure that Lennon and McCartney would be any more than a flash in the pan. The only assets the company had were Lennon and McCartney's untested songwriting talents. It wasn't as if they had a string of hits to their name. But what had James to lose? Dick James Music was struggling, and if Lennon and McCartney weren't the songwriting geniuses Epstein claimed they were, all he had to absorb were the start-up costs of the new company. The alternative was much worse: if Lennon/McCartney proved to be the greatest songwriting partnership since Leiber & Stoller and James lost them he would also lose a fortune.

James was taking a risk, but not a big one. George Martin, for one, was impressed by the scheme. "This was a radical idea, and Brian thought it was wonderful," he recalled. "It was unusual [at the time] for artists to write their own material … because the record business and publishing business in those days was a very rigid establishment and publishers were very strong. If you wrote a song and you had it published by somebody you expected to get 50 per cent of the performing rights, 50 per cent of mechanicals, and 10 per cent of sheet music, and that was the kind of standard contract. So you were giving away a lot. In today's terms if you accepted that you'd be considered to be an idiot. But that was the deal and it was against that background that The Beatles were signed to Dick James's companies."[11]

James recognised the brilliance of his idea and wasted no time in forming the company. Within weeks of his suggestion, Epstein had agreed to the proposition. "Before the end of February [1963] we had incorporated Northern Songs," he recalled, adding that Dick James Music was allowed to hold on to 'Please Please Me' in recognition of having done "such a fine job" on it.[12]

Like Epstein, James was no slouch when it came to making money. If he could form one company to publish songs by Lennon/McCartney then why not do the same for NEMS's other acts? The idea was too good to use just once, so James formulated a similar – although ultimately less profitable – company with Gerry Marsden called Pacermusic. He also formed a company with Epstein, Jaep Music Co, to handle publishing for the rest of the NEMS roster. Formed on May 17th 1963, Jaep published George Harrison's first composition, 'Don't Bother Me', and Alma Cogan's 'I Knew Right Away'.

The Northern Songs deal looked good on paper since very few songwriters owned their own publishing company. But then very few pop stars wrote their own songs. Lennon and McCartney only owned shares in the company: they didn't own it outright. The Beatles were breaking new ground and making the rules up as they went along. As co-owners of the company, Lennon and McCartney would still receive their earnings from copyrights, as well as company dividends, a share of the publishers' rights, and tax breaks. They were understandably impressed. "We said to them, 'Can we have our own company?'" McCartney recalled. "They said, 'Yeah.' We said, 'Our own?' They said, 'Yeah, you can. You're great. This is what we're going to do now.' So we really thought that meant 100 per cent owned. But of course, it turned out to be 49 per cent to me, John, and Brian and 51 per cent to Dick James and Charles Silver."[13]

In fact, Lennon and McCartney ended up owning considerably less than 49 per cent of Northern Songs. Not content with taking 25 per cent of their income from songwriting, Epstein also took ten 'B' shares in their new company. This was a shrewd move. Epstein's existing contract with Lennon and McCartney was for three years, but with a stake in Northern Songs he was guaranteed an income from their songwriting for as long as he remained a shareholder. He could, if he wanted, sell them – or acquire more shares. But the lion's share went to Dick James and Charles Silver, who owned 49 'A' shares in the company. This left Lennon and McCartney with 39 shares between them, of which Lennon was assigned 19 and McCartney 20.

Furthermore, Dick James Music was appointed to administer Northern Songs, for which it took ten per cent of the gross receipts. This meant that for every £1,000 earned by Lennon and McCartney's songs, DJM took £100. The remaining £900 was split 50/50. Income from mechanical royalties (record sales) and publishing as well as from the PRS was also split 50/50. Lennon and McCartney received ten per cent of sheet music sales, which was paid directly to NEMS Enterprises.

As The Beatles' fame grew, James began setting up publishing companies in other countries. He formed Maclen Music Inc in America, Northern Songs (Pty) Ltd in Australia, and Northern Songs SARL in France. Although Lennon and McCartney owned shares in these companies, the deal for overseas publishing royalties was similar to the deal offered by record companies – which amounted to a smaller slice of the income. At the time it was standard practice for the overseas company to take a 50 per cent administration fee and then transfer the remaining 50 per cent back to Britain. It was from this 50 per cent that the songwriters received their 50 per cent – which meant in practice that Lennon and McCartney received 25 per cent of the income from overseas publishing.

Unlike Epstein, who always consulted a lawyer before committing himself to a deal, Lennon and McCartney were given no legal advice before agreeing to form Northern Songs. "Brian was at the house with a lawyer-type guy, but nobody said to us, 'This is your lawyer and he's representing your interests in this thing,'" McCartney recalled in 1997's *Many Years From Now*. "We just showed up, got out the car, went into this dark little house, and we just signed this thing, not really knowing what it was at all about, that we were signing our rights away for our songs. [And] that is virtually the contract I'm still under!"[14]

Like many musicians, The Beatles relied on their manager to oversee their business arrangements, but they were also keen to learn as much as they could about the music industry. George Harrison was particularly inquisitive. Helen Shapiro, whom The Beatles supported on their first national tour, later described Harrison as "the most professionally intelligent" member of the group and "the keenest to know all the mechanics of the music industry". But Shapiro didn't have a huge amount of information to impart – she was after all only 14 when she first topped the British charts in 1961. "I was way out of my depth much of the time," she admitted, "because I don't get involved in royalties and stuff like that. I leave that to managers and record producers and the businessmen."[15]

Trusting your manager was one thing, but having to sign complicated contracts while all around you was chaos was quite another. As Pete Townshend of The Who later put it, "Can you imagine actually trying to sit down in the middle of a tour and explain a very complex bit of tax law to somebody as stoned as Keith [Moon] and I used to be most of the time, or as thick as Roger [Daltrey] used to make himself out to be?"[16] If Townshend was struggling, how were any of The Beatles supposed to cope?

Lennon and McCartney's publishing deal might have been draconian, unfair, and loaded in James's favour, but at the time they were probably more than happy with it. Most pop stars aspired to little more than a nice suit, a flashy car and, if they were very lucky, their first house. How many of Lennon and McCartney's peers could count a publishing company among their assets?

They were also fortunate that James was struggling to stay in business. Had he been more successful he might not have thought of forming a new company. As it turned out he was hungry for success in case Dick James Music failed, so worked The Beatles' copyrights for all their worth. James did more than sit back and watch the money roll in. He actively promoted Lennon and McCartney's songs, encouraging other recording artists and record producers to record them and thereby generate income from royalties. As Derek Taylor recalled: "Dick James was a good workmanlike publisher who wasn't [yet] rich like Chappell, so he worked those copyrights like buggery."[17]

Lennon and McCartney might not originally have been aware of the huge sums of money they could earn from songwriting, but by the middle of 1963 they must have felt like Midas. In 1963, during The Beatles' first package tour of the UK, they were asked by producer Norrie Paramor to write a song for Helen Shapiro. Paramor rejected the resulting 'Misery', but that didn't matter. The song was quickly recorded by another singer on the same tour, Kenny Lynch, and issued by EMI's HMV subsidiary.

It didn't take long for other A&R managers to catch on to the Lennon/McCartney phenomenon. The market quickly became flooded with versions of their songs. Duffy Power recorded 'I Saw Her Standing There', as did Johnny Halliday; Dick Rivers cut another version of 'Misery'; Del Shannon scored a minor American hit with 'From Me To You'; The Kestrels tackled 'There's A Place', 'Please Please Me', and 'All My Loving'; and Bobby Sansom gave the public his reading of 'There's A Place'. These cover versions were not only a valuable source of income, but they promoted The Beatles' own records, too. EMI couldn't release every single Beatles album track as a single even if it wanted to. But a hit cover of a Lennon/McCartney song promoted the original recording as much as it did the artist that covered it. Generating two sources of income from one product was a neat and very profitable trick.

Epstein wasn't slow to catch on to this either. He used Lennon/McCartney songs to launch several of his new acts. Billy J. Kramer debuted with 'Do You Want To Know A Secret', The Fourmost with 'Hello Little Girl', and Cilla Black with 'Love Of The Loved'. Since Lennon and McCartney had already written over 100 songs, Epstein had a ready supply of hits to draw on, from which he reaped the benefits twice: firstly as manager of the recording artist, and secondly by way of his share in Northern Songs. There was no way he could lose.

The Beatles scored hit after hit not just in the singles and albums charts but in the sheet music charts, too. 'Please Please Me' topped the *Record Retailer* sheet music chart in February 1963, while in May 'From Me To You' made it to Number 4. The popularity of songs had, prior to November 14th 1952, been measured by sales of sheet music. Although sheet-music sales decreased as more people began to buy records, the *New Musical Express* continued to publish a sheet music chart until February 1965. With the number of hits Lennon/McCartney were having with The Beatles and other artists, the income from this side of the business would have been considerable.

Within two years of signing Lennon and McCartney, James had built a nice little publishing empire. In April 1965, he was interviewed for *The Beatles Book* and enthused about the number of Lennon/McCartney copyrights being exploited. "Our latest survey showed 1,920 different money-making units of a Beatle song in the world," he explained, drawing on his 'bible': a book containing details of every known recording of a Lennon/McCartney song. "Take a song like 'A Hard Day's Night'. Its release in Britain on record is one moneymaking unit. Its release in America another ... it then earns dollars. Pesetas, drachmas, francs – each counts separately."[18]

James clearly knew the value of Lennon and McCartney's work, even if he was a little cagey about the amounts involved. "You can't value a song," he said. "You could say two million pounds ... but no, you can't be accurate with a song. I'd rather have this talent of John and Paul and George than several thousand feet of factory space, though."[19] That much was obvious. By comparison to running a factory, his overheads were minimal and he had nothing to manufacture. Copyrights are intangible, but the money kept rolling in and would continue to do so for as long as Lennon/McCartney songs were being recorded and played on the radio.

If James had A&R managers and record companies falling over themselves to record Lennon/McCartney songs, the same could not be said of the songwriters' American publishers. Capitol Records had been slow to realise The Beatles' potential, and its lack of enthusiasm for the group was mirrored by its publishing subsidiary, Beechwood.

Having been assigned the rights to 'Love Me Do' and 'PS I Love You', Beechwood wholeheartedly failed to exploit them. While Maclen Music Inc worked Lennon and McCartney's copyrights for all they were worth, Beechwood did nothing. "There was a lot of aggravation between Capitol and The Beatles so I had no instructions from anybody to exploit their songs," recalled Beechwood employee Sam Taylor. "We didn't work the two songs, didn't do a thing with them."[20]

Northern Songs on the other hand made huge profits. In its first six months the company made £17,000 (or around £250,000 today), which almost doubled over the next six. The forecast for 1964–5 was for profits to soar to £500,000. Northern Songs was performing so well in fact that its owners decided to list it on the London Stock Market.

The idea was probably Charles Silver's. As the accountant and financial brains behind Northern Songs, he would have known that floating Northern Songs on the London Stock Market would considerably reduce the company's tax bill. At the time The Beatles were paying tax at a rate of 83 per cent; according to *Time* magazine, they were making so much money that their tax contributions helped to balance Britain's shaky finances. The report quotes Board Of Trade president (and later Prime Minister) Edward Heath as admitting, "The Beatles have boosted our reserves."[21]

In an attempt to ease Lennon and McCartney's tax burden, it was decided that Northern Songs should be restructured, with a quarter of the company's five million shares to be sold on the Stock Market. The remaining shares were split between James and Silver (937,500 each), Lennon and McCartney (750,000 each), Harrison and Starr (40,000 each), and NEMS (375,000). This was just as unique a move as James's original idea to form a company to publish a pair of unknown songwriters. "There was no precedent for what The Beatles did," recalled Mitch Murray, the composer of 'How Do You Do It'. "They had already done what nobody had done before by conquering America, so anything was possible for them."[22]

In February 1965, each of the shareholders sold a quarter of their holdings in return for a percentage of the sale price of 7s/9d per share. Investors were required to buy a minimum of 200 shares at a value of £39, which would have put them out of the reach of most fans desperate to own a piece of The Beatles. As songwriter Bill Martin put it, "We couldn't afford a cup of coffee, let alone shares."[23] At the point of floatation, Northern Songs was valued at £2.7 million – more than £36 million today. Lennon and McCartney each received a tax-free £94,270 for the sale of their shares (Capital Gains Tax had yet to be introduced). As long as Northern Songs continued to perform well – and with Lennon and McCartney providing hit after hit there was no reason why it shouldn't – shareholders would also receive a handsome annual dividend.

Lennon and McCartney received a considerable financial windfall from the sale, but now that Northern Songs had been floated on the stock market it was liable to takeover attempts. Slowly but surely The Beatles were losing control of their greatest asset: their songs. By the decade's end they would have lost them completely.

Epstein had no taste for finance, so didn't attend any of the meetings about the flotation of Northern Songs. As he was a director of the company, one might have thought he'd have taken a little more interest, but he seems not to have. In his place he sent Geoffrey Ellis, who knew next to nothing about the proposed flotation, and left James Isherwood, The Beatles' accountant, to work on the financial arrangements. "He left the entire operation entirely in my hands," Isherwood later claimed. "I'd always felt that Brian was extremely efficient, but it soon became clear to me that while he was adept at arranging tours, he had no financial expertise of any kind."[24] (The only Beatle to show any interest in the flotation plans was Lennon, who attended at least one board meeting at the offices of Northern Songs' solicitors, Stephenson Harwood & Tatham.)

More restructuring of Lennon and McCartney's publishing empire took place later in 1965. The songwriters formed a new company, Maclen, to represent all future songs and collect royalties. It took over from Lenmac, which they had formed on May 12th 1964 to collect PRS royalties on songs written between 1962–4. Lennon and McCartney owned 80 per cent of the new company; the rest went to Epstein. As part of the general restructuring, Lennon and McCartney had their royalty rate increased to 55 per cent, but only for songs published after 1969. In return they agreed to deliver at least six songs a year to Northern Songs until 1973. They continued to receive a royalty rate of 33⅓ per cent for their American publishing, and an annual salary of £1,200 on top of their income from royalties.

On April 5th 1966 Lennon and McCartney sold their shares in Lenmac to Northern Songs for £146,000 each; Epstein also sold his shares in the company for £73,000. The sale of Lenmac to Northern Songs had been their accountant's idea. None of The Beatles liked paying tax, but George Harrison liked it least of all. "The Inland Revenue had been after him a couple of times," according to Geoff Emerick.[25] Harrison voiced his objections to the British tax system in the biting 'Taxman'. Northern Songs published the song; but unlike Lennon and McCartney the astute guitarist had negotiated a far superior royalty. While Lennon and McCartney were on a 50/50 split, Harrison received 80 per cent of mechanical royalties, 70 from overseas publishing, and 66⅔ from performing and broadcast fees. Ironically, most of the money he made from the song went straight to the Inland Revenue. No wonder he was annoyed.

As well as selling their shares in Lenmac, Lennon and McCartney sold their composers' royalties for the 56 songs published by Northern Songs. They would still receive a royalty from these songs, but at a reduced rate. At the time it seemed like a good idea, because it saved them from paying a considerable amount of tax. It was, however, a shortsighted move that would lose Lennon and McCartney millions of pounds in future royalties. Once McCartney discovered what had happened he was furious. "Brian did do some lousy deals and he put us into long-term slave contracts which I am still dealing with," he said three decades later. "For 'Yesterday', which I wrote totally on my own, without John's or anyone's help, I am on 15 per cent. To this day I'm on 15 per cent because of the deals Brian made ..."[26]

Had Lennon and McCartney received better advice they would have kept their composer's royalties, which would have provided them with an income for the life of the copyright. But if selling their composer's royalties was a bad move, selling Lenmac to Northern Songs – which then became a public company – was even worse. By doing so Lennon and McCartney effectively lost ownership of their songs. The only way they could get them back was to buy them. Had they realised this at the time, they probably wouldn't have gone through with the deal.

In the meantime, Northern Songs continued to perform well. By 1967 shares in the company had risen from their starting price of 17s/9d each. This came as a result of The Beatles' remarkable success, Lennon and McCartney's remarkable ability to write consistently popular songs (not only for themselves but also for others), and the company's considerable export earnings. Northern Songs was making vast profits for its shareholders, which inevitably attracted interest from other companies interested in acquiring a share in its profits. Not content with making a vast profit from selling The Beatles' records, EMI began to look into the possibility of acquiring shares in Northern Songs.

EMI had long considered publishing to be little more than a by-product of its main business of selling recorded music. It had shown little interest in publishing Lennon and McCartney, and lost hold of them after publishing both sides of The Beatles' debut single. But now that EMI realised just how much money could be made from publishing, it made plans to develop this side of its business. EMI offered £900,000 for a 50 per cent stake in Northern Songs in 1965, but the deal collapsed when the company attempted to change the terms of the agreement. Had EMI acquired Northern Songs, it would have consolidated its investment and control in The Beatles and ensured considerable long-term income for the company.

Further changes were to follow after the sudden death, on August 27th 1967, of Brian Epstein. The Beatles were in Bangor, Wales, studying with Maharishi Mahesh Yogi when they heard the news, and were understandably shocked. For almost five years Epstein had managed and arranged everything for them. But actually, since they stopped touring in 1966, his role had begun to diminish. He had initially spent most of his time planning complicated tour itineraries, but had never involved himself to any great extent in the group's financial matters or what they recorded.

Epstein still busied himself with other acts, notably Cilla Black, and began promoting concerts at the Saville Theatre, London, but this proved to be financially draining (as was his gambling, which had by then become excessive). To make matters worse, The Beatles were slowly growing away from him, both socially and professionally. Now that their hectic touring days were behind them, The Beatles started asking other musicians about contracts, percentages, and management deals, which pointed up flaws in Epstein's fiscal management skills.

Even more worrying for Epstein was the fact that his management contract with The Beatles was coming to an end. The group had already taken the first step toward self-management by registering Apple Music Ltd on May 25th 1967. Epstein was obviously aware of this and must have thought long and hard about what he'd do if the group decided to sign with another manager. His anxiety would have grown with the news that Allen Klein was making noises about managing The Beatles. Not that any of this mattered – by the time his contract with the group expired Epstein had died of an accidental drug overdose. News of his death sent shares in Northern Songs plummeting. According to a report in *The Times* on August 30th, over £250,000 was immediately wiped off the company's market value. Shares in Northern Songs recovered quickly once dealers in the city realised that the company would continue as before. But Epstein's death did more than just affect the share price of Northern Songs: it left the company open to hostile takeovers.

EMI had already attempted to acquire a 50 per cent share of the company. Now that Epstein was no longer there to protect his Beatles, investors began to circle like a pack of hungry hyenas. Dick James feared the worst. "There's no doubt that the decision to sell Northern Songs, and not necessarily to Lew Grade … [came as a result of] Brian Epstein's death," recalled James's son, Stephen. "My father realised that with Brian Epstein's death, The Beatles would probably break up."[27]

The Beatles had already started to develop their own independent business empire, Apple, and by early 1969 had installed Allen Klein as their business manager. But while they were at last attempting to take control of their career, they were also drifting apart. The future looked uncertain, and James began to think about severing his ties with the group before everything collapsed. According to his son, Dick James felt that "the city and the media" might fail to understand that Northern Songs would continue to earn money. "I think Lew Grade also realised that this was his moment," Stephen James continued. "There was an opportunity to make a very fast offer to Northern Songs at a time when the whole thing was vulnerable."[28]

Lew Grade, an influential show-business impresario and television executive, had already approached Northern Songs once with the intention of becoming a major shareholder, but like EMI had failed to acquire a stake in the company. However, in 1968 Dick James went back to Grade and began secret negotiations to sell. The two men had been friends for years: when James had tried to make it as a singer, Grade was his agent. This time James agreed to sell his share of the business to the cigar-chewing impresario.

On March 28th 1969 Grade's ATV company made an offer of 37 shillings

(£1.85) per share for Dick James and Charles Silver's 32 per cent holding in Northern Songs. A day later Grade told *The Times*'s Business News section that the deal had been "brewed up by both sets of directors over a cup of coffee last Monday". The deal made James an overnight millionaire, but EMI Managing Director John Reid felt that it was not very generous: "We have not yet considered making a bid but the board will be in touch over the weekend and will probably have reached a view by Monday."[29] (Ultimately, however, the view was that EMI was still unsure about music publishing.)

Unlike Clive Epstein, who gave The Beatles first refusal on NEMS Enterprises, James made no such offer to Lennon and McCartney. Neither Grade nor James had any meetings with them before making the deal. In fact, James waited until they were both out of the country – McCartney was in America and Lennon in Amsterdam. He didn't inform Northern Songs' other major shareholder, NEMS Enterprises, either. "Neither Dick James [nor] Charles Silver informed me or my co-director Clive Epstein of their plan in advance," said Geoffrey Ellis, "although I have no doubt that it should have been discussed by the full board."[30] James later claimed to have gone about his business in secret in order to avoid a leak to the press. "What I did, I did in their interests as well as mine, and the rest of the shareholders," he later said. "I was not acting behind their backs. I believed I was acting for them and for the whole future good of the company."[31]

The fact remains however that James *did* act behind their backs, and while he might have believed that he was acting in their interests, that most certainly was not the case. His arrogance typifies the way The Beatles were treated by their so-called advisers. "Nobody ever sat down with me," George Harrison told *Billboard* in 1996. "No manager or lawyers – we never had any lawyers and nobody ever gave us any advice."[32] Harrison might have been exaggerating slightly, but it probably was true that The Beatles received little in the way of good business advice to begin with. By the late 1960s they had learnt a lot and were taking business advice very seriously. Harrison, Lennon, and Starr had employed Klein to guide them, while McCartney had Eastman at his side.

The battle for control of Northern Songs was heating up. On April 11th 1969 Warburg & co made an official offer to the company's shareholders on behalf of ATV. The Beatles retaliated on April 20th with an offer of their own. Acting on The Beatles' behalf, Henry Ansbacher & co placed an advertisement in *The Times* newspaper stating why shareholders should side with the group. Chief among their reasons was that David Platz, an experienced music publisher, would be appointed to the Board Of Directors, as would a director from the group's merchant bank. Allen Klein would not become a director of Northern Songs; Lennon and McCartney would extend their contracts with the company for a further two years (and not, as was speculated, move to their own Apple Publishing). Most importantly, The Beatles were prepared to pay a higher price per share: 42s/6d.

In April 1969, The Beatles held just over 27 per cent of the capital in Northern Songs. To gain control of the company they needed to acquire a further 23.1 per cent, or 1.15 million shares, at a value of £2.4 million. The group would need to borrow two million pounds in cash to finance the deal, half of which would come from their investment bankers, Henry Ansbacher & co.

As The Beatles were attempting to purchase NEMS Enterprises at the same time, their finances would have been stretched to the limit, and they would have had to put up their own shares in Northern Songs as collateral. ATV, meanwhile, was adamant that its shares were not for sale to anybody. "We have 35 per cent of the shares and they will stay with us," Lew Grade told *The Times* in London.[33]

The battle to gain control of Northern Songs wasn't helped by tensions within Apple. Lennon and McCartney were as divided over the Northern Songs deal as they were over the NEMS Enterprises buyout. Allen Klein, representing Lennon, thought the deal could be improved, but John Eastman, representing McCartney, thought it too hazardous. The songwriters' relationship deteriorated further when it was discovered that McCartney had bought extra shares in Northern Songs without Lennon's knowledge. It seemed Dick James wasn't the only one acting secretively. McCartney had broken the verbal agreement he made with his songwriting partner to share equally in their endeavours. Lennon was understandably furious.

While Lennon and McCartney were slogging it out over the boardroom table, a consortium of investors holding 15 per cent of Northern Songs outmanoeuvred them. Both sides had begun negotiations to gain control of the consortium's vital 15 per cent. Klein approached EMI for assistance, but once again the company decided against investing in Northern Songs. He also approached Capitol in America, but it too declined his offer. In an attempt to encourage shareholders to deal with The Beatles, the group issued a statement to the press. On April 30th *The Times* printed an article entitled 'Beatles woo shareholders' in which it was claimed that The Beatles planned to invite a representative from ATV to join the board if they gained control of Northern Songs. The statement also claimed that "invitations to become directors" would be issued to: Henry Ansbacher; "an experienced solicitor"; and "a chartered accountant with experience of the entertainment industry".[34]

The Beatles were determined not to let ATV take control of Northern Songs. But while the statement appeared at first to be having the desired effect, its effect was nullified by Lennon's announcement that he wasn't going to be "fucked around by men in suits sitting on their fat arses in the city".[35] The men in suits were understandably put out and decided to withdraw their offer.

ATV was no more successful in its attempts to woo the consortium. The company's offer of ATV shares instead of cash failed to impress. In May the consortium made clear its position: that it wasn't happy with either ATV or The Beatles' offer, and was keeping its options open.

Negotiations continued for several months but without resolution. Klein met with Grade on several occasions in an attempt to broker a deal but Grade didn't like the way things were going. Growing tired of Klein's delaying tactics he called Peter Donald, a major shareholder in the consortium, and made an offer of 40 shillings (£2) per share – less than The Beatles' offer – for their 15 per cent of Northern Songs. Donald accepted, and by September Grade owned 54 per cent of the company.

With no chance of gaining control of a company that was originally intended to safeguard their financial future, all that was left was for The Beatles to sell their shares to ATV. But even this wasn't as simple as it should have been. Klein brokered a deal with ATV for loan stock and cash that stated that Lennon and McCartney would re-sign with Northern Songs and buy back Lenmac, and that Apple would have sub-publishing rights for America – only for the deal to be rejected out of hand by Eastman simply because he had played no part in the negations. Instead Lennon and McCartney received £3.5 million in ATV loan stock in return for their shares in Northern Songs. By December 1969, ATV had managed to acquire 92 per cent of Northern Songs.

Disputes between Lennon, McCartney, and ATV rumbled on throughout the 1970s. No sooner had Lennon and McCartney gone solo than they began to claim that they were collaborating with their respective partners. McCartney's second solo record, *Ram*, was issued as a joint Paul and Linda McCartney album. McCartney claimed that several songs on the album were co-written with his wife, Linda. Lennon didn't go quite as far as McCartney, but still claimed that he too was writing with his wife, Yoko. Not surprisingly both found themselves in conflict with ATV.

As Linda and Yoko were not signed to Northern Songs, their share in royalties would not be paid through the company. To collect these royalties McCartney established McCartney Music Inc and Kidney Punch Music, while the Lennons set up Lenono Music. The dispute led to problems with both McCartney's *Ram* and Lennon's 'Happy Xmas (War Is Over)', which was delayed by a year. The dispute was eventually settled with publishers' royalties being divided 50/50 between Northern Songs and McCartney Music and Lenono Music. But with Lennon and McCartney both still dissatisfied with the terms of their agreement with ATV, each continued to fire legal broadsides at the company in the years that followed.

McCartney was particularly irked at having lost his songs, but had learnt a valuable lesson. Determined to never lose control of his material again, he established McCartney Productions Ltd (MPL) in 1970, which has become one of the world's largest privately owned music publishers. Over the years MPL has acquired the work of Buddy Holly, Frank Loesser, and Harold Arlen.

In 1981 McCartney made another attempt to buy Northern Songs. Lew Grade was in financial trouble at the time and needed to offload some assets quickly. He offered Northern Songs and ATV Music to McCartney and Yoko Ono for £30 million. McCartney, however, was only interested in Northern Songs, which he claims Grade duly offered for £20 million. Grade gave McCartney a week to think it over, during which time the ex-Beatle decided that Ono should also be part of the deal. Bringing Ono in meant that he wouldn't have to find £20 million on his own or pay the full amount for what he considered was, by rights, already his. But despite offers of £21 million and £25 million, the deal fell through. McCartney has since put this down to the fact that Ono refused to offer more than £5 million, but others have suggested it was because McCartney was only interested in Northern Songs, not the whole of ATV Music, which Grade wanted rid of.

Stephen James, who discussed the possibility of acquiring Northern Songs with McCartney, has since recalled telling him that this would be the only chance McCartney would get to buy back Northern Songs, and that he could in any case sell ATV or have someone else manage it for him. McCartney, however, told him he only wanted Northern Songs, and for no more than £25 million. Now, of course, it's worth somewhere in the region of £500 million.

At around the same time that McCartney was attempting to acquire Northern Songs he started working with the self-styled King Of Pop, Michael Jackson. Jackson had recorded a version of McCartney's 'Girlfriend' for his 1979 album *Off The Wall* before deciding that it would be a good idea to get together with McCartney to "write some hits". The pair duly met in early 1981 and wrote 'Say Say Say' together. The song was subsequently included on McCartney's *Pipes Of Peace* album in 1983.

McCartney didn't just help Jackson write some hits, but also advised the diminutive pop star on what to do with the mountain of cash he was earning: invest it in songs. Songs were after all the investment that keeps on giving, so he really couldn't go wrong. Jackson thought it was a great idea and told McCartney he just might buy the Lennon/McCartney catalogue. McCartney thought he was joking, but should have known better.

Jackson had more business savvy than McCartney realised. With McCartney's words ringing in his ears he began acquiring copyrights to add to his own small but profitable catalogue. Jackson's people then made contact with McCartney and Ono's people to inform them of his intentions to purchase ATV and Northern Songs. It's alleged that at the time neither McCartney nor Ono had any plans to acquire ATV, so Jackson began negotiations with the owners of ATV. After several months of talks, during which the asking price steadily rose, Jackson eventually acquired ATV and the Lennon/McCartney catalogue on August 10th 1985 for $47.5 million (£34 million at the time). Besides acquiring the Lennon/McCartney catalogue, Jackson also got more than 5,000 copyrights to songs by artists including The Pretenders, Little Richard, and Kenny Rogers.

Jackson paid a lot of money for the Lennon/McCartney catalogue but – if inflation is taken into consideration – no more than its original 1969 valuation. He also acquired a large catalogue of work by other artists that weren't part of the Northern Songs catalogue. When Jackson bought ATV, CBS Songs took over administration of the catalogue, which the singer began to exploit. One rumour that circulated after he'd bought ATV was that his next album would consist of covers of Lennon/McCartney songs, but all that materialised was a version of 'Come Together', as featured on Jackson's 1995 album *HIStory*.

It has since been suggested that McCartney didn't buy ATV because he had no great desire to exploit the Lennon/McCartney catalogue, which would have made it difficult for him to recoup the huge capital outlay involved in buying the company. Jackson of course had no such qualms, and began to exploit the catalogue as soon as he'd acquired it. Although he could only issue licences for songs and not the original Beatles recordings (which remained with EMI), it wasn't long before Lennon/McCartney songs began to appear in commercials.

As the owner of the Lennon/McCartney copyrights, Jackson didn't have to ask permission from McCartney or Ono before licensing songs to companies like National Panasonic ('All You Need Is Love') or Oreo Cookies ('Good Day Sunshine') for use in commercials. The Beatles were being used to sell everything from computers to cookies. Unsurprisingly, the surviving Beatles were less than happy about having their work used to sell other companies' products. It was bad enough that they'd had their songs misappropriated first time round. To have them exploited a second time was too much. "If it's allowed to happen," George Harrison complained, "every Beatles song ever recorded is going to be advertising women's underwear and sausages."[36]

It all became too much when Nike used The Beatles' recording of 'Revolution' to advertise sports shoes. Nike licensed the song from ATV, but rather than use a cover version it received permission from Yoko Ono to use The Beatles' recording. As a member of the Apple board, Ono should have consulted the other Beatles before giving permission for their recording to be used. Likewise, Capitol should have checked with Apple before issuing a licence. Apple sued Capitol and Nike for £15 million, but it didn't make a lot of difference. Nike continued to use the Beatles' recording while waiting for the case to go to court. When the case did reach the courts, Apple, EMI, and Capitol agreed that in future no Beatles recordings would be used in commercial advertising.

A year after losing the majority of the Lennon/McCartney catalogue to Jackson, McCartney lost another two songs, 'Please Please Me' and 'Ask Me Why', while Harrison waved goodbye to 'Don't Bother Me'. Dick James Music, the company to which these songs were assigned before the publisher registered Northern Songs, was sold to PolyGram Music (now Universal). Of all the songs he wrote with Lennon, McCartney owns just two, 'Love Me Do' and 'PS I Love You', both originally assigned to Ardmore & Beechwood Ltd. Unlike Jackson, McCartney has done little to exploit them, bar recording a dire medley entitled 'PS Love Me Do' for the Japanese edition of his *Flowers In The Dirt*.

Although EMI had decided against acquiring Northern Songs on several occasions, the company inadvertently ended up administrating the catalogue on Michael Jackson's behalf. CBS Songs, which owned the administration rights to the Northern Songs catalogue, was sold to SBK in 1985, while EMI acquired SBK's publishing interests for $295 million four years later. Jackson renewed the administration deal with EMI in January 1993 for a further five years. While McCartney was receiving a little over 15 per cent in royalties, Jackson walked away from the deal with a cool $70 million in advances over a five-year period. Like any good publisher, Jackson continued to develop his business to the extent that by 1993 ATV was making $30 million per year.

Jackson might have had money to burn, but he was living a profligate lifestyle, with some rumours suggesting he spent a million dollars per month. Like The Beatles before him, Jackson turned to his business advisers for help. They suggested that by selling a share of ATV he could generate a large cash windfall. So in 1995 Jackson merged ATV with Sony Music for $110 million and a 50 per cent share in Sony Music, as a result of which Northern Songs became part of an even larger corporate publishing company, Sony ATV.

Jackson continued to earn vast sums from his music publishing empire, but then things took a turn for the worse. First his 2001 album *Invincible* failed to recoup the vast $40 million advance and $25 million promotional budget, leading him to have to arrange a $200 million loan with Bank Of America Corp – which he secured with his 50 per cent share in Sony ATV. Then he was charged with child molestation. During the trial the prosecution claimed that he was $30 million in debt. Jackson was fine as long as he kept up his debt repayments, but in April 2005 he reportedly missed one. Instead of calling in the loan, Jackson's bank sold it to the Fortress Investment Group. The King Of Pop was being slowly sucked into a financial black hole that made The Beatles' problems with Apple pale into insignificance.

In December 2005 the UK's *Independent* newspaper claimed that Jackson had "a mountain of legal debts arising from his heavily publicized child molestation trial", which ended in June 2005 with his acquittal, and "is having trouble making the mortgage payments on the Jackson family home in the San Fernando Valley in Los Angeles".[37] Four months later *The Times* newspaper reported that Jackson had signed a new deal to reorganise his vast debt "by relinquishing his joint control over the $1 billion Beatles back-catalogue".[38]

Like Lennon and McCartney before him, Jackson was losing control of the greatest song catalogue in the world. Jackson gave Sony the option of acquiring his half of Sony/ATV for a fixed price of $200 million. When McCartney heard about the deal he seemed ambivalent. "The thing is," he told *The Times*, "I get some money from the publishing already. And in a few years more of the rights will automatically be reverting to me. It's not like I'm getting nothing at the moment."[39]

Jackson wasn't the only one plotting to sell his share in Lennon and McCartney's legacy. The value of song catalogues has soared in recent years, and anyone who owns a share in a publishing copyright is likely to be sitting on a nice little nest egg. But in April 2007 it was reported that Julian Lennon had sold his share in his father's publishing royalties to US music-publishing firm Primary Wave. While Sony/ATV Music Publishing owns the publishing rights for the Beatles catalogue and EMI the rights to the group's master recordings, Primary Wave told the *Boston Herald* in 2007 that their deal gives them "a significant share of Julian Lennon's economic interest" in the songs Lennon wrote with McCartney.

McCartney might have come to accept the fact that he will never own the songs he wrote with Lennon, but he and The Beatles now face another problem. In Britain the copyright on sound recordings expires after 50 years. What this means is that when the copyright on the recording of 'Love Me Do' expires on January 1st 2013, EMI will lose exclusive rights to the recordings, making them available to whoever wants to issue them. After the copyright expires none of The Beatles will receive a penny for sales for this or any recordings more than 50 years old. With the boom in the digital delivery of music, musicians could stand to lose a considerable slice of income.

This isn't so much of an issue for The Beatles and their heirs, all of whom are already multi-millionaires. Royalties from Beatles songs and records will continue to make millions for years to come. But if The Beatles' trials and tribulations sound unfair, spare a thought for Neil Innes, who like Lennon and McCartney lost a sizable chunk of his royalties to Sony/ATV. In 1978, his group The Rutles issued the soundtrack to a spoof documentary about The Beatles, *All You Need Is Cash*. Innes's fictional group first appeared in the opening episode of the second series of Eric Idle's BBC television series *Rutland Weekend Television*, the success of which led to the idea of a full-length parody.

"One of the things I thought would be cheap and cheerful to do was a parody of *A Hard Day's Night*," Innes recalled, "and Eric [Idle] had an idea for a documentary maker who was so boring that the camera ran away from him. We showed this on *Saturday Night Live*, and before I knew where we were, could I write 20 more Rutles songs by next Thursday lunchtime?"[40]

With the help of an ex-Python, Innes's idea developed into a feature-length television documentary. Innes fashioned parodies of songs from every phase in The Beatles' career for the documentary soundtrack, issued by Warner Bros Records in 1978. "I didn't listen to one Beatles song, I wrote songs based on my memory of them," he recalled. "The hardest part was coming up with genuinely affectionate songs like 'Hold My Hand', working in stories from your own adolescent experience. We needed something from each period, because The Beatles never did the same thing twice. That was the brief. The thing was to make the lyrics just parallel, or askew, and not use the same tune."[41]

Despite the songs being Innes's and obvious parodies, ATV Music didn't get the joke and sued Innes's publisher Chappell & co/Pendulum Music for copyright infringement. "Somebody at ATV thought it would be fun to see if they could clobber [the album]," Innes recalled. "That's what they did. Most people who know music think it was grossly unfair and I tend to agree."[42]

Rather than fight the mighty ATV through the courts, Chappell and co simply gave in and assigned ATV half ownership of all the Rutles songs that had been issued by Warner Bros. With just the threat of legal action, ATV found itself with 50 per cent of the publishing. Nice work if you can get it. "In the end they took 50 per cent of the copyright," Innes said. "I had nobody to stand up for me. It reminded me of school. There are big boys and if you've got sweets they'll take them away from you."[43]

Sony/ATV is very big indeed. In a recent documentary for BBC Radio, Paul Russell, former head of Sony/ATV, suggested that the company, which is still half owned by Michael Jackson, is valued at more than $2,000 million. Trying to fight a company with that much financial clout must be daunting. It's no wonder that Chappell just gave in. But the story then took another bizarre twist. Not content with taking 50 per cent of the publishing, ATV insisted that Lennon/McCartney or Harrison would be listed along with Innes as co-authors of the songs. Lennon, McCartney, and Harrison are now credited as co-composers of songs they had no hand in writing, and continue to profit from them. (What's perhaps even more disturbing is that a new generation of music fans could grow up thinking that Lennon and McCartney got together with a member of The Bonzo Dog Band and wrote a song called 'Cheese And Onion'.)

When Lennon and McCartney began their careers they had no idea how valuable their copyrights were. Things have changed a lot since. Now companies will do almost anything to acquire copyrights. The amount Primary Wave paid for a share in the publishing of Julian Lennon's stake of the songs his father wrote with Paul McCartney wasn't disclosed. But whatever it paid, Primary Wave must clearly think that its share in Lennon's royalties – already split several ways – will provide a good return on its investment. From now on Primary Wave will receive a royalty every time a Lennon/McCartney song gets played on the radio, used in a film, or sold on a CD (or, eventually, downloaded).

Trying to keep track of who owns what is becoming increasingly complicated. If Lennon and McCartney had known in 1962 that a company that "tastefully markets intellectual property through opportunities for re-uses in film and television"[44] would end up owning a share in their songs – songs they thought they could leave to their children – perhaps they might have thought twice before signing on the dotted line.

I Read The News Today

Meeting the press in the UK and the USA

Playboy: *"How do you feel about the press? Has your attitude changed in the last year or so?"*
Ringo: "Yes."
Playboy: *"In what way?"*
Ringo: "I hate 'em more now than I did before."[1]

magine a world without MTV and MySpace. A world with only two
television channels and one 'popular music' radio station. A world without
blogs, iPods, and text messaging. That's what Britain was like when The
Beatles issued their first single. Getting yourself noticed wasn't easy. Before
you could appear on either of Britain's television channels you had to pass
an audition. The same applied if you wanted to appear on BBC radio. Today,
signed and even unsigned bands can communicate with their fans instantly –
and globally – at the click of a mouse. But while The Beatles might not have
had websites and blogs with which to promote themselves, they did have the
power of the press.

In the early 1960s, the weekly popular-music press was a relatively new
phenomenon. Its arrival was driven by the emergence – by way of American
market researchers – of the teenager, who by the mid 1950s symbolised
everything that was at the cutting-edge of leisure-orientated consumption. In
1957, the year that the BBC launched *6.5 Special*, its first programme dedicated
to popular music for teenagers, the *Daily Mail* reported on "a new world of
young people with their own self-made heroes" – a new world populated by
students and dreamers; by bank clerks, typists, nurses, factory workers, and so
on.[2] By the late 1950s young people had more money, more to spend it on, and
more leisure time to enjoy. It was this new spending power as much as The
Beatles' undeniable talent that made the group so successful. Youth culture
had arrived, and nothing would ever be the same again.

Liverpool was similar to other British cities in that it had a thriving
entertainment industry. Few others, however, could boast of having over 300
clubs.[3] Some sources suggest that there were as many groups on Merseyside as
there were venues for them to play in. If there were, then the majority had no
real impact on the local music scene. But there's no denying that few places in
Britain had as many social clubs, dancehalls, and dedicated music-venues in
which to enjoy live music as did Liverpool.

Not only were there more music venues, there was also more music to
listen to. British record companies began to issue American recordings in
unprecedented numbers as popular music quickly became by far the biggest
outlet for teenage consumption. Several weekly music-papers emerged in

Britain to exploit teenage spending and dole out the latest pop gossip. Pop stars such as Bill Haley and Buddy Holly were fast becoming as commercially successful as Hollywood film stars. Their popularity was used to sell a raft of new publications, initially aimed primarily at girls. But why target just girls? Publishers weren't slow to realise that they could, with a little tweaking, sell their magazines to boys, too. There wasn't much for fans to buy besides records, but they could always get their weekly pop fix from music papers. It wasn't long before British newsagents shelves were creaking under the mountain of magazines and newspapers aimed at the pop fan.

Melody Maker was the most established of the British music weeklies, and the most conservative, too. Founded in 1926, it was favoured by 'serious' musicians and was often dominated by its coverage of jazz. Its combination of reviews of musical instruments and equipment and articles on playing techniques gave it a substance that some of its competitors lacked. But it was also slow to cover rock'n'roll – continuing instead to focus on jazz and folk well into the 1960s – and consequently lost ground to its great rival, the *New Musical Express*.

The *New Musical Express* (also known as the *NME*) was originally called *Accordion Times And Musical Express*, until it was bought and renamed in March 1952. It was the first British music paper to feature a singles chart, and was more finely attuned to public taste than its more conservative competitor. Better placed to react to change, it not only reflected new trends but also helped to shape them. Unlike *Melody Maker* it championed the new 'beat' groups and promoted a highly successful series of *NME* Poll Winners' Concerts from 1963–6, each of which was broadcast on British Television. While a feature in *Melody Maker* might have given a group gravitas, it was the *NME* – which sold 200,000 copies per week – that would make them popular.

New Record Mirror had a far smaller circulation but it too reported on popular trends, and in 1956 became the first British music paper to publish an album chart. The discerning pop fan had plenty of other choices, too, including *Pop Weekly*, *Disc*, *Hit Parade*, and, of course, Liverpool's own *Mersey Beat*, founded by Bill Harry and first published on July 6th 1961. A passionate fan of the local beat scene, Harry had originally planned to write about jazz but got sidetracked by local groups such as Cass & The Cassanovas, Kingsize Taylor & The Dominoes, and The Beatles. Harry was keen to promote local talent outside of Liverpool, but, like Brian Epstein, found himself up against a wall of indifference. "I decided to write to national newspapers, such as the *Daily Mail*, to inform them that what was happening in Liverpool was as unique as what had happened in New Orleans at the turn of the century, but with rock'n'roll groups instead of jazz," he recalled. "No one took any notice. Liverpool, it seemed, was isolated."[4]

Undeterred, Harry decided to publish his own paper – a local paper about local groups for local people. *Mersey Beat* was originally little more than a well-produced fanzine, with Harry responsible for everything from writing the copy to organising distribution. But music was big business on Merseyside and the first printing of 5,000 copies sold out quickly. According to Harry, the paper was more than just a commercial success. "*Mersey Beat* became a catalyst for the scene and groups, managers, and anyone connected with the music took to visiting the office."[5]

Harry was determined to use his paper to promote his friends, The Beatles, and encouraged them to contribute to the paper. "I made it a policy," he later recalled, "to request bands to write features and creative articles which would give readers more of an insight into [their] working life."[6] Both Lennon and McCartney wrote short articles about their group for *Mersey Beat*. The first edition featured an article on its front page by Lennon entitled 'Being A Short Diversion On The Dubious Origins Of Beatles'. It might have been a shameless piece of self-promotion, but it helped pad out the paper and gave an early insight to Lennon's quirky sense of humour.

The Beatles were obviously the flavour of the month on Merseyside. Harry featured the group heavily not just because they were so popular but also because they helped sell his paper. Not everybody was best pleased. Bob Wooler, a champion of the local beat scene, once complained to Harry that The Beatles' extensive coverage came at the expense of other groups. "He said that *Mersey Beat* was plugging the Beatles to such an extent that we should rename the paper *Mersey Beatle*," Harry recalled, "and in fact I later introduced a special section called just that."[7]

The Beatles were keen to supply Harry with news in order to maintain their public profile. This made simple business sense: the more people they attracted to their concerts, the more bookings they were likely to get. The articles and stories the group gave to Harry serve as an early example of Beatle branding. They built on the group's reputation and established their credentials as experienced, professional musicians, and gave the group the perfect opportunity to develop their image in the public mindset.

The Beatles' image was as important as the songs they wrote and the records they made. Buying a Beatles record wasn't just about the record itself but about an image and a lifestyle that said as much about the buyer as it did about the group. That image was built – by the group themselves at first and later by their management – on a combination of promotion, publicity, press reports, and criticism, all of which was disseminated by the print media. Promotion included advertisements, press releases, and television and radio appearances. Even the way the group dressed and wore their hair formed part of the way they promoted themselves.

In terms of publicity, the standard was set at The Beatles' first American press conference, which was given at Kennedy Airport on February 7th 1964. Even though the questions were banal, it established The Beatles as cheeky, quick-witted, fresh, and youthful – and it was this image that remained virtually unchanged until Lennon's claim in 1966 that they were "bigger than Jesus". The Beatles' concerts, songs, records, and television, radio, and film appearances helped develop their image, too. The group's early songs – 'Love Me Do', 'I Want To Hold Your Hand' – were written to appeal to a mainly female audience, and their image initially based on the established teen-idol model. But it didn't take long for The Beatles to mature and begin to manipulate and distort their image, which made it much more difficult for journalists to pigeonhole them.

The way The Beatles were written about and the unsophisticated nature of music criticism at the time also contributed to the group's image. Journalists constantly referred back to the bandmembers' humble beginnings while reinforcing their star quality. In Britain, The Beatles received more coverage in the music press at first than they did on radio and television. It was through this, as much as from their records and television appearances, that the group's image was built.

The Beatles were lucky to have Bill Harry as a friend and fan. With him on their side they were sure to get good reviews and could keep him up to date on how the group was progressing. The second issue of *Mersey Beat*, published on July 20th 1961, featured the group on the front page alongside the headline, 'Beatles Sign Recording Contract!' This must have caught Brian Epstein's eye. He sold *Mersey Beat* at his NEMS shop, and as the manager of a busy record department he would have been keen to read it in order to stay abreast of local developments. Even if he only glanced at the front cover he couldn't have helped but notice The Beatles on it.

Mersey Beat continued to promote The Beatles as local heroes. In January 1962 the group topped *Mersey Beat's* first popularity poll and once again appeared on the front cover. "That the first four groups were most popular was a foregone conclusion," Harry remarked about the poll. "All signs have indicated their popularity; the crowds that flock to their performances, the regularity of their bookings, the letters and requests for photographs and news concerning them."[8] The Beatles didn't top the poll simply because they were good. They worked hard to promote themselves and stay at the 'toppermost of the poppermost'. The runners-up in the poll – Gerry & The Pacemakers, The Remo Four, and Rory Storm & The Hurricanes – were all competing with The Beatles for bookings. This rivalry kept each of the groups on their toes and maintained the local beat scene's vitality.

Most of the popular groups on Merseyside had some sort of manager, and when The Beatles acquired one of their own he wasn't slow to use *Mersey Beat* to promote them. The May 31st 1962 issue carried the headline 'Great News Of The Beatles'. The paper reported that the 'impresario' Brian Epstein – note that he's no longer a mere shop manager – had secured the group a recording contract with EMI. On May 9th, Epstein had sent the paper a telegram from London that claimed he had "secured for Beatles to record for EMI on Parlophone label. First recording date set for June 6th".[9]

Mersey Beat duly reported the news and asked fans to send in their suggestions for songs The Beatles might record for their debut single. Whether or not Epstein really had secured the group a recording deal or just an audition is open to debate. He didn't actually receive a contract from George Martin until sometime around May 26th, and hadn't signed and returned it to EMI until June 5th. But he was certainly confident that Martin would sign the group, and wasted no time in promoting The Beatles as a 'Parlophone Recording group' in an advertisement in the same issue of *Mersey Beat* for their June 28th gig at the Majestic in Birkenhead.

Parlophone issued 'Love Me Do' four months later. One might have expected *Mersey Beat* to give it a glowing review, but instead the paper described the single, in its October 18th issue, as "monotonous". The single still topped the Merseyside Tops chart in the same issue, as well as the chart compiled by Disker (Tony Barrow) for his Off The Record column in the *Liverpool Echo*. Barrow had access to a pre-release copy of the single, and wrote a glowing review for it in the *Echo* that drew attention to its "exceptionally haunting harmonica accompaniment"[10] and which was then reproduced in The Beatles' first press release.

Epstein turned to Barrow for advice on how best to promote the single. George Martin's entire annual budget of £55,000 for his label didn't stretch too far: he wouldn't be spending a fortune advertising an unknown group. Epstein had to do everything he could to promote The Beatles and their single. If 'Love Me Do' was to receive any publicity at all, a professionally produced press release was essential. With this in mind Epstein paid Barrow to write it for him. But because Barrow was employed by Decca, and couldn't be seen as promoting a competitor's record, he had to sub-contract Tony Calder, a former Decca employee, to send the press release out to radio, television, and newspapers.

Like The Beatles themselves, Barrow's press release was groundbreaking. Although he had, like George Martin, planned to follow convention and pick one of the group members as the leader – John Lennon & The Beatles, as it were – he was talked out of the idea by Epstein, who insisted that Barrow present them as a group of equals. Barrow's press release emphasised The Beatles' achievements: that they had been voted the north west's top group, that Lennon and McCartney were prolific songwriters, and that advance orders for 'Love Me Do' on Merseyside were in the thousands. (Perhaps this is where the oft-repeated story about Epstein ordering 10,000 copies of the single for NEMS came from.)

During the summer of 1962, the British music scene was very dull indeed. The charts were dominated by established acts such as Elvis Presley, Cliff Richard, and Ray Charles, who between them held onto the Number 1 spot for 23 weeks. "For pop writers such as myself, nothing seemed to be happening, at least musically," recalled Peter Jones, then editor of *New Record Mirror*. "With no obvious potential superstars coming through," he said, "and no clear musical direction, the pop music industry was simply a rat race."[11]

The Beatles were the right band in the right place at the right time. They were new, original, and different – a breath of fresh air in an otherwise stagnant pool of talent. As if to wipe the slate clean, Barrow's press release featured striking black-and-white photographs of four unsmiling Beatles – the very opposite of what was expected of early-1960s pop stars. Although Epstein dressed them in suits, the group's visual image was far removed from the contemporary pop style. Unlike happy-go-lucky but ultimately unobtainable stars such as Adam Faith and Billy Fury, The Beatles were presented as a down-to-earth alternative to the established pop hierarchy. By presenting the group with matching suits and mop-tops, Epstein hid their working class origins, turning them into the kind of cheeky chaps you could take home to meet your parents. Crucially, although The Beatles looked odd, they didn't look scary.

Barrow's press release was sent out with promotional copies of 'Love Me Do', but few of the music papers picked up on the record. *Record Retailer* declined to review the single, despite the fact that EMI had placed an ad for it in the paper. So too did the *New Musical Express*, *Melody Maker*, and *Pop Weekly*. The only national music paper to review 'Love Me Do' in fact was *Disc*, which found the single "deceptively simple" but no more than "ordinary". *Disc*'s reviewer also noted that The Beatles "sound rather like the Everlys or the Brooks [depending on] whose side you're on".[12]

EMI included 'Love Me Do' in its New Pops advertisement in the October 6th issue of *Pop Weekly*, while Ardmore & Beechwood placed an ad for the single in the same paper a week later. Epstein did his bit by placing a small advert in the *NME*, which he continued to run until The Beatles' next single was released. (He later used these adverts to alert readers to the fact that NEMS Enterprises represented The Beatles and Gerry & The Pacemakers.)

The *New Musical Express* might have failed to review 'Love Me Do' initially but wasn't slow to pick up on The Beatles once the single entered the charts. On October 26th it ran an article by Alan Smith headed 'Liverpool's Beatles wrote their own hit'. According to his report, when Smith asked about the origins of the name The Beatles, "the boys" evaded the question by saying: "The name came to us in a vision!" Calling The Beatles 'boys' helped reinforced the group's youthful freshness. Epstein referred to them in the same way, too, and it wasn't long before the rest of the media caught on as well.

Alan Smith's short article drew rather obviously on Barrow's press release. As well as the old chestnut about their name appearing to them in a vision, Smith reported that "the boys" had already written "more than 100 of their own songs". This 'fact' was ruthlessly exploited. The Beatles were the first British group to write their own songs, and Lennon and McCartney's ability to write hit after hit was an important selling point. Having two songwriters in the group made The Beatles doubly unique. Even Elvis didn't write his own songs. When their second single entered the *NME* chart in the first week of February 1963, McCartney claimed: "We also wrote 'Please Please Me', but that hasn't exhausted our supply of compositions. We've nearly a hundred up our sleeves, and we're writing all the time."[13] Whether or not Lennon and McCartney really had 100 songs in the bag was a moot point. They were truly successful songwriters, and until Ray Davies and Pete Townshend emerged a few years later would remain a unique British phenomenon.

A year after running its first popularity poll, *Mersey Beat* published another. It came as no surprise that The Beatles topped it for a second year running. But in the 12 months between the polls, the Merseyside beat scene had changed dramatically. Proof that it had developed into a highly competitive and professional business can be found in an editorial that Bill Harry wrote for *Mersey Beat*'s November 29th 1962 issue. Under the heading 'The Rat Race', Harry reported that the once-friendly rivalry between Liverpool's groups, managers, and promoters had given way to acrimonious backstabbing and muckspreading. Citing an unnamed local compere, Harry noted that competition between groups "is motivated by petty jealousies, a form of 'one-upmanship'" in which certain people "proceed to conspire to manipulate groups and others to their advantage".

There were bound to be a few greedy players on Merseyside, and a few more who sought success at any cost, but this sense of disenchantment might ultimately have resulted from the music scene's rapid growth. The scene had, only a few years earlier, been populated by amateur groups, managers, and promoters. It was run by music fans for music fans. People made money from it, of course, but not as much as would be made once beat music took off.

From a musical and cultural perspective, Liverpool was ahead of every other city in Britain. It was bound to change, and those who were there at the beginning were liable to feel alienated by what followed. Bill Harry was clearly one of them. "The people who wish to make quick money from the local scene [are] spoiling it in their attempts," he wrote. "For, in their excitement and greed, they forget the most important people of all. In their blindness they are ignoring the youngsters who attend dances – and they are the people who count. Without them there would be no entertainment scene."[14]

The entertainment scene was changing and The Beatles were the engine of change. Merseyside was about to become very fashionable. Harry might once have struggled to convince London-based papers to cover Merseyside's flourishing music scene but would soon find himself having to beat them back with a stick. The emphasis was shifting from London to Liverpool, and as if to prove the point both the *NME* and *Mersey Beat* reported that George Martin might record The Beatles' debut LP in their hometown. "I'm thinking of recording their first LP at the Cavern," Martin was reported as saying in *Mersey Beat*, "but obviously I'm going to have to come and see the club before I make a decision. If we can't get the right sound we might do the recording somewhere else in Liverpool, or bring an invited audience into the studio in London."[15] Martin eventually decided against recording at the Cavern but had clearly noticed, even at this early stage of The Beatles' career, how inextricably the group was linked to this dank cellar club – and how important it was to their early success. (In the end he decided that there was no great value in recording at the club as few outside of Merseyside would have heard of it yet.)

With the success of 'Love Me Do' still ringing in their ears, The Beatles began to attract more press coverage. *Mersey Beat* naturally continued to cover their every move. The January 3rd 1963 edition carried a report by Alan Smith on their November 26th recording session for EMI. Smith, who had previously written about the group for the *New Musical Express*, compared The Beatles to The Drifters, while George Martin suggested they resembled "a male Shirelles". *Melody Maker*'s Chris Roberts thought the sound the group made was "straight out of Nashville, or anywhere you like in America's Southern music belt".[16]

Journalists were clearly finding it difficult to describe The Beatles. Drawing comparisons to American groups was the obvious thing to do because they were very much influenced by US rhythm & blues acts. But The Beatles were British and had a new, unique sound. According to a *Pop Weekly* article: "Their talent is obvious [because] they are the first British group to reach the charts with their first release – something which even The Tornados or Shadows could not do!" The article ended with a McCartney quote that summed things up better than most journalists of the time could. "We think our success is due to the fact that we are not a copy of anyone else," he said. "We have found a distinctive name, a distinctive sound and a fresh stage act."[17]

McCartney was right: The Beatles were distinctive. But that gave the press the problem: finding a way to describe a group without any obvious points of reference. If comparisons to American acts didn't quite fit, some of the references to other British groups were bizarre. *Pop Weekly*, again, described The Beatles as "probably the weirdest bunch to hit show biz since The Temperance Seven waxed their out-dated but hilarious numbers".[18]

The Temperance Seven were among Britain's first art school groups and played a raucous form of trad jazz that would later be picked up by The Bonzo Dog Do-Dah Band. But why were The Beatles being referred to, in the words of *Pop Weekly*, as "the Temps' younger brothers"? Perhaps it had to do with their sense of humour, since The Beatles neither sounded nor looked like the spat-wearing Temperance Seven. The only other links between the two groups were that they shared a record label, and that George Martin had produced The Temperance Seven's UK Number 1 hit 'You're Driving Me Crazy'.

Perhaps it was just that there wasn't anybody else to liken The Beatles to. They might have sounded American but they didn't look it, nor did they look like any group Britain had yet produced. But these attempts to describe and categorise the group were still useful as they generated yet more press coverage. The Beatles were pop's avant-garde, and their influence was already being felt. In February, *Melody Maker*'s Jerry Dawson foresaw the popularity of the Beatles mop-top, noting, "Barbers in Liverpool are rapidly becoming expert in this new style."[19] A month later, the same paper's Chris Roberts wrote: "Even their clothes and hair styles have been swept up by the club crowds, who wear black polo-neck sweaters and dark clothes as a sign of hipness."[20]

Roberts wasn't just describing The Beatles, he was helping to disseminate a visual style that defined membership of an exclusive but growing club. It was easy to be hip: all you needed was a black polo-neck sweater, a mop-top haircut, and a copy of The Beatles' latest single. As strange as it might seem, the way The Beatles wore their hair was almost as important as their music. Most pop stars of the time still kept theirs short and swept back; The Beatles' was much longer by comparison. To the press, this was a fascinating evocation of rebellion and self-expression. The way you wore your hair was important. It signified membership (or not) of a particular group, and helped the wearer stand out from the crowd. A Beatle haircut was a mark of modernity and, when the group hit America, became *the* talking point. It was imitated to such an extent that toy manufacturers began to produce Beatle Wigs – which Capitol Records, keen to draw attention to its ties to the group, had some of its employees photographed wearing.

A few years later a wannabe pop star by the name of David Jones tried to use the length of his hair to generate publicity for his band The Manish Boys. Jones and his bandmates grew long, Beatles-style hair, formed the Cruelty Society For The Preservation Of Long Haired Men, and appeared on a BBC television show to discuss the subject. The fact that the BBC granted valuable airtime to the subject says a lot about public interest in The Beatles' hairstyles. It did little to help The Manish Boys' push for fame, however – the group's lead singer would have to wait several years and go through numerous changes of image before hitting the big time as David Bowie.

Once The Beatles had become a successful chart act, reviews of their next single, 'Please Please Me', came in thick and fast. The group sent shockwaves right through the music scene. There really hadn't been anything like them before and the music press were still struggling to find a way to write about them. In *New Record Mirror*, 'Please Please Me' was described as a song with "plenty of guts, and good tune, vocalising, and some off-beat sounds".[21] Modern listeners might question the final point, but then we are listening with 21st century ears better accustomed to everything from thrash metal to gangsta rap. In January 1963, the repertoire of popular-music styles was much smaller. The Beatles' early recordings might sound ordinary today, but at the time they must have sounded like something from another planet. As *New Record Mirror* noted, 'Please Please Me' contained sounds "that other British groups [just] can't reproduce".[22]

Melody Maker reviewed 'Please Please Me' on January 26th. Although the paper gave more coverage to British groups than others, most singles by UK acts were given one-line reviews. 'Please Please Me' was reviewed by Janice Nicholls, the schoolgirl panellist from *Thank Your Lucky Stars*, who felt it had "more quality" than 'Love Me Do' and should perform better on the charts, but still surmised: "A lot of people don't like it." She was wrong on that score: a lot of people *did* like it, to the extent that it topped almost all of the music papers' singles charts, except the one in *Record Retailer*, where it reached Number 2. *Record Retailer* did at least review the single this time, predicting that, after the success of 'Love Me Do', "the group are destined to be regular chart entries. Certainly this second record has chart written all over it and seems sure to do well". That, however, was the sum total of the paper's attempts to entice its readership of record retailers to stock the single. EMI placed its regular advertisement announcing its new singles, with The Beatles and The Four Seasons at the top of the list, but there was no further coverage.

After The Beatles had chalked up their first hit EMI became more willing to spend money on advertising the group. 'Love Me Do' was featured in EMI's New Pops advertisements in the January 18th and February 1st issues of the *NME*, although 'Tell Him' by The Exciters and Jess Conrad's 'Take Your Time' were given priority. One way that American retailers got to hear of the group was through the paper's Top 30 singles chart, which was also published in both *Billboard* and *Cash Box*. National coverage in America was still a long way off, but both magazines reported on The Beatles even before they'd issued a record there. As the group became a regular fixture on the *NME* chart – on which 'Please Please Me' hit Number 1 – the group must surely have caught the attention of retailers and record company executives alike. It was a shame that nobody at Capitol noticed what was happening on the other side of the Atlantic. *Cash Box* and *Billboard* certainly did.

Cash Box was quick to pick up on The Beatles and published news of their signing to Parlophone and the release of 'Love Me Do', noting that George Martin "sees a bright future for The Beatles" – three months before 'Please Please Me' came out in the USA on Vee-Jay. The British Invasion was taking shape. Mr Acker Bilk had become the first British artist in some time to reach Number 1 on the *Billboard* Hot 100, with 'Stranger On The Shore', and was quickly followed to the top of the charts by The Tornados' 'Telstar'. American pop fans were becoming more receptive to music recorded by British artists, who were also becoming more popular in their native country. The January 19th 1963 edition of *Billboard* took note of British artists' domination of its "annual single chart summation", noting that, while Elvis Presley "had a clear lead", the likes of The Shadows, Acker Bilk, and Billy Fury weren't too far behind.

Both *Cash Box* and *Billboard* carried news of The Beatles signing to Vee-Jay, with *Billboard* reporting that the group had already "taken [Britain] by storm", providing "yet another triumph for [Parlophone] A&R manager George Martin and the first major hit for publisher Dick James".[23] 'Please Please Me' wasn't a success for Vee-Jay, but the label obviously saw something in The Beatles as it subsequently picked up the option for the follow-up, 'From Me To You'. *Cash Box* reviewed the single and praised a group capable of doing "a bang-up sales job" with "a real catchy cha-cha twist romantic novelty that the fellas deliver in attention-getting manner".[24] While it took the best part of a year for 'From Me To You' to top the US charts, *Cash Box* was right in its prediction that the single would do well. Despite Capitol's scepticism, it was clear that other sections of the American music industry recognised The Beatles' potential. All they needed was the right song and a bit of luck.

Back in Britain The Beatles found themselves becoming the most written-about band in the country after only two singles. Potted biographies written in gushing prose popped up in several music papers. In *Pop Weekly*, Linda L'Aventure announced that "these guys" – note how they are no longer mere 'boys' – "are so wonderfully exhausting that I wonder what type of fuel they fill up with". The rest of L'Aventure's article – which claimed "millions of fans" on The Beatles' behalf and described 'Love Me Do' as "selling like Wow, Man, Wow!" – might have been a little over the top, but she knew how to sell the group, and was clearly excited by them. The Beatles, she wrote, "are beating us a different kind of music, a kind of music which we hear apart from the rest".[25] (L'Aventure also recounted the standard rags-to-riches story, which helped to establish The Beatles as ordinary working-class people – just like *Pop Weekly's* readers – while contextualising their rise from obscurity to stardom. The Beatles were sold, just like Elvis Presley and every other star of the day, as boys next door, with whom teenage girls could easily identify.)

It has long been claimed that the British national press didn't pick up on The Beatles until their appearance at the London Palladium on Sunday October 13th 1963, after which it was reported that the group caused a near riot. But with 'Please Please Me' working its way up the charts the group began to receive more nationwide press. Maureen Cleave of the *Evening Standard* reviewed the group's performance at the Grafton Ballroom, Liverpool, while Vincent Mulchrone of the *Daily Mail* wrote about them, too.

Fleet Street's finest were still a long way behind the music press. *New Record Mirror* had taken note of the increasingly frenzied behaviour of Beatles fans as early as February 1963. The paper described how "fans went mad" after a BBC recording and "tried to tear the door of The Beatles' taxi off its hinges", and how, at a concert in Manchester, "the audience refused to go until the boys came back for an encore".

This was not just one of the first reports of Beatlemania, but also one of the first examples of negative press about the group. "Soon people will be saying that The Beatles incite violence,"[26] the paper warned. The Beatles certainly didn't want to be associated with violence, but it was a growing problem. And now that the group were famous, the press would be looking for anything to write about, good or bad. Epstein's press office would be rushed off its feet as it attempted to manage the media.

The Beatles were everywhere. If journalists weren't writing about them, they were using them as an excuse to write about beat music or Liverpool. The Beatles were leading a 'beat boom' with Liverpool at its epicentre. Dick Rowe might once have claimed that "guitar groups are on their way out" but all that changed with The Beatles. Or as the *New Musical Express* put it: "Groups Are In!"[27] The charts were full of 'non-vocal' and 'singing-team' records, and it was the solo singer who seemed to be on his way out. If your name was Adam Faith, John Leyton, or even Cliff Richard, it was time to rethink your act. The statistics spoke for themselves. In 1962 the *NME* charts featured just 13 groups, but by the sixth week of 1963 eight had already appeared in the listings. The *NME* put this change down to the emergence of "some really exciting new groups, among whom we number our Beatles".[28]

The Beatles weren't the first beat group to form in Liverpool, nor were they the first to issue a record, but they were the first to make it big. Their dramatic rise to fame meant that for a while Liverpool became very fashionable. An article by Chris Roberts in *Melody Maker*, entitled 'The Beat Boys', claimed The Beatles – "the only group so far to spotlight the talent-soaked northern scene by collecting a Number 1 hit and rave reviews" – to be solely responsible for the beat boom. They didn't change Britain's music scene on their own, of course, but they did lead the charge. "I never realized how dull the pop scene was becoming until The Beatles crashed into it," read a fan's letter to the *NME*. "They are full of zest and life, which so many other acts lack."[29]

For all the good press The Beatles' phenomenal rise to fame brought, it was inevitable that there would be a backlash. There were plenty who disliked The Beatles and beat groups in general. By the summer of 1963 there was a growing concern that beat groups – and the merseybeat scene – had already passed their best. The June 5th edition of the *NME* featured a letter from a reader who felt that The Beatles' "new sound" had "disappeared under a welter of Pacemakers, Dakotas, Flamingos, Dreamers and others" and that "Liverpool now has nothing new to offer to beat fans!"[30]

This was true in a sense. There were scores of beat groups competing for attention and the shock of the new had worn off. Many of them looked and sounded very similar, and opinion was divided as to whether they were any good. While film-music composer John Barry declared himself to be "100 per cent in favour of beat", longtime bandleader Ted Heath thought beat music "adolescent", and jazz saxophonist Tubby Hayes felt that it was "bad for youngsters to be brought up on this kind of music". For the maverick record-producer Joe Meek, The Beatles were in "a class of their own", but he was still concerned by the number of recording managers "trying to get a Beatles sound on other records".[31]

If Britain's fickle pop fans were growing bored of the seemingly endless stream of lookalike beat groups flooding the country they could always look to America for inspiration. Britain's new wave of beat boys might have usurped the old guard of greasy US rockers, but there was another trend developing on the west cost of America that threatened the beat boom for popularity. In June *Melody Maker* reported on how beaches and ballrooms were buzzing to a new American craze: surf. "Wild, thrill-happy American youth are getting their kicks in a new way," the paper reported, "on the west coast of the US, where the ocean surf is tricky, rough, and challenging and where the muscular heroes of the beaches accept the challenge every day."[32]

The new surfing scene was glamorous and exciting, and had its own soundtrack every bit as dynamic as British beat. The Markets had already had hits with 'Surfer's Stomp' and 'Balboa Blue', and if the paper was to be believed the British charts would soon by awash with tanned, muscular surfers. "The music has become all-American already with national sales action on many of the records," the paper reported. "With summer here, surfers in the East are expected to latch on to the action, as the waters of the Atlantic warm up to swimming temperatures."

It was almost as if the two countries had entered into a musical exchange-programme, which would only benefit acts on each side of the Atlantic. British beat groups out-performed their surfing rivals, but there was room for both to exist without fear of the other collapsing. At least one group emerged from the surf to rival The Beatles for popularity: The Beach Boys, who were as successful and inventive as The Beatles, and by the mid 1960s had entered into a friendly rivalry with them that pushed both groups to even greater creative and commercial heights.

While America had yet to feel the full impact of Beatlemania, Britain was experiencing the phenomenon with growing infatuation. The Beatles had proved that they were more than a mere flash in the pan, and there were plenty of people keen to exploit their success. In August 1963 a new monthly magazine entirely devoted to the group made its debut appearance on newsstands: *The Beatles Book* (later known as *The Beatles Monthly Book* and *Beatles Monthly*), published by Beat Publications. Beat Publications was owned by Sean O'Mahony, who first heard The Beatles while working for *Pop Weekly*. He wasn't too impressed by 'Love Me Do', but after hearing 'Please Please Me' became convinced that beat music was the sound of the future. O'Mahony decided that the time was right to leave the rather predictable world of *Pop Weekly* and start a magazine of his own. That was *Beat Monthly*, which published its first issue in May 1963. But O'Mahony wasn't content just to report on the beat scene as a whole. Within a few months he was publishing another magazine dedicated to just one group, The Beatles.

O'Mahony had already established a working relationship with Brian Epstein while employed at *Pop Weekly*. In February 1963 he approached him with the idea of publishing a Beatles magazine. Epstein liked the idea, but wouldn't commit to it without first consulting 'the boys'. After a couple of months of negotiations, Epstein proposed a deal whereby NEMS Enterprises received 50 per cent of the profits.

O'Mahony thought that this was a risky strategy on Epstein's part, and that he would be better off with a royalty. In the event, however, it wasn't. The first issue easily sold its print run of 80,000 copies, while at the height of its popularity the magazine was selling 330,000 copies per month – over 100,000 more than Britain's bestselling music weekly, the *New Musical Express*. *The Beatles Book* was one of the most successful music magazines of the era. The Beatles did well from its success – as did O'Mahony, who went on to create a magazine dedicated to Gerry & The Pacemakers.

The Beatles weren't the first pop act to have their own magazine. The idea of producing a magazine exclusively for fans of a particular star or type of entertainment was already well established. Fan magazines aimed mostly at female audiences flourished during the 1920s. Magazines such as *Photoplay, Love Story Magazine*, and *Argosy* included news, gossip, and lots of photographs of Hollywood stars. The relationship between magazines and the movies developed to such an extent that by the 1950s the two were in direct competition. To survive, publishers had to find more diverse audiences to target.

Rock'n'roll provided a new market to exploit. Newsstands and newsagents were full of magazines aimed at teenage girls: *Valentine, Roxy, Marilyn, Mirabelle*, and so on. These were styled on earlier American publications and contained photographs of pop stars to "cut out and keep" or "real photograph[s] of Elvis autographed for you". The articles tended to focus on the 'Love Secrets Of Your Favourite Stars' or 'The Film World's Most Thrilling Love Stories'. Elvis Presley naturally had his own magazine, but so too did Billy Fury. These too were aimed predominantly at female fans. Few males, it was assumed, would be willing to spend their hard-earned cash on such trivialities.

The Beatles Book followed this established template but also featured in-depth articles full of exclusive photographs of "our heroes" – the kind of thing that male fans could read without feeling too embarrassed. O'Mahony's magazine received exclusive access to areas of the group's working and private lives that other publications could only dream of. It covered recording sessions, followed the group backstage, and even went into their homes.

Although NEMS Enterprises had a press department, it couldn't control what the press wrote about The Beatles. It could, however, manage the way the group was promoted in *The Beatles Book*. There would be no negative reviews or stories, only up-beat articles sanctioned by the boys' team of PR advisers. But that's not to say the magazine didn't evolve and respond to change.

O'Mahony (who used the pseudonym Johnny Dean to edit the magazine) had an instinctive feel for what the fans wanted and even went as far as to replace his original choice of photographer, Philip Gotlop, with somebody closer in age to The Beatles, Leslie Bryce. *The Beatles Book* initially stuck with convention and didn't even hint at the fact that any of the group might have girlfriends, let alone be married. Pop stars had to be 'available', so any mention of wives or girlfriends was strictly taboo. But when the national press began to cover this part of The Beatles' lives, O'Mahony responded by acknowledging the group's partners and even including them in the photographs he published. He employed Beatle insiders such as road managers Neil Aspinall and Mal Evans to write exclusive articles, and made clear the magazine's ties to The Official Beatles Fan Club.

From The Beatles' perspective, the magazine gave the group another way to communicate with their fans. Lennon and McCartney wrote songs that their fans – particularly their female fans – could relate to. *The Beatles Book* was a further extension of that dialogue, even if the group's input was minimal. It strengthened the bond between band and fan and created a community wherein fans could ask the group questions, buy exclusive 'fab' merchandising, and swoon over photographs of their heroes. It was part of an armoury of Beatles-related artefacts that gave the fans a sense of belonging.

The rest of the music press was rather less partisan. *Melody Maker*, which had already described 'From Me To You' as "Below Par Beatles", suggested that 'She Loves You' was creating controversy among Britain's disc jockeys because it too was not up to standard. That didn't seem to fit with the public response to the record. 'She Loves You' became Britain's biggest-selling single to date – a record it held until 1977, when it was overtaken by Wings' 'Mull Of Kintyre'. It remained on the charts for 33 consecutive weeks, spending 18 of those in the Top 3 and five at Number 1. The only apparent controversy was that *Melody Maker* didn't much like it (nor, the paper reported, did The Temperance Seven – as if that made any difference).

Melody Maker wasn't alone in its criticisms of 'She Loves You'. BBC disc jockey David Jacobs found the record "rather disappointing", while Brian Matthew, the presenter of *Saturday Club* and a friend of the group, said: "It is the first Beatles record that hasn't knocked me out, and it strikes me they've rested far too much on the success they've already had."[33] It did seem, however, that the paper was simply stirring things up to sell more copies. Rather than give the single – which it knew would be a hit – a positive spin, it couldn't resist criticising it. Having built The Beatles up, it was time to knock them down – despite the fact that an article by Chris Roberts a few weeks earlier had proclaimed Britain to be "on the brink of the biggest boom in beat music since Bill Haley's crude, socking off-beat gave young people a new social role in 1955".[34] (Exactly what kind of social role this new beat generation would have – aside from antagonising parents – was not yet clear.) Roberts felt that the beat bubble would eventually burst, but that, unlike most of their peers, The Beatles would survive the inevitable slump. So did Ray Coleman, cited in the same article as saying that the beat boom "has produced two groups to cherish – The Shadows and The Beatles".

By September 'She Loves You' had sold almost a million copies in Britain alone, the *Please Please Me* album had been at the top of the charts since May, and *Twist And Shout* had become the most successful EP ever. Few other acts, aside from the likes of Cliff Richard, were able to sustain their popularity without bowing to the changes The Beatles had brought. Some were happy to continue with the same tried and tested formula, but others were only too keen to adapt to meet current trends. Adam Faith's 'The First Time' was described by the *NME* as having out-Beatled The Beatles. It certainly marked a change in style for Faith who, prior to its September 1963 release, had specialised in teen ballads sung in an affected Buddy Holly style. 'The First Time', however, sounded as if it could have been recorded by any number of merseybeat combos. At times Faith sounds remarkably like Gerry Marsden, while the backing of heavy drums and guitars has a solid beat that bears more than a passing resemblance to The Beatles. As Joe Meek noted, record producers wanted to replicate The Beatles' sound because it sold so well. If you wanted a hit, you needed more than just a Beatles haircut: you needed the sound to go with it.

Imitation might be the sincerest form of flattery, but The Beatles weren't happy. The front page of the August 3rd edition of *Melody Maker* carried the headline, 'Boiling Beatles Blast Copy Cats'. "Some other groups around are climbing on this rhythm & blues bandwagon they're talking about and pinching our arrangements," Lennon complained. "And down to the last note, at that."[35] But bandwagons are there to be jumped on. Adam Faith wouldn't have been too concerned about replicating The Beatles' sound – even down to the last note – if it gave him a hit record. The Beatles themselves had started out by adapting somebody else's style, but had reshaped it with such skill and imagination that they ended up with something of their own. They had created something more than just a new musical style: they'd fashioned a complete cultural shift. Lennon might have considered imitation to be a lazy option, but it was all that some of his less-talented peers had.

While coverage of The Beatles had reached saturation point in Britain, in America news of their fame was only just beginning to spread. *Billboard* and *Cash Box* both continued to report the group's progress in their International News sections. The November 2nd 1963 edition of *Billboard* reported on the group's appearance at the Royal Variety Show under the headline 'Beatles Soar To Success'. "The group's rise to fame is being compared here to the early success story of Elvis Presley," wrote Chris Hutchins.[36] If that was true, then The Beatles must really be something. *Billboard* had already noted the changes in Britain's music scene, but this was something else. Comparing The Beatles to Elvis, at least in terms of their impact, made clear the group's potential to American music-industry insiders. There was no point in referencing other successful British acts, as few were well known in the USA. Never had a British group come close to replicating the success of an American act – never mind one as popular as Elvis Presley.

A week later *Cash Box* carried a report on The Beatles' Christmas Show. It described how news that the group would be putting on the show brought "hundreds of teenagers to the box office, some of whom queued all night for tickets. Such was their enthusiasm that a police guard had to be called – a regular feature now of all Beatles personal appearances".[37]

In *Billboard*, Chris Hutchins used The Beatles' unprecedented sales figures to impress his American readers. "As sales of [*Please Please Me*] soar towards the half-million mark, EMI is readying another [album] for issue this month," he wrote, making it sound as though the label was planning a military campaign. In a sense, it was. Releasing a Beatles record was becoming a major logistical operation. British record shops would be besieged by fans when *With The Beatles* went on sale. And if that wasn't enough, Lennon and McCartney were providing hits for other British stars at the same time. "Other new releases from The Beatles' pen," Hutchins wrote, "include a Parlophone single by Billy J Kramer (for whom they have already written two chart toppers), 'I'll Keep You Satisfied', and a Decca record by The Rolling Stones 'I Wanna Be Your Man'."[38] The Beatles might have made little impact in America thus far, but they were certainly worth keeping an eye on.

As Hutchins noted, the British music scene was in the midst of significant change. "British record sales continue their astonishing increase," he wrote. "In August, manufacturers' sales were valued at $5 million – an increase of almost one third on sales in the same month last year."[39] Britain's pop fans were buying more records, and most of them were by homegrown acts. America's grip on the British music scene was beginning to weaken. It wouldn't be long before the US charts were dominated by acts from the UK in much the same way American acts had dominated the British charts during the late 1950s and early '60s.

The proliferation of beat groups in the British charts should have sounded an alarm throughout the American recording industry. Not only were American acts no longer able to guarantee a place on the British charts, they were now finding it difficult to sell records in their own country. An article in the December 14th issue of *Billboard* concluded that the "British disk industry [is] in better shape than ours". The rock'n'roll America gave the world in the 1950s had grown safe and boring. Britain's new wave of beat groups had grabbed it by the scruff of its neck and given it a firm shake. The Beatles might have looked respectable but the music they played was new, exciting, and dangerous. It was also selling like there was no tomorrow.

America couldn't fail to take notice. *Time* magazine ran an article about the group in mid November. So too, a month later, did *Life*. In the days before national music magazines such as *Rolling Stone*, this is how The Beatles were introduced to their American audience. Even Capitol Records had woken up to the group's potential. It took three UK Number 1 hits and a court case with Vee-Jay, but by December 14th *Cash Box* was reporting that "Capitol Gets The Beatles". The label scheduled the release of 'I Want To Hold Your Hand' – which, as *Cash Box* noted, had received pre-release orders of more than a million copies in Britain – for January 13th 1964, but then brought it forward to December 26th.

'I Want To Hold Your Hand' was an instant hit. It sold 250,000 copies in its first three days, and had passed the million mark by the second week of January. This level of success was virtually without precedent. The only British group to have topped the American charts before The Beatles was The Tornados – and they had proved to be a one-hit wonder.

If The Beatles' rise to fame in Britain had been fast, in America it was instantaneous. *Billboard* put the group on the front page of its January 25th edition. Much of the article was about the Vee-Jay lawsuit, but elsewhere in the magazine the group was described as "Britain's hottest record act in history" and as the potential saviours of the failing American record-industry. The same issue also featured a report on The Beatles' recent visit to Paris. The French press response to the group had been mixed, but it was clear that The Beatles had gone down well with the public. Odeon Records rush-released three EPs and three albums to coincide with the group's French jaunt, while a shop in Paris had imported Beatles wigs 'direct from New York'. If staid Parisians were willing to risk their cool by donning Beatles wigs, then the group could surely conquer American hearts and minds with ease.

Perhaps surprisingly, the first American reviews of the group were rather mixed. Jack Gould of the *New York Times* felt that The Beatles were "dated" after watching a clip of the group performing on *The Jack Parr Show*, while after the group appeared on *The Ed Sullivan Show* a few weeks later another New York critic wrote: "We can put away the spray-guns, The Beatles are harmless."[40]

Being "harmless" worked in the group's favour. The first reports about The Beatles in the US press had sent American parents' minds boggling. The group's name suggested something dark and unpleasant, and all that hair seemed rather unnatural. Whatever these Beatles were, it didn't sound nice. But when they eventually appeared on American television, The Beatles didn't look like deviant outsiders. They were civilised, asexual, and homely. Or, as *Time* put it, "teddy bears ... as wholesome as choirboys".

All of a sudden there was nothing to fear about these cute, charismatic mop-tops. America's daughters were safe. But while their parents could sleep soundly, others were busy thinking up ways to squeeze as much money out of Beatles fans as possible. It wasn't just Parisian department stores that sought to cash in on The Beatles' ability to sell anything from records to wigs. As Vee-Jay did battle with Capitol, the Cameo Parkway label rushed out a 'tribute' single, 'The Boy With The Beatles Hair Cut' by The Swans.

But The Beatles were responsible for more than just selling t-shirts, wigs, and novelty records. The success of 'I Want To Hold Your Hand' opened the doors for other British recording artists to take America by storm. As a February 1st 1964 article in *Billboard* entitled 'Beatles Boom Cues Others' reported: "The astonishing success of The Beatles' first Capitol single in America ... [is] regarded as a possible breakthrough for the other groups who found fame here in 1963."[41] The Beatles impact on America was likened to the events of 1775 – but this time the British might win. American record companies were desperate to sign British groups. "The fact that the Swan and Vee-Jay records are selling now," *Billboard* concluded, "indicates to many industry observers that Liverpool is ready to break as a full-fledged trend."[42]

The Beatles were responsible for American record companies investing heavily in British groups, including some whose earlier attempts at breaking the US market had failed. Gerry & The Pacemakers, The Dave Clark Five, The Searchers, The Fourmost, Freddie & The Dreamers, Dusty Springfield, Kathy Kirby, The Hollies, and The Rolling Stones all secured American record releases thanks to The Beatles. Although he didn't really have the right sound or attitude to compete with the beat boys, even Cliff Richard managed a US hit.

The Beatles transformed American attitudes to British music. American record companies, including Capitol, had long considered it impossible to sell British records in the USA. British acts didn't have it all their own way, as there were plenty of dynamic American groups in the charts, from The Beach Boys and The Trashmen to The Rivieras and The Temptations. But it was The Beatles who were seen to be responsible for rejuvenating the American entertainment industry. Even *Billboard* seemed to overlook the impact that Tamla Records was having on the charts. Like everyone else, it was too caught up in Beatlemania.

The front page of the February 15th edition of *Billboard* featured a photograph of the group and two reports on the impact they were having on the American music industry. Chicago had apparently flipped its wig over the group, with dealers describing their influence on record sales as "the most virulent form of record fever" since Elvis Presley's heyday, while "retailers and broadcasters alike" in Hollywood were reporting that "Beatles fare is getting top attention from buyers and listeners".[43]

The Beatles were generating huge amounts of money for American businessmen, and it was this – just as much as the fans' hysteria – that excited record label executives, retailers, and radio stations. The group made headlines precisely for this reason. *Billboard* reported that in the six months prior to breaking America The Beatles had earned $17.5 million (more than $115 million today) – and that figure didn't include US sales for the first quarter of 1964. The Beatles had earned a staggering amount of money for their record company but – as we've seen already – saw very little of it themselves.

America's infatuation with The Beatles led to some within the music business to complain that they were struggling to get their records played on the radio. The Beatles got so much airplay that there wasn't much left for anyone else. In the week of April 4th 1964 The Beatles occupied the first five places in the *Billboard* singles chart, and had another seven singles in the Top 100. (The records in question were 'Can't Buy Me Love' at Number 1; 'Twist And Shout' at Number 2; 'She Loves You' at Number 3; 'I Want To Hold Your Hand' at Number 4; 'Please Please Me' at Number 5; 'I Saw Her Standing There' at 31; 'From Me To You' at 41; 'Do You Want To Know A Secret' at 46; 'All My Loving' at 58; 'You Can't Do That' at 56; and 'Roll Over Beethoven' at 68.)

The Beatles dominated the charts in a way that has never been equalled. Their success was such that *Billboard* created a new 'Across The Board Award', which it presented to the group in London on March 6th. Radio stations vied with each other over coverage of the group. On New York's WINS, Murray The K called himself "The Fifth Beatle", while according to *Billboard* numerous other stations across America "hyped The Beatles excitement with offers of fan club cards, free records, [and] Beatle contests of all sorts" and continued to push each of the group's US releases.

When The Beatles first started out in Britain, the BBC had only one single to play, and interest in the group took months to develop. But when the group broke – overnight – in America, radio stations had half a dozen singles and three LPs to chose from. For some even that wasn't enough, and they started importing British Beatles records to supplement those issued in America. The Beatles' domination of American airwaves angered some, but to others it came as a blessing. Record companies with British groups on their books looked forward to what became the British Invasion. They didn't have to wait long: by March 1964 The Dave Clark Five, The Searchers, and The Swinging Blue Jeans were all picking up lots of airplay on American radio.

The Beatles had become a huge money-making machine. Not only did they boost British and American record markets, they bolstered publishing markets as well. Magazines and books about the group began to fill the shelves of newsagents and bookshops. Some were hasty cash-ins; others were more carefully considered. But each was published with one thought in mind: making money.

The first book about the group appeared in 1963. Issues two to seven of *The Beatles Book* featured 'A Tale Of Four Beatles' by *New Record Mirror* editor Peter Jones (writing under the pseudonym Billy Shepherd). Sean O'Mahony compiled the articles and published them as the first authorised Beatles biography, *The True Story Of The Beatles*. It wasn't the first book aimed at the growing pop market, but it was one of only a handful of similar publications available at the time. It was of course advertised in *The Beatles Book* and like the magazine itself presented the group as clean-cut boys-next-door.

Jones had been the first London journalist to interview The Beatles and follow them on tour. He later told Bill Harry that he was in "a difficult position" because he had been "expected to 'gloss over' The Beatles' tawdry indiscretions": "If one of them, without mentioning any names, wanted to have a short orgy with three girls in the bathroom, then I didn't see it."[44] If Jones did witness scenes of debauchery, he certainly didn't report them in the music paper he edited, *New Record Mirror*. But then he would have known that, had he done so, Epstein would surely have sued and ensured that The Beatles never talked to *New Record Mirror* again. In any case it wasn't in Jones's interest to dish the dirt on The Beatles, whose fans probably wouldn't have believed the stories anyway. (Such revelations were much more in keeping with the up-and-coming Rolling Stones.)

While Epstein controlled what was written in magazines and books published by Beat Publications, he couldn't control what other publishers said about the group. *The True Story Of The Beatles* didn't exactly open the floodgates, but it did lead the way for a steady flow of magazines and books about The Beatles of variable quality and dubious accuracy. Four Square Books was first off the mark, having already published books about Adam Faith and Jet Harris. *Top Twenty*, compiled by Phil Buckle, featured short biographies of contemporary stars, including two pages on The Beatles. This was followed by the tacky *Here Are The Beatles*, which *Mersey Beat* called "tedious", "tiresome", and "the worst Beatle book yet".

Unlike *The Beatles Book*, which had the group's best interests at heart, *Here Are The Beatles* was exploitation of the worst kind. *Mersey Beat* drew attention to the lack of "fresh or original ideas"[45] available to publishers of books about the group. The same tried and tested formulae were churned out over and over again. Why spend time and money trying to reinvent something that already had a proven track record? The Beatles were big business, and publishers weren't slow to take advantage of that. In February 1964, *Billboard* carried an advertisement for the new *Beatles Round The World* magazine. "If you can't beat 'em ... join 'em," the tagline read. "Jump on the profit bandwagon, sell the new 40-page Beatles magazine."

Nobody knew how long The Beatles might last. There was nothing to say that they wouldn't disappear as quickly as they had arrived. Unlike manufacturers of other forms of merchandising, publishers could print whatever they wanted (as long as it wasn't libellous), and that they did. But they were, in fairness, only giving the fans what they wanted. Had there not been a demand for these products, they wouldn't have been printed.

One exception to the litany of trashy cash-ins came when Jonathan Cape published John Lennon's *In His Own Write* to great acclaim. Lennon had been writing silly short stories since his school days, when he would fill his schoolbooks with writings and drawings (which he called *The Daily Howl*) instead of doing his homework. Some of his writings had already appeared in

Mersey Beat – Small Sam and *On Safairy With Whide Hunter* – but the rest of what appeared in *In His Own Write* was new to the public. Published in 1964, the book topped the bestsellers lists on both sides of the Atlantic, and earned Lennon the title The Literary Beatle. The *Times Literary Supplement* considered the book to be "worth the attention of anyone who fears for the impoverishment of English language and the British Imagination",[46] but *Time* magazine's response was more measured. Although Lennon's work was deemed to be "startling" and "post-Joycean", it might prove too clever for "all those jellybean-lobbing, caterwauling Beatle fans".[47]

Whether they understood it or not, plenty of those fans bought the book. It sold more than 100,000 copies in its first printing and has since been reprinted and repackaged many times. *In His Own Write* did more than just make its author money; it gave him and his group credibility. How many pop stars had written a book? None. And this wasn't just any book, but one, according to *Time*, that bore comparison to Lewis Carroll and James Thurber.

Encouraged by the success of his first book, Lennon wrote a second, which was published in June 1965. *A Spaniard In The Works* also sold well and led to another first: a stage play. Lennon adapted both books for the stage with the help of Victor Spinetti, who had featured in *A Hard Day's Night* and *Help!*. The play was also called *In His Own Write* and opened at the Old Vic Theatre, London, on June 18th 1968.

Hundreds – if not thousands – of Beatles-related books have followed in the years since. Sean O'Mahony might not have realised, when he published *The True Story Of The Beatles*, that he was starting a whole new industry, but that's effectively what he did. In the years since, a small library of books have been written and published about – and occasionally by – the group.

A quick check on Amazon reveals more than 1,300 Beatles-related titles. In recent years fans have taken it upon themselves to add to the already creaking shelves by self-publishing books about The Beatles, the demand for books about the group having apparently outstripped the supply offered by commercial publishing houses. These titles range from fanzines to exquisitely produced hardcover books, while plenty more writing about The Beatles has since been published online.

The Fabulous
BEATLES

I Wanna Be Your Fan

The strange tale of The Beatles Fan Club

"This might sound corny but I mean every word of it. I feel
very grateful, very honoured by the way our fans treat us."

Something about Britain changed after the Second World War: people got younger. Birth rates soared and the youth became the focus of attention. Young people began to drive social and cultural change like never before. The pace of these changes and the impact they had on society had rarely been felt so strongly. Self-expression became a priority. As the British film theorist Laura Mulvey notes, the "pre-60s generation [had] turned against the values of British culture [and] British political traditions" and found themselves drawn towards popular culture: principally the cinema and rock'n'roll.[2]

As British Prime Minister Harold Macmillan famously announced in 1957, the country's youth had "never had it so good". If Macmillan was to be believed, young people had more money in their pockets and a wider variety of things to spend it on. Exactly how true this was is open to debate. Writing in 1959, the sociologist Mark Abrams suggested that teenagers were spending twice as much on 'leisure' as their parents had.[3] But research carried out during the 1960s suggests that these teens were nowhere near as profligate as Abrams thought. The myth persists; nothing colours our view of the 1960s more than popular music and its resplendent consumerism. But even so, without a newly affluent generation to patronise it, the Merseyside music scene could not have developed as it did. It needed groups of relatively well-paid individuals who could afford to buy expensive musical instruments; venues for them to play in; and an audience that was willing and able to pay to see its groups perform.

Virtually every great musician, writer, or artist has been reliant to some extent on the patronage system, without which they couldn't have produced the work that they did. The Beatles were no different. They might have been an unknown quantity beyond Merseyside, but their local popularity was such that by early 1962 they had their own fan club. In January 1962 the group topped the *Mersey Beat* readers' poll and were attracting a large following of (mostly female) admirers. Most of the girls who watched The Beatles in Merseyside's seedy venues were more interested in being chatted up by a Beatle than listening to the group's music. As one fan later admitted, "All of us just wanted to get off with one of The Beatles ... if one of the boys actually took you home afterwards, you knew you'd really scored."[4]

One such admirer, Roberta 'Bobbie' Brown, was the founder of The Beatles Fan Club, which she ran from her home in nearby Wallasey. To begin with the club involved little more than simply collecting the names and addresses of other fans and sending them information about upcoming gigs. But the club occupies a unique place in The Beatles' business empire in that it was not formed by Brian Epstein and not run as a business. It was never intended to make money, and never did – in fact it ended up running at a loss.

Brown started the fan club as a gesture of support to The Beatles and their fans. It would keep fans happy by maintaining a constant supply of up-to-date news, and help the group by continuing to promote them to their core audience. It also helped to form a community of fans that would in itself become just as important to its members as the group they supported.

Although they weren't in change of it, Epstein and The Beatles were aware of the importance of having a fan club. Everybody else had one – from local stars such as Billy Fury to international icons such as Elvis Presley – so it made sense for them to have one, too. Beatles fans played a key role in the group's early development. The group talked to their fans, and knew many of them by name. They responded to requests, played songs they knew their fans liked (and dropped those they didn't), and dressed in a way that they knew would appeal to them. It was a mutually beneficial relationship.

"We never thought of the girls at The Cavern as fans," Lennon explained. "They were friends we'd met and chatted up in the clubs."[5] Fan clubs aren't there simply to massage a group's collective ego. They cater to the desire of fans to know everything they can about their idols. Speaking in 1964, Paul McCartney noted: "Sometimes I get talking to groups of fans and I realise they know all about me and my family just as though they were close relatives."[6]

When Roberta Brown started The Beatles Fan Club it was simply to provide fans with information about the group's activities, but it soon developed into something bigger than just an information service. On April 5th 1962, the club organised a fan night with The Beatles as the headline act. Tickets were priced at six shillings and sixpence, which included a free photograph of the group and membership of the club. The poster for the concert, like the free photograph, showed The Beatles wearing their black leather gear, which, as

Pete Best recalled, was "misleading". But although the group had long since abandoned the leather look in favour of suits, they knew that the "old Cavern crowd" wasn't so keen on their new, smartly suited image. "So on fan night we came out with our leathers to wild cheers from our fan club girls," Best said.[7] One such fan, Bernadette Farrell (who later dated George Harrison), described the atmosphere as electric. "The place was so over-crowded and badly ventilated that condensation was dripping off the walls and ceiling," she recalled, but she didn't care much: "As long as The Beatles stayed we were happy."[8]

Fan night at the Cavern was a neat way to promote the group. The Beatles were able to give the fans what they wanted while also demonstrating how they were progressing; fans got the opportunity to meet the group and socialise with each other. By now Epstein was involved with the fan club, and his influence was clearly visible in the way the event was organised and advertised, and in the theatrical nature of the concert – notably the costume change, from leathers to suits, during the interval. The free photos given to each club member also reek of his intuitive show-business sensibilities.

The Beatles were becoming objects of desire that could be purchased for a few shillings. Beatles fans didn't passively consume the group: they used them actively to give their lives meaning and to define themselves in relation to other 'non fans'. You didn't have to wear a badge or t-shirt to let people know you were a fan of beat music and The Beatles. The Cavern's unique smell, which stuck to your clothes and hair, was enough to alert others to the fact. Bernadette Farrell recalled dashing to the Cavern during her lunch hour and then rushing back "hot and smelling of disinfectant, which let everyone know where I'd been".[9] All of this signalled membership, literally and symbolically, of a club. The way you looked and smelled and the meanings and values you constructed with other followers of the group were all part of your identity as a fan. If you met somebody who smelled of disinfectant, it meant either that they were fans of beat music or cleaned toilets for a living.

Some girls simply wanted to grab themselves a Beatle, but this clearly wouldn't be possible for all of them. The next best thing was to dream about and discuss them with other fans. One American fan interviewed for *The Subculture Reader* confessed to spending hours wondering if Paul "sleeps with a different girl every night" or if George "really [is] more sensitive". There had been fans and fan clubs before, but few groups had had such a demanding audience. Helena Harding tried to quantify her devotion to the group in the fourth issue of *The Beatles Book* by describing herself as "a complete Beatle Parasite". Her entire existence, she wrote, had become dependent on "receiving regular Beatle transfusions" in the form of records, news, TV appearances, pictures, and so on. "It's all something to do with their music," she said, "their looks, their personalities, Ringo's rings, Paul's eyebrows, George's hair, their grins ..."

Collecting information about The Beatles, whether in the form of records, pictures, or news articles, was a way for fans to record the pleasure they got from the group: a way of documenting a personal history that could be shared with other fans. It reinforced a sense of individual identity, while belonging to the fan club instilled a sense of cohesion and community. The Beatles gave meaning to the lives of fans. As Edward Hulton had written a decade earlier in *Picture Post*, fans "prefer [the actor] Victor Mature to God because they can understand Victor – and he relieves the monotony of their lives; as far as they know, God doesn't." To some fans, The Beatles *were* gods, which perhaps brings into context Lennon's later remark about the group being 'bigger than Jesus'.

Those who worshipped The Beatles, as so many did, invested a lot of time, effort, emotion, and money in the group, and as such became very passionate in their opinions about them. When Pete Best was sacked, cries of "Pete Best forever – Ringo never!" were heard at the Cavern, leading to a scuffle outside that resulted in George Harrison receiving a black eye.

Beatles fans took a lot of satisfaction from their discussions about the group's relative merits. This in turn extended beyond fan communities to publications such as *Mersey Beat* and the weekly music papers, which contributed to debates about which group was the most popular by organising polls to rate and rank them. But although fans had already begun to organise themselves into distinct groups, it wasn't until 1964 that the music papers attempted to create a classification system that mirrored the growing interest in marketing and consumerism that had recently begun to arrive in Britain from the USA. In the August 15th 1964 edition of *Melody Maker*, Ray Coleman,

Bob Dawburn, and Chris Roberts invited fans to "read all about yourself" in an article that split them into three camps: pop fans, jazz fans, and beat fans.

The pop fan, *Melody Maker* revealed, was aged between five and 40, but most likely to be in his or her twenties, and constituted 50 per cent of the British record-buying public. She attended between six and ten package concert tours per year, listened to *Saturday Club, Easy Beat,* and Radio Luxembourg, and supported artists as much for their reputation as for their music, with a tendency to form "frantic fan clubs with unbelievable dedication, fervour, and sincere belief that, for instance, Elvis Presley would be a better bet than Barry Goldwater for president". The jazz fan meanwhile was a bit of a "square", and part of a minority interest group drawn to contemporary fashions. Where once, according to the *Melody Maker,* he might have bought any LP with 'soul' on the cover, by 1964 the jazz fan had abandoned it for rhythm & blues.

The beat fan shared many of the pop fan's interests. She was "a difficult specimen to squeeze under the microscope", since the term covered "a multitude of musical tastes – from The Beatles to John Lee Hooker". The beat fan was aged between 14 and 26; likely to describe herself as a mod, a mid, or a rocker; and spent one fifth of her wages on records. Beat fans tended also to be active members of fan clubs. "I grew out of my Cliff Richard days a couple of years ago," revealed Jeanie Parkin, a 20 year old interviewed by the paper. "When I look back, I think how soppy I must have been. The groups now like The Beatles and the Stones have really got something, and I can't see me getting tired of them. Not until I'm old anyway."

The Beatles held an advantage over many of their peers – including Cliff Richard and The Rolling Stones – in that their combination of pop sophistication and a rhythm & blues edge appealed to both pop and beat fans. Their fans were mainly girls, but they also appealed to boys. The group's male following was slower to develop, but had grown considerably by the mid 1960s, by which time pop had begun to metamorphose into rock.

The Beatles Fan Club however was largely run by girls for girls. For a while, the burden of running the club – printing membership cards, producing posters and photographs, replying to fan letters – was shared by Roberta Brown and Freda Kelly, who became one of its best-known secretaries. But none of this came cheap. From the outset, The Beatles helped finance the club with their own money. Brown and Kelly would meet the group backstage at the Cavern where, according to Kelly, "Paul would have a whip-round amongst the lads and hand over what I needed."[10]

Epstein began to take control of the fan club soon after he took over management of the group, at which point it became more business-like. Brown and Kelly passed the fans' subscription fees on to Epstein, who paid the club's additional running costs. To begin with it's likely that Epstein met these costs out of his own pocket. But as the club grew into the biggest fan club in Britain – and by extension the most expensive to run – The Beatles found themselves having to foot the bill. Epstein employed Kelly as a secretary, with the fan club being her primary responsibility. Running the club had initially been a part-time job, but that would soon change. Under Epstein's direction it began to do a lot more than just provide information about upcoming Beatles shows. The club started organising bus trips to the group's gigs outside Merseyside, which not only ensured that the group took an audience with them but also brought in extra money for NEMS.

The dedicated fan followed The Beatles everywhere. But if they didn't live on Merseyside they could still enjoy an authentic Beatle experience. Brian Epstein wasn't the only person to have realised that The Beatles were a neat moneymaking machine. By late 1963 Beatles-themed holidays were being offered to fans. The November 27th edition of *Variety* reported on how a Liverpool-based hotelier, Ben Usher, had started offering fans a "$36 Beatle vacation with bop and board" – a holiday package that included accommodation, concert tickets, and a trip to the Cavern. In recognising that teenagers had a lot of disposable income, Usher instigated perhaps the first example of rock tourism.

Usher was way ahead of his time. Forty-four years later, VisitBritain announced an exclusive partnership with EMI to drive interest in the UK's rock heritage, claiming in a press release that "21 per cent of potential visitors are inspired to choose a [holiday] destination because of the music or bands of that country" and that "half of potential visitors were also 'very likely' to attend a live music concert or event". The people of Liverpool, of course, had long since become aware of how big a draw The Beatles were, and that the group's potential to make huge amounts of money wasn't limited to selling records and concert tickets.

While The Beatles' fans all headed to Liverpool, the group's fan club moved to London in June 1963 to share office-space with their press office. Membership was growing rapidly. Until 1963, it had been divided into two branches, for the north and south of England, run by Freda Kelly and Bettina Rose respectively, but as its membership grew so did the number of full-time staff required to run it. The two branches were combined and put under the control of a fictitious National Fan Club Secretary, 'Anne Collingham'. In reality, the club had set up a network of Area Secretaries, who organised local activities, but all applications and queries were redirected to the London office. Freda Kelly still found herself with a fearsome workload. "I seldom leave the office before seven," she told *The Beatles Book*, "and then both Bettina and I take work home to do in the evenings – but I wouldn't swap my job."[11]

Although The Beatles Fan Club had initially been run by young girls it was taken over from mid 1963 onwards by Tony Barrow, who joined NEMS as head of press and PR. Like Epstein, Barrow wanted the fans to feel that they were getting value for money, but was troubled by how much time and money it took to run the club. Fortunately, help was at hand, in the form of *The Beatles Book*.

By August 1963 the two ventures had become affiliated to the benefit of both parties. Sean O'Mahony gave the fan club a few pages in his magazine, which not only encouraged more fans to buy it but also meant that the fan club no longer had to produce costly mail-outs for its members. This was one of Brian Epstein's better business decisions. He had managed to reduce the fan club's expenditure while also boosting NEMS's income, since the company received a percentage of the profits earned by *The Beatles Book*. Beatles fans, meanwhile, were more than happy to carry on paying their fan-club membership fees while also buying the magazine.

As well as keeping Beatles fans informed of the group's activities, the club also organised a pair of 'get-together' sessions at which the fans could meet their idols. Two such conventions took place: at the Empire Theatre, Liverpool, on December 7th, and the Wimbledon Palais, London, on December 14th. Tickets were sent to a random selection of applicants, some of whom were given free entry. (The remainder paid 3s/6d.)

The Northern Area Fan Club Convention was attended by 2,500 fans. The Beatles made use of their ready-made audience for the filming of two BBC television shows: a special edition of *Juke Box Jury* and a live concert. A week later 3,000 fans attended the London get-together and were treated to a 30-minute mid-afternoon performance. Later the same evening, the group put on a Grand Public Dance, for which tickets were priced at ten shillings.

These two events were essentially the next step up from the fan-club night the group had held at the Cavern 18 months earlier. It was becoming impossible for The Beatles to communicate with their fans as they had in the past, but they were still keen to have some sort of personal contact with them. "I only wish we could be on friendly first name terms with every fan we've got," Lennon claimed in 1964, "like a sort of enormous Cavern club where everyone knew everybody else."[12]

The group hoped that these get-togethers could be the next best thing to sitting and chatting with their fans. But even relatively small-scale events such as these were difficult to manage. In Wimbledon, the group had to play behind a six-foot-high steel fence. It would also take literally hundreds of get-togethers for The Beatles to 'meet' all of their fans. The group continued to hold smaller-scale events for their Area Secretaries, but the rest were quietly dropped.

The fan club conventions did, however, provide a model of sound business management. The Beatles might have appeared to have been giving their fans something for nothing, but the events were combined with paid engagements. The group received £1,750 just for the *Juke Box Jury* appearance taped at the Liverpool get-together, while the London event was followed by a concert that brought in £1,500 in ticket sales.

Maintaining personal contact with each and every one of their growing army of fans would not be possible, but there was something that The Beatles could do for those who had taken the trouble to join their fan club: record a special Christmas message. 'The Beatles' Christmas Record' was issued in the

UK on December 9th 1963, having been recorded two months earlier, on October 17th, at the same time as 'I Want To Hold Your Hand'. It was issued as a one-sided flexi-disc in a yellow gatefold sleeve alongside a note that called it "your own special Christmas gift" – a fan-club exclusive with "exceptional souvenir value", since only 25,000 copies were pressed.

Things got even busier the following year. The Beatles' National News Letter Number 4, issued in December 1964, announced that the club now had 65,000 members. But as impressive a figure as 65,000 members might sound – particularly given that the number had doubled in less than a year – it was only a fraction of the million-plus people that had bought 'I Want To Hold Your Hand' in Britain alone. That was about as big as it got, too: total membership peaked at around 70,000 during 1964–65. Income from subscriptions brought in around £17,500 during 1965 – not an insubstantial figure, but not enough to cover the cost of printing the National Newsletter and producing a Christmas single.

"The club runs at a loss," wrote 'Anne Collingham' in the April 1965 edition of *The Beatles Book*, in an attempt to explain why existing members were being asked to re-subscribe ("for the first time since 1963"). "Any fan who enrolled in, say, September 1963, has received a big return on her original payment of five shillings," she wrote, before listing the various gifts members had received over the past two years, among them "two special records", "a 32-page glossy magazine", and "a large glossy photograph" – items which, in total, have cost the club "more than ten shillings per member".

The "glossy magazine" was produced as a way of appeasing fans who were unhappy about the amount of time they were having to wait both for their membership requests to be processed and the lack of Beatle action in the UK. (The group had spent much of the early part of 1964 in France and the USA, and then in London filming and recording the soundtrack to their first film, *A Hard Day's Night*.) The magazine came with a voucher that could be redeemed for a photograph of the group with a "special handwritten message to members" on it. This was a costly exercise that Epstein only sanctioned on the condition that it was self-funding. The magazine's production costs were met by selling advertising to companies that produced Beatles merchandising.

Although The Beatles Fan Club could now be seen to be endorsing merchandising – something it had rarely done – it did not handle sales. Instead fans had to apply directly to the manufacturers of their Beatles souvenirs.

By the end of the year The Beatles Fan Club had taken over the whole of the group's Monmouth Street office, which meant that the press and publicity department had to move to nearby Argyll Street. But while the cost of running the club continued to rise, the potential for income fell. The Beatles were so big, and so busy, that there was little chance of them appearing at conventions, while as the demand for merchandising nosedived the opportunity to generate income from advertising all but disappeared.

The free records and magazines sent out by the fan club to keep its members happy cost NEMS and The Beatles £25,000. While The Beatles might have been earning a lot of money, they weren't cash rich. Royalties are generally paid annually, 12 months in arrears. The fan club therefore became a considerable burden on the group's finances.

One of the major expenses that the general public tended to overlook was the cost of sorting through the mountains of mail the group received. This would often become overwhelming to the staff at The Beatles' Monmouth Street offices, particularly if it was somebody's birthday. When George Harrison turned 21, the office was flooded with 60 mail sacks containing somewhere in the region of 30,000 birthday cards. The problem grew to the extent that another five staff members were taken on to work evening shifts in an attempt to clear the backlog.

Even that wasn't enough. Eventually, unable to cope with the volume of mail coming in to the office each day, somebody made the decision to dispose of it all, without opening it – even though some letters contained subscription payments. Given that the fan club was running at a loss, this seems rather shortsighted. They were literally throwing money away. It would admittedly have taken quite some time to process the backlog of membership requests, but the club needed as much money as possible to keep running. And when it came to light that Beatle fans' subscription payments had been sent to a waste-disposal company, the press response was understandably negative.

The Beatles Fan Club was coming under a lot of pressure and finding it difficult to cope with the demands placed on its staff. If they weren't snowed under with letters and membership requests, they were struggling to keep pace with The Beatles' frenzied work schedule. By the time each of the club's quarterly newsletters was published, there was often, as the fourth issue admitted, "very little fresh information" to be added to the endless sequence of news stories about the group. But while the newsletters were something of a failure, the club continued its efforts to widen the fan community by encouraging its British members to become pen pals with their American counterparts. One could argue that this was an early example of viral marketing, in that it became another useful way of promoting The Beatles – particularly in the USA. "We're still getting sacks and sacks of mail from America," wrote Bettina Rose in October 1964, "and we think Beatles People in Britain are telling their overseas pen-friends about the Club."[13] The Beatles didn't necessarily need much help in the way of promotion and marketing, but every little helped.

When The Beatles broke in the USA, the group's British fan club received more sacks of mail from American fans. An American fan club was formed, and by August 1964 had more than 60,000 members, but still many of the group's American fans sent their membership requests to the British headquarters. Their letters had to be sorted and returned to the USA at the club's expense, leading 'Anne Collingham' to make a statement, in *The Beatles Book*, to the effect that the club would no longer accept membership applications from abroad "if there is a branch of the club organised in the country concerned".[14] With official fan clubs running in 35 countries by the summer of 1965, returning unwanted mail to the correct Beatles outpost was an expense the club could well have done without.

While The Beatles developed as musicians and people at a remarkable speed, their fan club remained largely unchanged. It continued to keep fans informed of the group's activities and issue annual Christmas records, but there was little else it could do. The Beatles' audience was changing. They were attracting more male fans, who were more interested in the group's music than glossy photographs of them. If girls wanted to have a Beatle, boys wanted to be one.

In December 1965, a little over a year after the paper had split its readers up into pop, jazz, and beat fans, *Melody Maker*'s Bob Dawburn presented his 'Four Faces Of Fandom'. The first stage was the schoolboy who "knows the words to every Beatles song before it reaches the shops" and listens to Radio Luxembourg in bed; the second had turned his attentions to The Rolling Stones, grown his hair long and scruffy, and started to think of himself – probably mistakenly – as a bit of a rebel; the third was a fully fledged Carnaby Street dandy who spent his money on clubbing, clothes, and a broader spectrum of lesser known groups; and the fourth an "intellectual" whose tastes stretched from jazz to The Animals to Ravi Shankar.

The interesting thing about Dawburn's article isn't the way that he defines fan development, but the fact that he completely ignores girls – on whom the article from a year earlier had been almost entirely focused. Girls still made up a large proportion of the record-buying public, but things were beginning to change. The music business had always been a very male industry, but until the mid 1960s was targeted almost exclusively at a female audience. From that point on, however, it began to focus increasingly on male fans, who expected much more of their favourite groups than nice haircuts and songs about holding hands.

The Beatles started out as teen idols without much of an opinion about anything, but as the decade progressed they found themselves addressing such weighty issues as apartheid, the Vietnam War, and drugs. They became cultural leaders, and their fans grew with them. But their fan club stayed exactly as it was. It continued to report on activities and events such as new records and films, births and holidays, and changes to the fan-club personnel, but said nothing about the culture that The Beatles had come to represent.

Having reached the peak of its popularity in 1965, was there really any need to keep the fan club going? Perhaps not, but it continued until the bitter end, despite moving its offices back to Liverpool in 1966. Six years later, George Harrison and Ringo Starr met with Freda Kelly, whereupon they decided to close the club down. There has been no official Beatles Fan Club since, but several unofficial organisations have emerged to take its place and keep the Beatles flame burning.

Songs, Pictures And Stories Of The Fabulous Beatles

The birth of an image

"The thing is, we're all really the same person. We're just four parts of the one."

PAUL McCARTNEY[1]

The Beatles arrived in America in 1964 as the perfect pre-packaged pop group. They had it all: the haircuts, the wit, the cheeky grins, the cute accents, and, above all, great songs. But it had taken years for the group to evolve from scruffy rockers into teen idols. They appeared at New York's Kennedy Airport dressed impeccably in smart suits, immaculate shirts, and highly polished Chelsea boots, looking for all the world like a quartet of modern-day Apollos – gods of ordered beauty, clarity, and restraint. But beneath that polished exterior lurked the rebellious spirit of Dionysus, the wild god of music, passion, excess, and instinct. All at once The Beatles were safe but dangerous, sophisticated yet vulgar, smooth and composed yet coarse and frenzied. Familiar, but somehow different.

The Beatles' pictures were everywhere by the time the group hit America. They had appeared in the pages of national magazines, and on television screens, record covers, posters, and t-shirts. In an age of mass visual communication, image was everything. But like everything else in this modern world, it had to be constructed, and was both complex and contradictory. What it meant was dependent on the age, sex, and sensibilities of the beholder. It could be manipulated (and indeed it was), but it was also carefully controlled. By the time Capitol Records decided to start issuing Beatles records there had been plenty of careful consideration of how the group could and should be presented.

The American music industry had already been alerted to The Beatles' potency by coverage in *Billboard* and *Cash Box*, after which mainstream magazines such as *Time* and *Newsweek* helped introduce the group to the public. When television eventually caught on, it spread the word in a way that no other medium could. US radio helped to push the group, too.

Before the media hype took hold, however, The Beatles found themselves in the hands of Vee-Jay, an independent label that specialised in gospel and rhythm & blues, and which issued 'Please Please Me' and 'From Me To You' to an indifferent American public. Unlike Capitol, Vee-Jay didn't have the financial clout or marketing skills necessary to promote an unknown beat-group to an uninterested public, nor did it really know what to do with the group. (Capitol, on the other hand, reputedly spent $40,000 on the promotion of its first Beatles release, 'I Want To Hold Your Hand'.) In Britain, the admittedly conservative BBC welcomed all types of popular music, but America had hundreds of radio stations, each of which catered to a different niche audience: blues, country, 'Top 40', and so on. This gave Vee-Jay a problem: to which stations should they pitch The Beatles' records?

To a lot of people, particularly in America, The Beatles were a novelty act – and they were British, which didn't bode well for success in the USA. They didn't look or sound like anybody else, which made it hard to know what to do with them. Jack Parr, the first television host to broadcast footage of the group in America, later confessed that he "didn't know they were going to change the culture of the country", but merely "brought them here as a joke".[2] Parr wasn't the only one laughing at The Beatles. When Dick Clark played 'She Loves You' on *American Bandstand*, he showed the audience a photograph of the group. "When the kids saw a photo of the four long-haired lads," Clark later recalled, "they just laughed."[3] America, it seems, still wasn't quite ready for The Beatles.

Still unsure of exactly what The Beatles were, Vee-Jay covered its bases and promoted the group as a crossover act that would appeal to country, rhythm & blues, and pop audiences. This was both a blessing and a curse. On the one hand, it meant that the single could potentially be played on radio stations specialising in three different types of music. But it also meant that the programmers of a country station might turn up their noses at something they considered to be a rhythm & blues record.

Capitol employed the same marketing strategy when it issued The Beatles' first American album, *Meet The Beatles*. The sleeve notes describe how Lennon, McCartney, Harrison, and Starr "write, play, and sing a powerhouse music filled with zest and uninhibited good humor" that is "not exactly rock'n'roll" but "their own special sound".

For Vee-Jay, however, this genre-defying marketing ploy failed to generate either airplay or audience curiosity, the result of which was that 'Please Please Me' sank without a trace. The label persevered with 'From Me To You', which it promoted on the back of Del Shannon's recording of the song, a Number 77 hit on the *Billboard* chart. The Beatles' single, therefore, was "the original hit version!" But while Vee-Jay had at least narrowed down its target market this time, the single still failed to make much of an impression.

Vee-Jay's failure to make a success of The Beatles came down in part to the label's inability to put together or fund a sophisticated marketing campaign. But it was also the case that, at this stage, the group had yet to really prove themselves in Britain – something they had to do before they could succeed in the USA. America had enough pop stars of its own, so had little interest in British imitations of its own teen idols.

It wasn't until The Beatles started to make a big noise in their home country that the American media took notice. American trade papers had reported on The Beatles as early as November 1962. But the general public didn't read *Billboard* or *Cash Box*. Only when it became apparent that something truly remarkable was happening in Britain did the rest of the American press pick up on the group. By November 1963 each of *Time*, *Newsweek*, and *Life* had reported on The Beatles' success in the UK.

Had America had the kind of weekly music-papers that Britain enjoyed, Vee-Jay might have stood a better chance of breaking The Beatles. But what Vee-Jay needed – the help of the national press, radio, and television – was much harder to acquire. And what The Beatles needed was a record label with good distribution, an experienced marketing department, and money to spend. That label, of course, was Capitol, which eventually gave in to the inevitable and planned a comprehensive campaign to promote its first Beatles single, 'I Want To Hold Your Hand', that involved traditional press advertisements, window displays, promotional buttons (or badges, as they are known in the UK), Beatles wigs, and even a fake tabloid newspaper, *National Record News*. By this stage, however, the $40,000 marketing budget was barely necessary, since the national press had started to do Capitol's job for it by promoting the group for free. Capitol's campaign was simply the icing on the cake, a reinforcement of a media image already in circulation.

Magazines and colour supplements were extremely important in the way that they transmitted information to large audiences. They allowed cultural activities such as art and music to find a much wider audience than they otherwise would. The American press laid the foundations for Capitol's marketing campaign with a series of articles about The Beatles and their fans that gave a flavour of the hysteria about to erupt once the group set foot on US soil. In a sense these press reports provided a model of behaviour for American fans to emulate.

The American press also placed a lot of emphasis on the group's working-class roots. An article by Frederick Lewis in the December 1st 1963 edition of the *New York Times Magazine* entitled 'Britons Succumb To Beatlemania' claimed that "the most important thing about The Beatles is that they come from Liverpool" and that they had eclipsed "the prospects of a general election, Christine Keeler, even football" in the national consciousness. Lewis made a lot too of The Beatles' "shattering of the English peace", citing events such as those in Carlisle, where "400 girls fought the police for four hours while attempting to get tickets for a Beatles show", or in Dublin, where "young limbs snapped like twigs in the tremendous free-for-all during The Beatles' first visit to the city". Sometimes the results of Beatlemania were more benign. "A woman news reporter had her left hand kissed repeatedly," Lewis wrote, "simply because the hand had accidentally brushed the sleeve of a Beatle."

An indication of how important the national press was to The Beatles' success in America can be seen on the back of the group's first Capitol album, which mirrors the layout of the front page of a newspaper, with liner notes that echo the key themes of Lewis's article. "You've read about them in *Time, Newsweek, The New York Times*," the jacket announces. "Here's the big sound of that fantastic, phenomenal foursome."

By retelling the familiar rags-to-riches story, Capitol's Beatles campaign followed a long-established pattern. In America, the idea that anybody might succeed on talent and effort alone has been popular for well over a century. Americans had plenty of great role models to choose from, but now you didn't have to aspire to be a great industrialist to be rich and successful. If you could sing or play guitar, it could happen to you. Elvis Presley, Little Richard, Johnny Cash, Bobby Darin, and Chuck Berry all represented the idea of the poor boy made good. Berry even based his biggest hit, 'Johnny B. Goode', on the idea.

Capitol was keen to emphasise the similarities between The Beatles and their new audience, while also reinforcing their status as the new kings of rock'n'roll. Stars had to be seen as extraordinary, but they needed a certain ordinariness, too, in order that the entertainment industry might perpetuate the idea that regular people could be rewarded for their talents and abilities.

Hard work and dedication were also part of the deal. Few became stars without first paying their dues. Before The Beatles, pop stars such as Tommy Steele and Joe Brown made their 'ordinariness' part of their act. Both traded on their working-class origins on record. Brown recorded a rocked-up version of 'I'm Henry The Eighth I Am', while Steele cut the childlike 'Little White Bull' – which in some ways was a 1950s version of McCartney's 'Frog Chorus'.

There was little difference between Brown and Steele and the comedians who had entertained their parents – they just happened to play guitar. Writing in 1967, Kenneth Allsop noted how acts such as these had turned their "'commonness'" into a "cheerily vulgar style", but that The Beatles approach was rather different. According to Allsop, they neither "put their sludgy Liverpool through any refining filter" nor used it "as a comic prop".[4]

The Beatles were not like the pop stars of yore. They didn't look or speak like typical teen idols, and the music they made didn't sound like the usual chart fodder. They were part of a new wave of working-class musicians, artists, writers, and actors beginning to make themselves heard in a society still bound by a rigid class system. The fact that The Beatles came from Liverpool but were also glamorous teen idols was important to Capitol as it allowed the label to sell the group as a standardised product (teen idols) with a unique twist (the group's working-class roots) that made them stand out from the crowd.

Among the giveaways Capitol produced was a four-page fake tabloid newspaper, which it called the *National Record News*, and which was filled with stories about and pictures of The Beatles. Capitol's publicity director, Fred Martin, then instructed the label's sales reps to distribute copies of it to major retailers, radio stations, and high school students. Inside the paper, alongside stories about the group's working-class roots, the individuality of the four members, their haircuts, and the importance of Brian Epstein to their success, fans were encouraged to "Be A Beatle Booster" by buying a two-dollar Beatle wig, a button, or an autographed picture. (Capitol, it seems, had a better idea of the value of merchandising than Epstein.)

The Beatles' mop-top hairstyles played a significant part in Capitol's marketing of the group. As well as reproducing a story about a Beverly Hills hairstylist who had suggested that the "Beatle-cut" was the "biggest thing in women's hair styles in 1964", Capitol had its sales reps wear the wigs during business hours. The mop-top also featured prominently on stickers the label produced. The Beatles' hair – still considered long for the time – became a kind of shorthand for the group. It was adopted as the standard beat-group hairstyle, and even had songs written about it ('The Boy With The Beatle Haircut'). Capitol used the mop-top hairstyle as a unique sales point, encouraging its staff to "get those Beatle wigs around properly, and you'll find you're helping to start the Beatles hair-do craze that should be sweeping the country soon".[5]

The hairstyle wasn't actually quite as unusual as Capitol might have thought. French and German youths had worn their hair in such a way long before The Beatles adopted it. "Lots of German boys had that hairstyle," recalled Astrid Kirchherr. "Stuart [Sutcliffe] had it for a long while and the others copied it."[6] As George Harrison later admitted, "Astrid and Klaus [Voormann, the artist and musician who later designed the jacket for *Revolver*] were very influential. I remember we went to the swimming baths once and my hair was down from the water and they said, 'No, leave it, it's good.' ... They gave me the confidence and when it dried it dried naturally down, which became 'the look'."[7]

The Beatles' hairstyles certainly got them noticed in England, where most pop stars still kept their hair short or swept it back, but it caused much more of a storm in America, where most men had crew cuts. The very first advertisement Capitol placed for The Beatles in *Billboard* was a small image of a shaggy head of hair over the label's logo with the words "The Beatles Are Coming" – an homage to Paul Revere's famous phrase, "The British Are Coming!" The British Invasion had started, and this time there would be no prisoners taken.

The Beatles' hairstyle was more than just a sign of their difference. As the *New York Times*' Frederick Lewis noted, "one shake of the busy fringe of their identical, moplike haircuts is enough to start a riot".[8] The Beatle-cut was also a potent symbol of their sexuality, and it drove girls crazy. As the song says, "Give me a head with hair / Long, beautiful hair". But while magazines such as *Time* took note of this, they decided it was all part of The Beatles' harmless charm. "There is a considerable difference," *Time* claimed, "between the coleopteran flight of these four English boys and the phenomenon of Elvis Presley or Frank Sinatra in his swooner phase. Presley made his pelvis central to his act, and the screams of his admirers were straight from the ranch. Sinatra's Adam's apple bobbed in Morse code, and no lass misread the message. But the Beatles are really teddy bears, covered over with Piltdown hair."[9]

Having a Beatle haircut became a symbol of rebellion and nonconformity, and no doubt helped its wearer get a lot of girls. Long hair grew to signify a certain individuality and, as the decade progressed (and hair got longer), became associated with counterculture values and alternative lifestyles. Just as the Teddy Boys of the 1950s had the DA, beat fans of the 1960s had the mop-top, which gave American boys another option aside from the crew cut, the short-back-and-sides, or the 'Tony Curtis'.

The Beatles needed more than just Capitol behind them to succeed in America. If the press played a significant role, then so did radio. With the help of DJ Dick Biondi, Vee-Jay had managed to get 'Please Please Me' to Number 35 on WLS Chicago's chart. Similarly, 'From Me To You' made it to Number 32 on KRLA in Los Angeles. These were, however, rather isolated successes. With stronger airplay, Vee-Jay might have done better with those first two singles.

Capitol wasn't too worried about the same thing occurring when it came to issuing 'I Want To Hold Your Hand' – quite the opposite, in fact. In *Billboard*, Jack Maher reported on how some record labels were becoming frustrated by The Beatles' dominance of the airwaves. When the group released their first single, radio stations had two songs – the A-side and the B-side – to choose from. But when The Beatles broke in America, radio stations had two albums worth of material to pick from, as well as eight single sides. Some US stations even imported copies of *With The Beatles* to play on air, leading radio pluggers to complain that they were "having a tougher time than ever getting radio time for new releases".[10]

American radio stations competed with one another to provide the most exhaustive coverage of Beatlemania. New York's three leading Top 40 stations, WINS, WABC, and WMCA, sent DJs and journalists everywhere The Beatles went. Murray (The K) Kaufman spent hours with the group and then, making the most of his tenuous relationship with them, proclaimed himself to be the Fifth Beatle. Numerous other stations such as WWDC in Washington and WFUN in Miami featured exclusive interviews of their own with the group.

If you switched on a radio in early 1964, chances are the first song you would have heard was 'I Want To Hold Your Hand', but things could have turned out very differently. In December 1963 a young fan named Marsha Albert saw The Beatles performing 'She Loves You' on the *CBS Evening News*. She wrote to her local Top 40 station (the aforementioned WWDC) asking to hear the record. Keen to keep its listeners happy, WWDC responded by ordering a copy of The Beatles' latest single, 'I Want To Hold Your Hand', from the UK. A week later, Albert was on hand to introduce the record when it was first played. The response from WWDC listeners was extremely positive, and the single was added to the station's playlist.

One might have expected all concerned to be glad that 'I Want To Hold Your Hand' had been playlisted, but not Capitol. The label was less than pleased to find that the Washington station had started playing the record four weeks ahead of its American release. Brian Epstein's New York attorney, Walter Hofer, served WWDC with a 'cease and desist' order, demanding the station stop playing the record. But Carroll James, the DJ who had given the record its first spin, refused to stop playing it. In the end, Hofer persuaded Capitol Records head Alan Livingston that little could be done to stop James playing the record, and that it was only one radio station out of hundreds anyway. What difference would it make?

What neither Hofer nor Livingston realised was that, in his fanatical desire to get the song heard, James had made a tape copy of the single and sent it to another DJ in Chicago. From there it was passed on to a station in St. Louis. Everywhere it was played, 'I Want To Hold Your Hand' got the same reaction: listeners loved it. Within weeks it had become a radio hit despite not yet having been issued in America.

With so many radio stations playing the single, Capitol realised that it couldn't issue 'cease and desist' orders to them all – and that its job was to generate airplay, not restrict it. With 'I Want To Hold Your Hand' receiving unprecedented airplay for a song by a British act, Capitol had little choice but to bring forward the release of the single from January 13th 1964 to December 26th 1963.

The Capitol release differed from the British single as it featured 'I Saw Her Standing There' on the B-side (British listeners got 'This Boy'). This was another attempt by Capitol to manipulate The Beatles' image. The label wanted up-tempo songs on both sides of the disc as a way of presenting The Beatles as cute but tough rockers – not typical teen idols, who tended to issue softer material. Capitol saw 'I Saw Her Standing There' as the best of what was then available – and surely had the right idea, given that Paul McCartney continues to perform the song in concert well into the 21st century.

Just as The Beatles arrived in America as perfectly formed pop stars, their debut Capitol single was the perfect pop record. 'I Want To Hold Your Hand' fused a rock'n'roll aesthetic with a classic pop sensibility, setting considered group dynamics against rich vocal harmonies. It sounded great blasting out of a transistor radio, while its twee lyric was pitched directly at the group's female fans. "There was a little trick we developed early on and got bored with later," McCartney later revealed, "which was to put 'I', 'me', or 'you' in it, so it was very direct and personal."[11]

The B-side, 'I Saw Her Standing There', was representative of The Beatles' tougher, live sound. A classic beat-group rave-up, it appealed to the group's male fans, many of whom considered the group to be 'tough', or in the words of one such fan: "Tough like when you don't conform. It's not hoodlum. A leather jacket that's tailored – that's tough."[12] Although Epstein had tried to steer The Beatles away from this sort of image, there were still benefits to be had from courting a rebellious edge.

Before The Beatles, rock'n'roll had seemed to be on its way out. Elvis Presley had deserted music in favour of a spell in the army, and once demobbed had returned with a string of films and records that lacked the conviction of his earlier work. Buddy Holly was dead, Jerry Lewis had been disgraced, and Chuck Berry was in jail. Pat Boone had somehow transmogrified the raw sexual power of rock'n'roll into something as bland and safe as a drugstore soda pop. Rock'n'roll's progenitors had been replaced with pretty boys such as Bobby Rydell, Frankie Avalon, and Bobby Darin, or pale imitations such as Tommy Steele, Marty Wilde, Johnny Gentle, and Cliff Richard. These performers took the edge off something that was once new and dangerous and made it safe and dull.

Although they were marketed as squeaky-clean teen idols, The Beatles represented an alternative to the clean-cut all-American boys that dominated the charts. Their music was sharp and loud and it had attitude. This third quality seemed to stem from the group's time in Hamburg. "We didn't worry about arrangements of anything," McCartney recalled of The Beatles' time on the Reeperbahn. "If we had trouble with overworked amplifiers – we had to plug two guitars into one – I'd just chuck everything in and start leaping around the stage or rush to the piano and start playing some chords ... it was noise and beat all the way."[13] The success of the few records that broke the mould of the early 1960s – The Kingsmen's moronic hit 'Louie Louie', for example, of The Trashmen's equally dumb 'Surfing Bird' – showed that America's youth was open to fresh talent, even in its rawest form.

Within days of The Beatles appearing on *The Jack Parr Show*, Vee-Jay started producing promotional copies of a new Beatles single, 'Please Please Me', backed with 'From Me To You'. The sleeves of these promo discs called 'Please Please Me' "the record that started Beatlemania", and alerted radio stations to the group's upcoming appearance on *The Ed Sullivan Show* and to the articles about them in *Time*, *Life*, and *Newsweek*. The first pressing of the single, which misspelt the group's name as Beattles, sold a paltry 7,500 copies; reissued, it sold a slightly more respectable 55,000 copies in 15 days. It would eventually sell over a million copies and peak at Number 3 on *Billboard*.

The same thing happened to 'She Loves You'. Issued by Swan Records in 1963, it sold poorly and failed to connect with American teenagers. When it was played on the Rate-A-Record section of Dick Clark's *American Bandstand*, it received a decidedly average score of 73 (98 being the maximum). It didn't fare much better on WINS, as DJ Murray The K later recalled. He included it on his daily record review contest, for which "the audience would vote on which records they liked best, and the winners of each week would be played next Saturday". 'She Loves You' placed third out of five. Murray continued to play it, but to little apparent effect: "Nothing happened. I mean really no reaction. Absolutely nothing! Two months later I received an urgent call from my station manager in New York telling me 'The Beatles are coming!' 'Fine,' I said, 'Get an exterminator.'"[14] But while 'She Loves You' made no impact first time around – even on the man who would later call himself the Fifth Beatle – it eventually sold over two-and-a-half million copies and topped the charts.

On Monday February 10th 1964 The Beatles gave their first formal press conference for America's print media in New York City. Capitol issued a press release in advance that highlighted the remarkable sales and press coverage the group had generated without even setting foot in America, and announced plans to record the group's forthcoming appearance at Carnegie Hall. (The recording never took place.)

The press conference was held at the Terrace Room at The Plaza Hotel on Fifth Avenue on the day after The Beatles' record-breaking appearance on *The Ed Sullivan Show*. Reporters, columnists, and magazine writers came out in force to question the group; disc jockeys and television reporters got their turn later in the afternoon. The first of many press conferences The Beatles would give over the coming years, it allowed for maximum media coverage with minimum effort. Everyone in attendance was given a specially prepared promotional pack consisting of the *Meet The Beatles* LP, the *National Record News* tabloid, glossy photographs, and biographies of the group and each individual member. United Artists, which had recently signed The Beatles to a movie deal, also distributed a biography of the group.

Alongside the usual facts and figures, the Capitol press release reproduced the remark Lennon made before the Queen Mother when The Beatles played the Prince of Wales Theatre, London on November 4th 1963 – "People in the cheaper seats clap, the rest of you just rattle your jewels"[15] – while his individual biography described him as "a determined 23-year-old whose somewhat stern face gives the impression of an angry young man".[16]

Angry young men had been making themselves heard in Britain for the best part of a decade before Lennon elected to have his say. The times had been a-changin' – albeit rather slowly – since the mid 1950s. There was a growing desire to do something to bring about a change in the country's suffocating, class-ridden society. With the threat of Mutually Assured Destruction hanging over their heads, young people started to make the running. The time had come to cast off the mantle of repression and find a new way of living. John Osborne's play *Look Back In Anger* was so shocking and passionate in its condemnation of the status quo that it earned him the label 'angry young man', something to which he would forever be linked. But he wasn't the only one. The country seemed full of them, and they were all writing books and making films peppered with angry young male characters.

Alan Sillitoe created Arthur Seaton for his novel *Saturday Night And Sunday Morning*, and gave him a catchphrase – "Don't let the bastards grind you down" – seven words that could have been written by or for Lennon. The fact that Lennon was soon to become a published author (and therefore an intellectual) bolstered his association with the angry young men of the world, while his acerbic sense of humour was in keeping with that of a generation of angry young satirists, such as Peter Cook and David Frost in the UK and Lenny Bruce in America. To be young, intelligent, and funny was to be against the establishment.

Lennon's angry-young-man label gave The Beatles an edge that other groups lacked. The majority of entertainers of the time didn't have a voice; they toed the line and kissed the hand that fed them. Labelling Lennon an angry young man did more than just mark him out as a rebel: it installed him and his fellow Beatles as the leaders of youth culture. They weren't just style models but figures of social and cultural change – the physical embodiment of youth culture and, eventually, the counterculture.

Capitol's suggestion that Lennon was an angry young man – albeit a nice one you could take home for tea and cake with your parents – dovetailed nicely with the idea of The Beatles being 'tough' and rebellious. If Lennon, with his loosened tie and acerbic remarks, was tough, then so too was The Beatles' music. Lennon's voice was an important part of the group's early sound. His vocals on 'Twist And Shout' were delivered with such devil-may-care bravado that they moved the song on from an invitation to dance into a maelstrom of sexual desire and frustration. His hoarse cries of "C'mon, c'mon, c'mon, c'mon, baby now!" were enough to send any girl into a state of sexual abandon. This was as primal as it got in 1963. Lennon's raw power – as unacceptable to parents of the 1960s as Elvis Presley's primal hiccups had been to the previous generation's – evoked the perfect teenage combination of sex and rebellion and entranced The Beatles' male fans.

The Beatles were the epitome of modernity. When Capitol Records issued its initial press kit in 1964, one critic was moved to write that the group's sound "can only be written as 'Whoooo'".[17] The Beatles' image was more than just a photographic representation, but was composed of everything they did and everything written about them. It was everywhere: on magazine covers, television sets, posters, and record covers, or blasting from a transistor radio. If nothing else, Brian Epstein knew how to manage the image of his 'boys" and sell it to an expectant public obsessed with consumption. And what a job he did.

The Beatles were part of a larger cultural community that presented itself through modern communication mediums such as magazine covers, radio, and television. Artists such as Peter Blake and Andy Warhol, photographers such as David Bailey and Lewis Morley, footballers such as George Best and Bobby Moore, and pop groups such as The Beatles and the Stones all presented themselves in similar ways. The medium was the message, and everybody was a star. The Beatles existed in a world that thrived on advertisements, colour supplements, and articles about music, fashion, and style. Their image, therefore, was constructed and distributed in such a way as to mark them out as modernists: progenitors of new styles, fashions, and ways of being. This was the modern world and their image sat at its very core.

Theirs was an image of affluence and youth, of the glamour of show business and the profanity of the street. Although The Beatles were defiantly British, their image was gilded by American values. America was modern, affluent, romantic, and sexy – and so were The Beatles. They symbolized freedom and escapism, and offered an alternative to Britain's staid culture.

Their image was a product of publicity and promotion; it embodied pop culture, devoured it, and fed it back, changed and improved. And it was all done so effortlessly. The machine that manufactured The Beatles' image worked so smoothly that nobody noticed the sales pitch. In this sense, as a heavyweight sucker-punch that nobody saw coming, it was the perfect pop product, and one that met all but one of the criteria in Richard Hamilton's definition of pop art: it was popular, transient, low-cost, mass-produced, young, witty, sexy, gimmicky, glamorous, and big business. The only thing The Beatles weren't, by Hamilton's definition, was "easily forgotten".

You Never Give Me Your Money

T-shirts, wigs, toys, and more

Playboy: *"Don't you feel honoured to have been immortalised in plastic? After all, there's no such thing as a Frank Sinatra doll, or an Elvis Presley doll."*
George: "Who'd want an ugly old crap doll like that?"[1]

Although they didn't know it at the time, The Beatles were fast becoming a brand. Their style and personalities created a powerful image that could sell more than just records and concert tickets. But like most groups at the start of their career, The Beatles were more concerned with getting their first record released than having their names and faces plastered over everything from plastic guitars to tins of talcum powder. Brian Epstein hadn't given it much thought either, although he had included a clause about 'sponsorship products' in the group's contract and was happy to take his usual 25 per cent should they provide any income.

During the 1960s the variety of consumer goods aimed at young people mushroomed. Consumption was on the up, and big businesses were busy targeting a new generation of big spenders: teenagers, who spent money like it was going out of fashion. Elvis Presley's manager was the first to realise just how much money could be made from sticking his boy's face on t-shirts and panties. Now it was The Beatles' turn to squeeze every last penny from their fans' sweaty little hands.

A lot of thought goes into how an artist is branded today. Modern musicians and celebrities know exactly how valuable their image and its associated rights are, and for this they have The Beatles to thank. Few pop stars before them had exploited merchandising in the same way. Elvis was the first, but even Colonel Tom Parker's attempts to profit from his charge paled into insignificance compared to the way The Beatles were exploited. And in the case of The Beatles, that's 'exploited' in the worst possible sense of the word. The combination of incompetence, disinterest, naivety, and greed meant that millions of dollars were made and lost.

Merchandising has been around for a long time. Fourth-century pilgrims were offered genuine pieces of the True Cross and the bones of actual saints for sale. Centuries later, you could buy plates and mugs decorated with images of current and past monarchs. Entrepreneurs have long sought to make a fast buck from somebody else's likeness.

Until the 19th century what we now call merchandising was largely associated with the great and good. You had to be very special to get your name or face on a piece of commemorative china. Ten years before The Beatles invaded the national psyche, the only person associated with any kind of mass merchandising was Queen Elizabeth II. Cliff Richard and Billy Fury sold a few photographs and t-shirts, but they weren't kings or saints. (Neither were The Beatles, of course, but they seemed that way to some.) Merchandising wasn't unknown in Britain, but it had never really been linked to the pop music industry. There were no models for Epstein to base his business plan on – if indeed he had one, which seems unlikely.

Things were very different in America. While Britain had suffered rationing well into the mid 1950s, America was the land of plenty, full of 50-acre shopping malls offering a far more sophisticated retail experience than might be found in the UK. And while the world of merchandising wasn't anywhere near as well developed as it would be in subsequent decades, there were exceptions to the rule. The Disney company had developed merchandising into a fine art, having been among the first to license one of its likenesses to manufacturers. In 1929 the Disney brothers were offered $300 to put Mickey Mouse on writing tablets, and used the extra income to finance the production costs of future films. After that, realising they were onto a good thing, they licensed their characters for use on everything from soap and ice cream to Cartier diamond bracelets.

One thing Britain and America did share was a growth in relative affluence. After World War Two young people had more money to spend, which they used to distinguish themselves from their parents. Previous generations of children had dressed and acted in pretty much the same way as did their parents, but by the 1950s the teenager began to occupy a middle ground somewhere between the two. A new range of products and leisure activities emerged to cater for this new consumer group.

In the UK milk bars, coffee shops, and dance halls provided new places for teenagers to meet. Record companies gave them a soundtrack, and magazines offered up gossip and fashion tips. For those with a little more spare cash than they knew what to do with there were posters and t-shirts emblazoned with the likenesses of their favourite pop stars.

Although nobody else gave it much thought, it soon became obvious to

Epstein that merchandising was another seam in the vast Beatle money-making mine that could be opened up and tapped. Epstein had no knowledge or experience of merchandising, but that hadn't stopped him before. He entered into each of his businesses like a gladiator facing a pack of hungry wolves. When he was asked by Bill Grundy in 1964 whether he felt nervous about taking on things he had no knowledge or experience of, Epstein replied: "Not really, because one studies quite a lot from an outsider's point of view. After all, I started to manage The Beatles without any experience."[2]

In 1957, gross receipts for licensed Elvis Presley merchandise came in at over $20 million. Epstein had always said that The Beatles were going to be bigger than Elvis. Had he done his research, he might have realised he was sitting on a goldmine. But it was one thing to manage a local beat group, and quite another to enter into complex legal agreements with manufacturers for hundreds and thousands of pounds. Epstein's lack of interest in technical and legal matters didn't help. Yet as soon as The Beatles entered the charts he was inundated with businessmen knocking at his door, wanting to put the group's name or likeness on something or other. Sayers started baking Beatles cakes; Kangol made Beatles caps; and there was even Beatles wallpaper. The list went on and on. They were on jackets, boots, tea trays, toy guitars, packets of chewing gum, t-shirts, bags, stockings, record players – there was little, it seemed, that couldn't bear The Beatles' image or name.

A more astute manager would have realised that the number of requests pouring in meant something, but Epstein failed to grasp the magnitude of the situation. He simply couldn't see the bigger picture. While he insisted on checking the quality of every potential licence before authorising it, he didn't recognise (or act on) the huge potential they offered. All he did was arrange for a limited range of Beatles merchandise – photographs, sweaters, and badges – to be sold through the group's fan club and monthly magazine. The official Beatles sweater, manufactured by Epstein's cousin Raymond, was "designed specially for Beatles people" and only available in one size (which had been "fashioned to fit the widest possible range of average-sized girls").[3]

Epstein soon discovered that his limited resources were unable to cope with the huge demand for licences. He was in over his head. Once it became obvious that he needed expert help, Epstein did what he always did: he gave the job to someone else, in this case his lawyer, David Jacobs, whom he had met in 1963. Jacobs was a lot like Epstein. His family owned a furniture business and his mother doted on him. He was born into money and loved show business. And, like Epstein, he was a homosexual. Jacobs's clients included some of the biggest celebrity names of the day, among them Judy Garland, Liberace, and Diana Dors. He was extremely flamboyant, always wore stage makeup, and dyed his hair jet-black.

Licences to manufacture Beatles merchandise were making the group and Epstein a lot of money. Officially licensed products sold at an unprecedented rate. A bakery in Liverpool sold 100,000 'Ringo Rolls' in two days, while a company in Manchester sold the same number of rolls of Beatles wallpaper. Epstein's cousin Raymond sold 15,000 sweaters and 50,000 badges; two other companies shifted 150,000 plastic toy guitars and 50,000 tea trays.

Epstein and Jacobs took steps to protect their copyrights and rigorously prosecuted anyone who produced material without a licence. As early as December 1963, NEMS Enterprises sued two Blackpool companies over breach of copyright. In January 1964, they brought a High Court action against H. Vos Ltd to stop the Manchester clothing company from using the Beatles name and image. But that wasn't enough to stop companies making unauthorised goods. All a manufacturer had to do was spell the group's name 'Beetles' and they were free to put it on whatever they liked.

Official Beatles products continued to sell at a furious pace. Epstein might have been concerned at the sale of unauthorised Beatles merchandise, but he was content to let Jacobs manage all requests for licences. Jacobs however was overwhelmed by the scale of the operation and no better equipped to deal with it than Epstein had been – which is perhaps why he became increasingly and frustratingly taciturn about his management of it.

Epstein was well within his rights to assign the task of administrating licences to Jacobs. A clause in his contract with The Beatles allowed him to delegate his managerial duties and obligations to sub-agents. But Jacobs was no better resourced than Epstein, and within months of taking on the job had to pass it on to the chief clerk of his chambers, Edward Marke. The job of managing this important source of income was slipping further and further from Epstein's control.

Unable to cope with the demand from manufacturers, Jacobs followed the Epstein model and gave the job to someone else. One might have expected him to use his contacts and offer the job to a captain of industry. Instead, he took it out of Marke's hands and gave the opportunity of a lifetime to someone he met at a party: Nicky Byrne, a former member of The Horse Guards and a one-time nightclub manager. Jacobs was impressed by Byrne's enthusiasm and background. He had the right social standing and natural charm to ensure his place in the 'Chelsea Set', which cantered around debutantes, heiresses, and bohemians.

Surprisingly, when Jacobs first offered Byrne the job of administering the Beatles merchandising licences, Byrne declined. He had done some background checking and found that Epstein's incompetence was already getting him a bad name in the business community. But in the end Jacobs was able to persuade him to take the job on and to form a new company, Seltaeb, with which to manage The Beatles' American merchandising licences. (Epstein had already created Stramsact to manage European licensing.)

Seltaeb was formed by six partners, the oldest of whom was the 26-year-old John Fenton. Fenton did at least have some experience of merchandising, but the rest – all in their early twenties – had no more knowledge than Jacobs and Epstein. In fact two of the six partners were chosen simply because they were friends of Byrne and had the £1,000 required to invest in the company.

Epstein had delegated all responsibility for merchandising to someone he thought he could trust; Jacobs in turn had passed the job on to someone he'd met at a party. The company charged with running The Beatles' merchandising would need people with legal, business, and organisational skills, but Jacobs had entrusted its day-to-day running to a bunch of chinless Chelsea socialites barely out of school, whose only qualifications were that they all attended the same parties. They were hardly the best candidates for the job, and their reputation for hedonism would suggest that they were more likely to squander the easy cash that came their way than invest it or even account for it.

One might wonder how Jacobs was able to sell the idea to Epstein, but neither is around now to ask. Epstein probably had other things on his mind that he thought – mistakenly – were more important; Jacobs, like Epstein, was more interested in show business and his celebrity clients than Beatles bubblegum and bracelets. Perhaps Jacobs didn't tell Epstein exactly what he was doing. He had power of attorney, and might simply have done the deal alone. This seems unlikely, however, since the two men were good friends and would surely have discussed the matter at some point, even if only informally. What is clear is that, in the space of a few months, Epstein went from rigorously policing The Beatles' merchandising rights to letting them slip through his fingers.

Further madness ensued. Jacobs didn't so much negotiate the contract between Seltaeb and NEMS Enterprises as give it away. Byrne was asked to name his own figure. As he later recalled, when it came to negotiating the finer points of the deal, Jacobs simply asked him: "What percentage do you think you should take on the deal?" Byrne put down "the first figure" that came into his head: 90 per cent. To Byrne's amazement, Jacobs didn't even question it: "He didn't think of it as 90 per cent to us, but as ten per cent to The Beatles. He said, 'Well, ten per cent is better than nothing.'"[4]

Jacobs' attitude was unbelievable – not to mention rather unprofessional. As Epstein's lawyer he should have researched similar administration arrangements. Had he bothered to speak to Dick James, for example, he'd have learnt that the standard administration fee was ten per cent – not the 90 per cent that Byrne plucked out of the air. James could also have put Jacobs in touch with Epstein's American lawyer, Walter Hofer, who administered American merchandising licences.

It wasn't as if Jacobs was ignorant of such matters. He'd issued licences to British companies and must have known how the percentages broke down and what to expect. And yet he blindly agreed to a contract that was so unevenly balanced in Byrne's favour as to be almost criminal. With business associates like Jacobs, The Beatles didn't need enemies.

The American Beatles merchandising was in a mess long before Seltaeb was launched. Walter Hofer was in charge of issuing licences and had already encountered problems due to imprecise wording and overlapping territories.

As a lawyer one might have expected him to have that covered. But as Geoffrey Ellis, who worked for Hofer at the time, later recalled: "We would issue to somebody, for example, a licence to make Beatles watches exclusively for the UK, and then to another manufacturer a licence would be issued to make jewellery world-wide. And the two could obviously be in conflict."[5]

If this was obvious to Ellis, then why weren't Epstein's lawyers more assiduous? Everybody involved in the licensing of Beatles merchandising appears to have been negligent in one way or another. It's no wonder that they got into such a mess. But things were about to get a lot worse. Once Seltaeb was launched it started to issue licences that conflicted with those already negotiated by Hofer and Jacobs.

When The Beatles landed at Kennedy Airport on February 7th 1964, they were greeted by hoards of fans and admirers who wanted to see – and, if they were lucky, touch – them. Most of them were teenage girls who wore Beatles sweatshirts and wigs and clung onto Beatles magazines and record jackets. One male fan interviewed for the television cameras looked just as intoxicated by the hysteria as the girls as he revealed that he wanted "a piece of The Beatles" – which from the look in his eyes meant more than just a handshake. The only thing stopping him from causing actual bodily harm to at least one member of the group was a very thin line of New York City policemen.

It wasn't enough just to see or hear The Beatles: the group's fans wanted to possess them. If the young man in question had really only wanted 'a piece of The Beatles', all he had to do was visit his local Woolworth's and buy one of the many fine Beatles related products available at the time. You could wear The Beatles, sleep with The Beatles, eat and drink The Beatles. (A real Beatle wouldn't have been much fun, and would have taken a lot more looking after.)

The pop business was about to take a giant leap into the unknown. The world of pop merchandising faced a revolution that would transform it from a small-scale operation confined to selling photos and necklaces to a business that could make millions overnight. "There's more to pop singers today," an editorial in the February 5th 1964 edition of *Variety* concluded, "than just warbling the big beat on discs." Modern pop stars of the day, the magazine continued, "represent a merchandising goldmine [with] royalties that can run into many thousands of dollars per performer and millions collectively". Merchandising had become such a big deal that certain performers could rightly claim to be "running a fair size industry outside their songwriting, disc royalties, and performing fees". As ever, one group stood out among the rest: The Beatles, who were "protecting the merchandising aspect to the forefront of their trade as never before experienced in this country".

If *Variety* had spotted the huge potential in merchandising, why was Epstein still blind to it? Perhaps it was just that merchandising was an industry, and Epstein was no industrialist – and neither were Jacobs and Byrne. Had Epstein employed a real expert in the field, he and The Beatles might not have faced the mess that was about to hit them. But as *Variety* noted, America had never experienced anything like this before. And if it was too much for America to take, how was a shopkeeper from Liverpool expected to cope?

Demand for Beatles merchandise in America was both instantaneous and unprecedented. On February 18th 1964, the *New York Times* reported that "sales of apparel and merchandising patterned after the popular English singing group continue to mount". The Reliant Shirt Corporation sold one million Beatles t-shirts in three days, which the company's president revealed had a wholesale value of $1.4 million (more than nine million dollars today). Meanwhile, REMCO had orders for half a million Beatles dolls, and the Lowell Toy Corporation struggled to match the demand for Beatles wigs despite the fact that it was producing around 15,000 per day.

"The suddenness of The Beatles merchandising boom can best be illustrated by the rise of Seltaeb," the *New York Times* continued. "It was formed in New York three weeks ago and has opened, or has plans to open, offices in France, South Africa, Australia, and Japan."

Seltaeb was "licensed by NEMS Enterprises Ltd of London", according to the *New York Times*, but in reality NEMS had no more control over Beatles merchandising than it did over the sun and the moon. Epstein had no idea how much money was rolling in until he visited Nicky Byrne in New York and was allegedly handed a cheque for $9,700. Epstein was slightly taken aback and asked how much he owed Byrne for his services, at which point Byrne had to explain that Epstein didn't owe him anything and that the cheque was for his ten per cent share of the profits. It was then that Epstein finally realised that Byrne was raking in 90 per cent for administering The Beatles' merchandising licences – and that he probably wasn't having to work very hard to get it. Every manufacturer in America was beating a hasty path to Byrne's door.

If that wasn't bad enough, Byrne revealed that Columbia had offered him one million dollars for his share in Seltaeb – just a few weeks after he had put down £1,000 (around $2,800 at the time) for his stake in the company. Epstein, one assumes, would have been even less happy after reading in the February 17th edition of the *New York Times* that "no one involved would say yesterday what cut of the profits The Beatles themselves got", but that "everyone concerned" had reported the group to be "happy" with the merchandising boom.

Epstein certainly wasn't about to correct this assumption by telling the press that he'd sold his golden goose for a handful of beans. He would also have been at pains to keep it from The Beatles themselves. When the group did find out they were incandescent with rage. "It's your fault," McCartney reportedly told Epstein. "We should be making millions out of this."[6]

According to Don Short, who travelled with The Beatles on tour, the group didn't think Epstein had been negligent, just careless. McCartney's attitude to the fiasco certainly seems to have cooled over the years. "You can't go back and change things," he later said. "I'm not upset, but now that I'm more aware of the way business works I can see one or two things we really should have done better." Epstein, McCartney felt, did "good deals" most of the time. "I think he looked to his dad for business advice and his dad really [only] knew how to run a furniture store in Liverpool. This was a little bigger than that."[7]

Epstein knew a few things about business but he wasn't an expert, nor was he aware exactly how much could be made out of merchandising. But he should at least have known that it was a valuable asset. While McCartney seemed to forgive Epstein over time, Harrison didn't. He was still complaining in *The Beatles Anthology* about "the fiasco where Brian's father gave away the rights to The Beatles' merchandising" – which he "didn't have any authority" to do. Harrison got the facts a little wrong, but he was clearly still furious – and justifiably so, given that, according to the *Wall Street Journal*, total sales of Beatles merchandise for the year 1964 reached around $50 million.

With this much cash at stake everybody wanted a piece of the action. The Beatles weren't the only group to exploit their merchandising potential. With The Dave Clark Five about to make it big in America, the group's frontman formed Dave Clark (London) to manage the group's merchandising. Like The Beatles, he expanded his merchandising opportunities to include clothing and footwear. In February 1964, *Variety* reported that Clark "expected to bring in between $150,000 and $300,000 in the next year". This was nothing compared to what The Beatles were earning, but by managing his own affairs Clark would see much more out of his licensing deals than The Beatles did from theirs.

Dave Clark wasn't the only one with an eye for business. The Beatles' American record label, Capitol, also wanted a slice of the pie. Byrne had already received an offer from Columbia Pictures; next it was Capitol Records' turn to approach him. Capitol offered him half what Columbia Pictures had but was prepared to let him keep a 'half-interest' in the company. "Part of the deal was that they were going to get me one of the top American merchandising men – a man who'd worked for Disney," Byrne later revealed. "Then I found out that Capitol had no intention of persuading this man to work with us. I turned them down because they lied to me."[8]

Was anybody prepared to take The Beatles' merchandising seriously? Seltaeb desperately needed a professional to sort out the mess it had got itself into. Had Capitol taken the matter seriously, it would have benefited the directors of Seltaeb, Capitol, and The Beatles. Instead Seltaeb stumbled on, creating chaos and lawsuits as it went.

For Epstein, it wasn't just that he had to admit to himself that he'd screwed up. He also had to contend with a mountain of bootlegged merchandising that came flooding into American stores (which the *New York Times* was reporting on as early as February 1964). At least 60 cases involving unlicensed Beatles merchandising were being investigated across America, from Rhode Island to California. The Reliance Manufacturing Company used its 200 sales reps to police the sale of illegal t-shirts. According to Reliance president Miles Rubin, "each salesman has to compile lists of stores in his area selling Beatles items", which were checked against a master list. "If we find a store that is not on our master list," Rubin continued, "we notify our attorney and he takes action."[9]

Nicky Byrne might have been quick to pay Epstein his first royalty cheque, but Seltaeb soon let its accounting slide. Not only were the payments late, Epstein believed, but they were also inaccurate. Seltaeb claimed that accounting was made difficult by the confusion surrounding the licences. Epstein grew increasingly frustrated by Byrne and the stories of his excessive lifestyle, which was effectively being paid for by The Beatles. As Geoffrey Ellis later recalled, "Brian and I ... decided that we ought to sue Seltaeb for unaccounting and [non-]payment. The writs were issued in New York with the inevitable result that Seltaeb countersued."[10]

NEMS Enterprises began legal proceedings against Seltaeb in early 1964. Epstein wanted a set of up-to-date accounts, payment for outstanding royalties, interest on money owed, and damages. Seltaeb responded by suing NEMS for damages caused by conflicting licences, which it claimed had led to a loss in income. With all these lawsuits flying about, both manufacturers and retailers of Beatles gear grew nervous. Woolworth's had planned to install special Beatles counters in its stores, but cancelled orders for Beatles products, as did Penney's, resulting, reportedly, in a loss of $78 million in revenue.[11]

Walter Hofer represented Epstein, but wasn't particularly interested in litigation. Once again, Epstein had chosen simply to employ somebody he knew. The lawsuit went badly, and got worse when Epstein declined the judge's request to go to New York to give evidence, fearing that he would be made to look like a fool. Rather than engage with the lawsuit – which he might have been able to influence – Epstein ignored it, and his lack of determination cost him. The case went against NEMS, which faced a bill for five million dollars in damages. Had Epstein attended to the problem rather than simply burying his head in the sand, the outcome might have been very different.

Epstein didn't seem to understand the magnitude of the situation. When another of his attorneys, Nat Weiss, called him to tell him about the outcome of the case, Epstein reportedly asked, of the five-million-dollar judgement, "Is that good or bad?"[12] Hofer was instructed to appeal the ruling, but Epstein wasn't out of the woods yet.

While the two companies were fighting it out in the New York courts, NEMS managed to renegotiate the royalty rate Seltaeb paid to administer the merchandising licences. It had previously been ten per cent, but rose in August 1964 to 46 per cent. But while this brought in more money for both NEMS and The Beatles, most of the extra income went on fighting the lengthy course case. The merchandising bubble, meanwhile, was slowly deflating.

Epstein's next move was one he should have made much sooner: he called Nat Weiss for advice. Weiss suggested that NEMS employ a more experienced litigation expert than Hofer, and suggested that Epstein meet with Louis Nizer, who had represented numerous individuals and companies in the entertainment industry. Nizer asked for a $50,000 retainer and then assigned the case to an Englishman, Simon Rose. But once Rose started to research the case, he discovered that Epstein had been negligent in his business dealings.

Things were about to get a lot worse for The Beatles' manager. He would now have to defend himself at pre-trial examinations. The depositions were given under oath in a private room in the New York State Courthouse. During the questioning, Epstein had to admit that he knew next to nothing about the contractual agreements, the terms of the various contracts, what money was being earned, or even which items were being manufactured. He was given quite a grilling. "Do you mean to say," Epstein was asked, "that you had no knowledge of such and such a contract, which could earn your clients, The Beatles, hundreds of thousands of dollars?"[13] Furthermore, could it really be the case that, on the same evening that a million-dollar merchandising advance was being negotiated, Epstein was "fooling about with an appearance in Brighton"?[14] Unfortunately for Epstein, it quite obviously could.

Epstein spent about two days giving evidence before returning to London with Ellis. Ellis was due to give evidence two weeks later and wisely spent the intervening period absorbed in the details of the case. Once the two men had given their evidence they worked hard to settle the case with Seltaeb. But Seltaeb continued to produce accounts and issued a writ in an attempt to delay the trial. The company sued Epstein, Jacobs, Hofer, and Ellis for libel as a result of written instructions issued by Hofer's office that allegedly contained libellous remarks about Seltaeb's lawyers. It also wanted three million dollars in damages on the grounds that Epstein's lawyers had reportedly written to various manufacturers claiming the licences Seltaeb had issued were invalid.

Epstein wasn't the only person to sue Seltaeb. Although all of the partners in the company had enjoyed lavish lifestyles, Byrne's was the most extravagant. Another of the partners, Lord Peregrine Eliot, grew increasingly worried that money destined for The Beatles and the IRS was being squandered on limousines, helicopters, expensive hotels, and personal expense accounts. (His main concern was that, if Seltaeb's huge tax bill was not paid, he might end up having his ancestral home in Cornwall repossessed.) He and another Seltaeb partner, Malcolm Evans, took Byrne to court on December 8th 1964, claiming damages of one million dollars. The company's flamboyant president was accused of spending more than $150,000 on his own 'personal comfort' over a five-month period. Peregrine and Evans claimed that Byrne had accumulated hotel bills of $1,900 per week and opened charge accounts for girlfriends on Fifth Avenue. More importantly, it was claimed that he had failed to pay The Beatles $55,000 in royalties. (The legal papers also state that The Beatles had threatened to cancel their agreement with Seltaeb, but if there was a clause in the contract between Seltaeb and NEMS that allowed them to do so then Epstein would surely have acted on it already.)

Litigation between NEMS and Seltaeb dragged on for the best part of 18 months before the case reached its conclusion. NEMS paid Seltaeb $90,000, which only just covered the company's costs. Feeling responsible for the entire fiasco, Epstein also paid NEMS's $85,000 legal fees. As generous a gesture as this might sound, it should be noted that most of the money Epstein earned came from The Beatles, which meant that the group had for all intents and purposes paid for the trial themselves. In fact, it actually cost them more than money, for they would never be presented with another opportunity like this again. By the time the Seltaeb business had been dealt with, The Beatles had changed. They were moving so quickly that it would have been difficult for manufacturers to match their pace. The Beatles did later produce 'high quality merchandising' for their Apple boutique, but it's unlikely that a line of mass-produced tie-dyed ponchos would have sold particularly well. The legal mess that Epstein got himself into left a bad taste in his mouth, and after it was over he felt even less inclined to license Beatles merchandise for fear of getting burned a second time. Instead he focused on the group's music, and renegotiating their contract with EMI.

A combination of inexperience, naivety, and disinterest meant that Epstein lost the group a fortune. "The Beatles never made any money on merchandising in the United States," the group's American lawyer, Nat Weiss, claimed. "It had all been dissipated by the time the level of Beatlemania that would have generated the merchandising was over. After 1965 there was no possibility of income." "[If one takes the view that] the buck stops here," Weiss said, "then it's Brian's fault." Although Epstein "never denied that he didn't know about merchandising", he took credit for so many other things that, in this instance, he "had to acknowledge his mistakes".[15]

In fact he did, but The Beatles never forgave him. Epstein hadn't been the only one to underestimate the value of merchandising. The Beatles were just as ignorant of its importance. They might have liked money, but they didn't like being made into dolls or containers full of bubble bath, and could hardly contain their contempt when asked about it by *Playboy* in February 1965. They equated merchandising with children's cartoon characters, and weren't happy about being represented as such.

Only two years into their career, The Beatles had grown out of their cute, mop-top image. They might never have dreamt that they'd be turned into one-dimensional characters, but that's exactly what happened. Beatles merchandising products took a few recognisable features – their hair, for example – and turned them into novelties. But The Beatles saw themselves as serious musicians and couldn't see how that related to the many products with their name on.

"They didn't understand merchandising," Tony Barrow later claimed. "They would get very upset when a photographer they trusted, such as Dezo Hoffman, would publish a book of his Beatles photos. He'd immediately be refused access in the future." Lennon's famous quote – "We'll look after the music, you look after the percentages" – was clearly accurate. "With the possible exception of George, they didn't want to know what was happening."[16]

Had it been up to The Beatles alone, they probably wouldn't have bothered with merchandising at all. And if they had, they would have made the same mistakes Epstein did. They had no idea how much their image was worth, nor did they have any interest in dealing with licences and manufacturers. When Lennon was asked by a US reporter what he had wanted to do before he became a Beatle, he replied, "Nothing really. I just wanted to be rich, but I wanted to be a Beatle mainly." Asked what 'being a Beatle' meant, he defined it as "what we are ... a group, singing and selling records". That was the full extent of The Beatles' ambition at the time. They hadn't given any thought to the fact that they might become rich from selling wigs and dolls.

Until Epstein and Byrne made inroads into merchandising, nobody in music management – with the possible exception of Colonel Parker – had attempted anything like it on the kind of scale associated with The Beatles. "It wasn't happening then," says Larry Page, manager of The Kinks and The Troggs. "The Beatles were the first ones with little dolls coming out. Everyone thought, 'Isn't that wonderful. Look at that. Everybody's bringing out little dolls of The Beatles.' But it was never regarded as a big money maker."[17]

Epstein's attempts to control Beatles merchandising failed because the market was driving the demand for products, which became so great that it eventually controlled him. Had he taken more interest in merchandising – and not simply relied on poor business and legal advice – he might have been better able to control it. But as it was he let it slip through his fingers. The further it slipped from his grasp, the less control he had over it. NEMS was eventually forced to buy Byrne's share of Seltaeb – a company it should have owned from the outset. NEMS then formed a new company, Maximus Enterprises, to deal with Beatles merchandising, but all it did was license a poster to *Look* magazine. Only when *Yellow Submarine* was released in 1968 did it fully engage with the idea, leading to a range of themed merchandise that ranged from lunchboxes to Corgi models of the yellow submarine itself.

This was the last great merchandising push undertaken while The Beatles were still together, but the story doesn't end there. By the mid 1980s the group's image was once again being commercially exploited. In early 1986 Apple signed an agreement with Determined Productions Inc, a San Francisco-based company also responsible for *Snoopy* and *Peanuts* products. Part of this new agreement involved Determined being tasked with the job of ridding the world of unlicensed Beatles merchandise, and suing the manufacturers of unauthorised products on The Beatles' behalf. Once this had been achieved, Apple set about reseeding the world's retail outlets with its own 'official approved' novelty items, which covered everything from boxer shorts to cookie jars. If you had enough money (and no sense of taste) you could quite easily decorate your home from top to bottom with Beatles-themed products. You could even dress in clothes covered with Beatles motifs.

Apple took a third bite of the merchandising cherry in the late 1990s when it issued *Yellow Submarine* on DVD. As well as releasing a remixed *Songtrack* CD, Apple licensed Corgi to recast its submarine model; Gartlan USA to produce a lava lamp, a range of porcelain figures, and a 'Pepperland' musical globe; and McFarlane to make a range of articulated action figures of The Beatles and other characters from the film, including the Chief Blue Meanie and the Flying Glove. Suddenly it was 1968 all over again.

Each of the recent batches of reissued Beatles albums and DVDs has been accompanied by a range of merchandise. As part of a very successful marketing campaign for the *Anthology* project, Apple launched a new mail-order clothing company, Apple Organics, which sold, in conjunction with EMI, a range of Beatles hats, t-shirts, and rucksacks made from environmentally friendly materials emblazoned with the Apple logo. The internet, meanwhile, is awash with places to buy Beatles products, not least the virtual Apple Boutique. (The bricks-and-mortar version closed down almost as soon as its doors opened.) At The Beatles' official website it's possible to buy anything from a £4,500 Beatles jukebox to a £1,250 print of the *Sgt Pepper* artwork signed by Peter Blake.

The merchandising bubble isn't as big as it once was, but it's still a nice little earner. It's not just Beatles merchandise, either: George Harrison has a nice line in *Dark Horse* t-shirts and bags; John Lennon's name is used to sell everything from cuddly toys to 'fine art' prints; Paul McCartney will gladly sell you a keyring or an expensive jacket when he goes on tour; and Ringo has a selection of necklaces and baseball caps. All you need is love? Maybe, but what you really want is a cookie jar that plays 'Piggies' when you lift the lid.

Act Naturally
The Beatles at the movies

BBC interviewer: "You said you want to be a film star. I don't believe that; you don't really want to be a film 'star', do you?"
Ringo: "No, no. I want to be a film 'actor'."[1]

P op stars and the movies go together like fake tan and cheap sunglasses. It's the perfect symbiotic relationship. Rock'n'roll came of age at a time when the mass media was just hitting its stride, opening the doors for all sorts of combinations of sound and vision. Television was one thing, but films were even better. They were bigger, brighter, louder, and sometimes even better than the real thing. Viewers could see, hear, and almost touch their heroes (which was often a lot more than they could do at a concert).

Although it might seem like a more modern phenomenon, the pop promo video is actually almost 70 years old. In 1940 the Mills Novelty Company introduced its Panarom 'movie machine', a 'video jukebox' that for 10 cents allowed its customers to watch three-minute musical films from the comfort of their favourite Hollywood bar or hotel lobby. These film clips (or 'soundies') weren't restricted to the hits of the day: they featured a broad spectrum of styles and artists from country to jazz.

As the manufacturer's name suggests, these machines were little more than novelties. But people like novelties, be they video jukeboxes or Elvis Presley's swivelling hips. Rock'n'roll, too, was something of a novelty when it first stumbled up from the wrong side of the tracks into the bright lights of the city. Nobody expected it to last, but it did.

Making 'soundies' for jukeboxes was one thing, but the biggest and best novelty one could aim for was to star in a proper motion picture. Buck Owens had the right idea when he sang, "They're gonna put me in the movies / They're gonna make a big star out of me". Appearing on the big screen could make a square look hip and propel a nobody towards stardom.

Simply having a song used in a film, in fact, could work wonders on a flagging career. Bill Haley had wandered the rock'n'roll wilderness for years without much in the way of success before Hollywood came calling. His 'Rock Around The Clock' had already been issued as a B-side once, in early 1954, but it wasn't until it featured under the opening credits of *Blackboard Jungle* that it became a hit and thrust Haley into the limelight. He might have been fat, balding, and blind in one eye, but Columbia Pictures knew a good thing when they saw it and quickly cashed in on his sudden stardom with two quickie exploitation films, *Rock Around The Clock* (1956) and *Don't Knock The Rock* (1957). Both were designed to reap maximum profits from minimum outlay – and that they did.

In the years since, the good, the bad, and the largely indifferent have all starred in their very own motion pictures. These films have been made for one reason and one reason only: to make money. In the six decades since Eddie Cochran wiggled his way through 'Twenty Flight Rock' in *The Girl Can't Help It*, pop stars have made more bad films than Ed Wood.

British filmmakers were just as keen as their American cousins on the idea of making fast money. Always on the lookout for novelties and trends to exploit, they too were quick to jump on the rock'n'roll bandwagon. Insignia Films rushed out *The Tommy Steele Story*, Willoughby Film Productions cashed in on Billy Fury's success with *Beat Girl*, and Amicus Productions' *It's Trad, Dad!* cornered the lucrative jazz market. Meanwhile Cliff Richard, Britain's answer to Elvis, followed The King's example and made a string of cheap and cheerful 'light entertainment' musicals.

As soon as The Beatles became a pop sensation it was inevitable that they would be approached to make a film. "We'd progressed to success in America," Paul McCartney recalled. Film was the next logical step: "We'd loved *The Girl Can't Help It* and we knew you could make a rock'n'roll film."[2]

McCartney wasn't the only Beatle dreaming of film stardom. "Doesn't matter if you're in a group or not," John Lennon explained, "at one time or another everyone has imagined themselves starring in either a rock film or a James Bond film. We weren't any different, except suddenly we got the opportunity to do just that ... make a movie!"[3]

But what did The Beatles know about making movies? "Absolutely nothing," Lennon admitted, "except that we all instinctively knew if something was crap. And there were a lot of crap rock films about."[4] (Lennon cited the example of *The Teenage Millionaire*, which starred teen idol Jimmy Clanton alongside Dion, Jackie Wilson, and Chubby Checker, but there were plenty of others.)

The Beatles had already been in a BBC documentary, *The Mersey Sound*, while Pathé News had filmed the group for a short newsreel called *The Beatles*

Come To Town, which was later incorporated into the feature-length *Pop Gear*. Granada Television, meanwhile, decided to commission the Maysels Brothers, Albert and David, to document the group's first trip to America. The Beatles were being filmed everywhere they went, and to begin with they loved it. McCartney and Harrison were so entranced by the idea that they bought cameras of their own. "Happily we've spent a lot of this year in front of television cameras," McCartney told the *New Musical Express* in September 1963. "Now George and I have got a yen to be on the other side of the cameras and we aim to take movies of our fans in various parts of the country."

Feature-length film offers came in thick and fast, but neither Brian Epstein nor The Beatles were impressed with the quality of the scripts they received. (Fortunately for the group the RADA-trained Epstein had a better eye for screenplays than contracts.) As bad as some of the proposals were, however, the group couldn't help but be excited by the offers as they came in. "We were offered one early on called *The Yellow Teddy Bears*," McCartney recalled. "We were excited but it turned out that the fella involved was going to write all the songs, and we couldn't have that."[5]

The Yellow Teddy Bears did still go into production, but without The Beatles' involvement. There was no way Epstein would have allowed his boys to be associated with a film with the tagline "What they learned isn't on any record card!" Neither he nor the group wanted to make the kind of trashy b-movies that Elvis and Cliff Richard were knocking out. "None of us liked the films we were being offered at first," George Harrison explained in 1964, "so we didn't make one until we did. We were determined never to make a film where we'd be stuck in it for five minutes, like so many artists are on these rubbishy film spectaculars with millions of names. They're awful."[6]

The Beatles' stubbornness saved them from the b-movie hell that so many of their contemporaries fell into. But then they weren't like other pop groups. Having already insisted on recording their own songs, they weren't about to be rushed into making somebody else's bad film. Good sense prevailed, but once again The Beatles got lucky. Had they decided to work with a British company, they would almost certainly have ended up making something along the lines of *Just For Fun*, a cheap exploitation flick featuring "29 great hits" (and very little in the way of plot). Fortunately, before they could fall into that sort of trap, The Beatles were approached by an American Company, United Artists.

United Artists was one step ahead of its competitors. It was not technically a film production company but a distributor, and with no studio to run was able to keep its overheads much lower than those of Paramount or MGM. Because of the way it worked, United Artists shared its profits with producers, writers, and stars – and even allowed the rights to its films to revert to the producers after a certain period. (In the case of *A Hard Day's Night*, the rights reverted to Walter Shenson after 15 years.)

United Artists had a strong presence in Europe in both the film and music worlds. Noel Rogers, the head of the company's music publishing division in London, was the first to recognise the potential profitability of The Beatles, and was quick to alert George 'Bud' Ornstein, who ran the UK filmmaking arm. Capitol Records might still have been happy to reject hit after hit by The Beatles, but United Artists saw that it was only a matter of time before the group made it big in the USA.

United Artists planned to offer The Beatles a three-picture deal with the intention of also securing the rights to the accompanying soundtrack recordings. A soundtrack record would, of course, feature several Beatles hits and make as much money for the company as the film itself. Luckily for United Artists, The Beatles' contract with EMI did not include soundtrack recordings. Although Parlophone had an option on issuing Beatles soundtrack albums in the UK, United Artists hit pay dirt in the USA.

Before Ornstein could agree a deal with Epstein, however, he had to get clearance from David Picker, United Artists' Vice President Of Production And Marketing. Ornstein told Picker that a Beatles film could be made for around £60,000, and that the deal would include publishing and a soundtrack. Picker was impressed. "I said, 'If we can get those rights there is nothing to lose, because those rights will be worth something even if the movies aren't a hit'," he recalled. "So I approved a three-picture deal with this group called The Beatles that of course I'd never heard of."[7]

It didn't matter that Picker had never heard of The Beatles. The percentages added up to a profit. And if the first Beatles film flopped, United Artists had a get-out clause that would allow them to drop the group in a flash. As long as Picker got the soundtrack album – which could potentially sell millions of copies – he was happy. "What we [might] lose on the film," Ornstein explained, "we'll get back on the disc."[8]

United Artists got another pleasant surprise upon being introduced to Brian Epstein, whom the company quickly realised was a naive former shopkeeper with no real idea of just how valuable his Beatles were. On making his initial overtures to Ornstein, Epstein insisted that he couldn't accept anything less than a £20,000 advance and seven and a half per cent of the net profits. Ornstein couldn't believe his luck: United Artists would have been prepared to offer as much as £70,000 plus 25 per cent.

Fortunately for Epstein (and The Beatles) there was not yet a contract to sign. Epstein passed the task of agreeing one on to his lawyer, David Jacobs, who was then in the midst of gifting The Beatles' American merchandising rights to his friend, Nicky Byrne. He saw better sense on this occasion and insisted that United Artists offer a cash payment of £25,000 and 20 per cent of the net profits[9] – much more than Epstein had initially suggested, but still significantly less than United Artists' upper limit.

United Artists wasted no time in putting its first Beatles film into production. One of the first people approached to work on the project was Walter Shenson, a former Hollywood publicist who had moved to England during the 1950s and produced a couple of low-budget comedies: *The Mouse That Roared*, which starred Peter Sellers, and *The Mouse On The Moon*, which was directed by Richard Lester. The company was working so quickly that Shenson was asked to produce the Beatles film even before either party knew what it would be about. "United Artists approached me and asked me if I'd make a film for them," he recalled. "I thought they had a script or a book or something." In fact, all United Artists had was a vague plan to "make a movie with The Beatles".[10]

Shenson was still keen, however, and brought Lester along with him to direct. Lester had moved to London in the early 1950s and, after catching the eye of Peter Sellers, was given the job of translating the anarchic BBC radio series *The Goon Show* to television. He was then called upon to direct Sellers's self-financed *The Running Jumping And Standing Still Film*, which also starred Spike Milligan. George Martin had produced group records by The Goons, and solo efforts by Sellers and Milligan, of which The Beatles – and Lennon in particular – were huge fans. Who better than Lester, then, to direct their film?

As well as working with The Goons, Lester had also directed the jazzploitation flick *It's Trad, Dad!*, so knew how to sidestep the pitfalls that The Beatles wanted to avoid. Lester didn't want to follow the established template of the rock'n'roll movie; he wanted to do something new with the genre, which was what The Beatles wanted, too. "I think The Beatles were more interested in not being like the other films than I was," he explained, "because I don't think I'd seen many of them."[11]

Although United Artists were committed to making the film, they weren't prepared to stretch the budget – which, according to Lester, was capped at £200,000.[12] Shooting began on March 2nd 1964 and was completed by April 24th, with United Artists angling for an early July release, eager for both film and soundtrack to be out before the Beatlemania bubble burst. "[United Artists] kept calling me saying, 'Do you think they'll still be popular when the film comes out?'" Shenson recalled. "I said, 'I don't know if they're going to last or not. Just put the picture out. Don't worry if they're going to last! Because they're popular now and that's what you put the money into.'"[13]

A Hard Day's Night premiered in Britain on July 6th and in the USA on August 12th. United Artists needn't have worried about The Beatles' popularity waning. The film was a spectacular success on both sides of the Atlantic. In America it opened in 500 theatres and earned around $5.8 million in its first six weeks. According to the *Motion Picture Herald*, only *Goldfinger* earned more at the British box office in 1964. The same poll did however place the group behind Cliff Richard and Elvis Presley in terms of popularity among cinemagoers, but they were, it seems, still more popular than Sophia Loren and Dirk Bogarde. "Strange days indeed," as John Lennon would later put it.

United Artists struck gold with the soundtrack album, too, just as expected. It was so successful, in fact, that the company made a profit even before the film was released. Under the terms of its contract with The Beatles, United Artists could issue all eight of the songs the group recorded for the film. This wasn't quite enough for a full-length album, so it was padded out with instrumental tacks recorded by George Martin.

Capitol had the right to issue the same material, but crucially wasn't allowed to market its release as an original soundtrack recording. This gave United Artists a distinct advantage, but the company still made sure of the success of its *Hard Day's Night* soundtrack by issuing it on June 26th, six weeks ahead of the film's release. Such was The Beatles' popularity that the album sold one million copies in its first four days, making it one of the fastest selling albums of all time. Soundtrack recordings were big business at the time, and held the three top spots on *Billboard* in the week that *A Hard Day's Night* entered the chart. The Beatles' soundtrack quickly rose to the top itself, and remained there for 14 weeks, despite Capitol's attempts to undermine its success with its own *Something New*.

Issued on August 1st, *Something New* was originally set to feature the seven soundtrack songs (excluding 'I'll Cry Instead', which featured on the United Artists album despite having been pulled from the film at the last minute) and five unreleased songs. But having been beaten to the punch by United Artists, Capitol had to rethink its marketing strategy, eventually deciding to pair five of the soundtrack recordings with six new songs instead. The album really did offer 'something new' to Beatles fans, who snapped it up in their droves. *Something New* sold 500,000 copies on pre-orders alone, eventually topping the two million mark, and spent nine weeks at Number 2 on *Billboard* (right behind *A Hard Day's Night*).

A Hard Day's Night sold well in Britain, too, although it was EMI and not United Artists that reaped the financial rewards as the film helped the record achieve unprecedented sales levels. "The group breaks every rule in the book on sales," an EMI employee told *Disc Weekly*. Where once the 'saturation point' for album sales in Britain was around 500,000, he said, the group's second album soon doubled that figure. "It wouldn't surprise us in the least if the *A Hard Day's Night* LP reached a million when the film makes its full impact."[14]

Capitol enjoyed one major advantage over United Artists in that it had the rights to issue the soundtrack recordings as singles. Whereas in Britain the film's title song had been issued with the non-soundtrack 'Things We Said

Today' as its B-side, Capitol opted to include 'I Should Have Known Better', which was included in the film, on the flipside of its own 'A Hard Day's Night' single. This was all part of a clever ploy to make as many songs from the *A Hard Day's Night* soundtrack available on Capitol as possible, even if it couldn't market an 'original soundtrack'. But while Capitol was keen to steal United Artists' thunder, it was also happy for the film to do well, as that could only be good all concerned in the long run. Despite being in direct competition with United Artists over the songs, Capitol still made mention of both the film and its distributor on the label of its 'A Hard Day's Night' single, which spent two weeks atop the *Billboard* singles chart.

Capitol wasted no time in issuing a follow-up to 'A Hard Day's Night', which was released on July 13th in the USA (three days after its UK release). A week later, the label put out two more film-themed singles, 'I'll Cry Instead' / 'I'm Happy Just To Dance With You' and 'And I Love Her' / 'If I Fell'. In the space of just two weeks, Capitol had issued six of seven songs featured in *A Hard Day's Night* on singles. 'And I Love Her' proved to be very popular not just with the public but with other singers, too. It peaked at Number 12 on *Billboard*, while several other artists recorded the song in the wake of The Beatles releasing it. 'I'll Cry Instead' wasn't quite as successful, but still reached Number 25.

United Artists fought back with two singles of its own. Although it couldn't release songs by The Beatles as 45s, there was nothing to stop the label putting out a version of 'And I Lover Her' backed with 'Ringo's Theme (This Boy)' as performed by "The Beatles' brilliant musical director, George Martin & His Orchestra". It was followed by another Martin single, 'A Hard Day's Night' / 'I Should Have Known Better'. Neither single featured an actual Beatle, but that didn't stop them doing reasonable business. 'And I Love Her' sold a respectable 200,000 copies and peaked at Number 105 on *Billboard*; the B-side made it as high as 53. Martin's version of the film's title track stalled at Number 122. (It was followed by a full album of *Hard Day's Night* instrumentals by Martin.)

A Hard Day's Night was a fantastic critical, financial, and marketing success. There was only one problem – the usual problem. Most of the money made from the film (and the related albums) went to somebody other than The

Beatles. Once again Epstein had let a small fortune slip through his fingers. In response he did what he always did: set up a new company (albeit rather too late). In January 1964 he became the director of Subafilms Limited, which subsequently produced an exploitation flick starring Gerry & The Pacemakers entitled *Ferry Cross The Mersey*. Not as inventive as *A Hard Day's Night*, *Ferry Cross The Mersey* cast Gerry and his Pacemaker pals as art students by day and musicians by night.

Subafilms' next act was to document the 5th National Jazz And Blues Festival in Richmond, England, from August 6th–8th 1965, which featured performances by groups such as The Moody Blues, The Animals, and The Who. A few days later, a 12-man American crew filmed The Beatles' first and greatest appearance at Shea Stadium in front of 55,600 fans (a record at the time for a rock'n'roll concert). The Beatles were paid $160,000 for their 30-minute set. The resulting film, a co-production by Sullivan Productions, NEMS Enterprises, and Subafilms, aired in black-and-white on the BBC on March 1st 1966, and in colour in the USA on January 10th 1967.

Making a few low-budget films and television programmes might have kept Epstein in champagne and caviar (and The Beatles in spliffs and bacon butties) but the real money was going to be made with The Beatles' next full-length feature. Talks had begun about a follow-up even before *A Hard Day's Night* was rushed out in August 1964. A month earlier, *Disc Weekly* had reported that The Beatles were already trying to come up with ideas for a second film. The trouble was that *A Hard Day's Night* – a kind of 'day in the life' of the group – had said it all. The follow-up needed a stronger plot, but by the time The Beatles got around to coming up with one their natural talents had disappeared into a cloud of oddly scented smoke.

There were also some financial concerns to resolve. *A Hard Day's Night* had made its producer, Walter Shenson, a millionaire. When it came to negotiating a contract for a second Beatles film, Epstein made sure that he and they received a bigger slice of the profits. United Artists would still distribute the film, but it would be a joint Shenson/Subafilms production this time. The intention of course was to bring in more money, but as ever it wasn't entirely straightforward. The Beatles were now having to pay the top rate of income tax in the UK, and needed to come up with a way to keep hold of their earnings. The obvious solution was to set up a tax shelter.

George Harrison wasn't the only Beatle to complain about the British tax system. Lennon was earning considerably more than Harrison, and therefore had to hand over even more of it to the taxman. Lennon considered himself to be a socialist, but told journalist Ray Coleman that he was thinking about voting Conservative because "you have to look after your money".[15] The Beatles had earned millions in record sales, merchandising, and film rentals in 1964. Even if they didn't receive all they were entitled to, their earnings amounted to a large fortune. Revenue services on both sides of the Atlantic were eager to take their cut.

On January 5th 1965 the *New York Times* reported that the group was set to "shun" America as a result of a "tax rift". The paper claimed that The Beatles were considering boycotting future US tours because the Treasury was blocking access to the $2.8 million they'd earned from their 1964 tour. A NEMS spokesman revealed that "negotiations about The Beatles' earnings are now going on with the American government".[16]

It wasn't just the US government that wanted a slice of The Beatles' American income. The group's American lawyer, Walter Hofer, confirmed that the British government wanted its cut, too. "Our position is that we await the two governments coming to a decision on the matter," he said. "We're not resisting the tax, we just don't want to have to pay it twice."[17] Until the matter could be resolved The Beatles looked elsewhere for employment opportunities. Ever vigilant, the group's accountants suggested that the Bahamas might offer suitable relief from Britain's acquisitive tax system.

When Richard Lester was called upon to direct the second Beatles film, he recalled there being "some nudges from The Beatles' tax people that it would be a good thing if it were made in the Bahamas". Lester wasn't averse to the idea, but was "keenly aware, throughout our time filming there, of a gentleman – I will not mention his name – in a dark brown suit and tie with a briefcase in either hand". Brian Epstein, Lester noted, "was clearly looking for somewhere to put a lot of The Beatles' money".[18]

In the end Epstein's plans to squirrel away large chunks of The Beatles' money in offshore bank accounts came to nothing. He got cold feet when he thought of the bad press that might appear should his scam be uncovered. While spending long periods of time abroad and setting up offshore accounts later became standard practice for rock stars, Epstein didn't want to see his boys' reputations tarnished by suggestions that they weren't law-abiding citizens.

In return for the hundreds of thousands of pounds they paid the British government in tax, The Beatles were awarded MBEs. The *Melody Maker* had already started a campaign for The Beatles to be honoured either with awards from Buckingham Palace or a national 'day of recognition'. (Considering the amount of money the government made from The Beatles, giving the group MBEs was probably the least it could do.)

"Somebody said it might have been [because of] that," McCartney admitted when asked if the awards had anything to do with the ten million dollars worth of records that The Beatles had sold in America. "But you never know."[19]

Because *A Hard Day's Night* had been so incredibly successful, United Artists doubled the budget for The Beatles' second film to £400,000. The group's fee was increased, too. According to Walter Shenson, they were paid three times as much for *Help!* as they had been for their big-screen debuts. Richard Lester was also given a pay rise, and received £30,000 in recognition of his remarkable job of directing four stoned Beatles.

Because The Beatles' first film had been so different to what came before it, nobody wanted to make *A Hard Day's Night II*. The follow-up needed to be similarly inventive. The Beatles' first film had been significantly different to previous big-screen rock'n'roll fare. "It will not be a pop musical," Shenson claimed in *Disc Weekly* in September 1964, adding that The Beatles would serve as "scriptwriters" this time around. In the event, Shenson was wrong on both counts: it did end up being a musical, but the group had nothing to do with the plotting of it. "With *A Hard Day's Night* we had a lot of input, and it was semi-realistic," Lennon admitted. "But with *Help!* Dick Lester didn't tell us what it was about."[20]

Lester didn't tell The Beatles what it was about because to begin with he didn't know himself. Alun Owen, who wrote the script for *A Hard Day's Night*, was dropped in favour of Marc Behm, whom Lester described as "a rather absurdist thriller writer who worked out of Paris".[21] (Behm was an American ex-pat who settled in France after serving in the Second World War.) Further complications ensued when another director, Philippe de Broca, happened by chance to make a film called *Les Tribulations D'Un Chinois En Chine* that had a very similar plot to the one Lester had planned for the Beatles film. Charles Wood was called in to do a quick re-write.

None of this made a lot of difference to The Beatles, however, who had by then decided that the only way to get through the long, tedious days on the set was to consume vast amounts of marijuana. "Nobody could communicate with us," Lennon admitted. "It was all glazed eyes and giggling all the time."[22]

Trying to make a film with four stoned and disinterested Beatles wasn't easy. Lester solved the problem by calling action and then having them repeat their lines after him. Other directors would have thrown their hands up in despair. But as was so often the case with The Beatles, they had ended up with just the right man in the right place at the right time. "We were lucky to meet Brian Epstein," George Harrison noted. "Then we got George Martin, lucky again, because there are so many bad A&R men. Same with the film. It made all the difference to work with Walter Shenson and Dick Lester. They have the perfect nature for us."[23]

Although they might have appeared to be rather ambivalent towards the making of *Help!*, The Beatles were actually starting to feel the strain of having to make a successful follow-up to their first film. They might have been riding a tsunami of success, but they were also, according to Lester, beginning to crack under pressure. "Ringo was the one I worried about," Lester said. "He developed a tic during the making of the film – and we kept having to cut away from his shots quite early to avoid it."[24]

Even before the start of filming Starr had seemed anxious. "It's just like doing your first one, only worse," he told the *Melody Maker* in February 1965. "People will be watching us and expecting better."[25] Even John Lennon – who tended usually to have a nonchalant attitude to these things – seemed worried. "It's much worse this time, having something to live up to," he said. "If nobody likes it, that's it."[26]

The Beatles were right to be concerned. The film received decidedly mixed reviews after its release in July 1965. The *New York Times* called it "a fiasco of whimsies" and described the group themselves as "awfully redundant" and "dull".[27] Another journalist, Chris Hitchens, warned cinema-goers not to "go expecting a GREAT picture because *Help!* is not that".[28] *Melody Maker* gave a more measured critique, noting that, while there was too much buffoonery and not enough witty dialogue, the songs and direction were both excellent. But that hardly compared to the response to *A Hard Day's Night*.

The Beatles had been expecting this kind of reaction, having been on the receiving end of a wave of criticism for some time already. "We're quite prepared for a knocking," Ringo Starr said in the week the film went on release. "We've had a hell of a lot of it lately, what with the MBE business. When you get popular, you must expect it."[29] Good press or bad, the film was still a hit. As with *A Hard Day's Night* there was a record demand for prints following the London premiere of *Help!* on July 29th. United Artists made and distributed more prints of *Help!* than any of its previous colour pictures.

Help! did very good business in Britain. Box office receipts at the London Pavilion, where it had its premiere, were up 37 per cent compared to when *A Hard Day's Night* had opened there a year earlier. All in all, *Help!* brought in ten million dollars worldwide. United Artists' other big hit for 1965, *What's New, Pussycat*, earned $12 million but had cost a lot more to make. The key to profitability, in the case of *Help!*, was the cost of production.

By the time *Help!* went on release the rights to issue a soundtrack album had reverted, under the terms of The Beatles' new recording contract, from United Artists to Capitol. The album Capitol issued followed the template that United Artists had established for *A Hard Day's Night*, matching seven new Beatles songs with five instrumentals. Never one to miss a trick, Capitol upped the price of the album by one dollar – despite the fact that its seven Beatles tracks amounted, by the standards of The Beatles' Parlophone LPs, to more like half an album.

Help! sold one million copies in its first week of release in the USA and topped the charts on both sides of the Atlantic. There wasn't much United Artists could do except sit back and watch as Capitol raked in the dollars. It did however issue its own *Help!* album of sorts: a collection of instrumental tracks from the film, scored by Ken Thorne but attributed, once again, to George Martin & His Orchestra.

Help! dropped The Beatles into a bizarre fantasy world. It was, in Walter Shenson's words, "a comic strip vividly brought to life and packed with colour, thrills, and that distinctive Beatles humour". Even if the critics didn't like it, it made a lot of money. And it encouraged another spin-off idea: if The Beatles could be made into caricatures of themselves, why not turn them into actual cartoon characters? Just as United Artists had turned The Beatles into two-dimensional characters, so King Features had secured the rights to produce a series of cartoons featuring the group for American television.

The television series was broadcast by the ABC television network and followed the formula of *A Hard Day's Night*. "The four lead characters will be based on the personalities of John, George, Paul and Ringo," a report in *Variety* read. "On the soundtrack, The Beatles will perform a minimum of two songs in each half hour, some of them new, some Beatles classics."[30]

The cartoon was the brainchild of Al Brodax, who had previously produced 220 episodes of *Popeye*. He had been looking for a way to combine original music and animation for some time. The tremendous success of The Beatles gave him the perfect opportunity. Brodax approached Epstein for the rights to animate The Beatles' likenesses and use their music and lyrics in the cartoons. Epstein seemed to like the idea and, as had become his custom, directed Brodax to Walter Hofer. Epstein had learnt his lesson with the merchandising fiasco and now insisted on a contract that favoured The Beatles. Brodax was told by Hofer that "any deal would be a matter of paying an onerous amount of money, granting majority ownership in the series, and certain special provisos that Brian is adamant about", such as that "commercials that have anything to do with depilatories, deodorants, etc would be prohibited".[31]

The Beatles could sell anything in 1964. An animated cartoon series was no different to a Beatles wig or a pair of sneakers. It was just another way to sell the group and their music, and to make money. If handled right the cartoon could make its producers a lot of money. All they needed to find was the right sponsor. As luck would have it (again), an ailing toy manufacturer, the A.C. Gilbert Company, saw the Beatles cartoon as the perfect vehicle to promote its toys and paid one-and-a-half million dollars. This bought the company three minutes of advertising per show, about which it was very pleased. "We have undoubtedly captured the television plum of the season in The Beatles," a company spokesman said.[32] (Quaker Oats and Mars also bought advertising.)

In terms of audience ratings the show was indeed a 'plum'. It opened with a 51.9 per cent share of the viewing audience and was the second most successful Saturday morning show of the season. In its first year the series grossed three million dollars, leading ABC to commission a further 13 episodes. From a critical perspective, however, *The Beatles* was disappointing. The kids might have loved it, but with a budget of only $30,000 per show, the animation and storylines played second fiddle to the music. "As far as I'm concerned, the sponsors have paid for The Beatles tracks and the kids want to hear them," supervising director Jack Stokes complained, "so anything else must suffer before the music."[33]

Suffer it did. King Features didn't have its own studio, so subcontracted the animation to studios in London and Sydney. Initial plans to have The Beatles lend their voices to the project were soon forgotten. Instead, the speaking parts were "done by actors in somewhat exaggerated voices". This was done partly because it was assumed that an American audience might struggle to understand the group's Liverpool accents. (Similarly, United Artists had wanted to overdub the dialogue for *A Hard Day's Night*.)

As banal as it was, the Beatles cartoon series played an important role in keeping the group in the public eye. It presented a consistent and safe image of the group to the kids and their parents. The real-life Beatles were changing, but in cartoonland they were still cute mop-tops. "This crucial aspect of the Al Brodax venture was not even considered, let alone appreciated, by Brian Epstein," Tony Barrow later noted, "but the rest of us saw it as a significant factor in prolonging the career of The Beatles in the commercially important teenyboppers' market."[34]

But as useful as *The Beatles* might have been in the USA, the group were so unhappy with the final product that they refused to let it air on British television. It wasn't shown in Britain until 1980 and wasn't repeated for another eight years (and even then only on the proviso that it aired late at night). The Beatles didn't want their British fans to see what had been done to them in America, and who could blame them?

The Beatles might not have liked their cartoon selves, but Al Brodax saw great potential in his animated mop-tops and kept thinking of ways to develop the idea further. He first tried to pitch the idea of similar cartoons about other British groups such as Herman's Hermits and Freddie & The Dreamers, but was unable to convince any television executives of their value. After going back to the drawing board, it occurred to him that rather than try to dilute the formula with lesser beat groups he should attempt to expand his Beatles television series into a feature-length film.

By 1967 Brodax had, perhaps surprisingly, managed to convince Epstein and The Beatles that such a film might work. The positive response was due in part to the fact that the group still owed United Artists a third film but had been unable to find a suitable vehicle for it. Various scripts had been submitted and commissioned, among them a western called *A Talent For Loving* and *Shades Of A Personality*, in which The Beatles would each play different parts of a character with a split personality.

None of these ideas made it very far. A whole year passed in a haze of marijuana and LSD without any sign of a suitable concept for a new Beatles film. "It's difficult to find a suitable script because we are all demanding a very high standard," Shenson told *Melody Maker* in May 1966. "We don't have to make a film at the moment and we are all agreed that it's better to make no film at all than make a bad one."[35] Another idea that didn't come to fruition was a script by British playwright and satirist Joe Orton entitled *Up Against It*, which Orton based on an earlier story of his own called *The Silver Bucket*. Orton's script was too provocative, however, even for The Beatles – in it, according to its author, the group would be "caught in-flagrante", "become involved in dubious political activity", crossdress, and commit murder – and didn't get any further than a first draft. After that things started to get desperate. It was even suggested that The Beatles might star in new versions of *The Three Musketeers* or *Lord Of The Rings*.

It was only then that Shenson, Epstein, and The Beatles realised that the answer had been staring them in the face all along. Al Brodax had been badgering Epstein for some time about his idea for a feature-length Beatles cartoon. This, Epstein eventually realised, would be perfect. Not only would it fulfil the group's contract with United Artists, it would also mean that they wouldn't have to do anything too tiresome. Rather than sit on a drafty film set they could do what they wanted, which was to disappear to India for a couple of months.

The Beatles didn't take much convincing, and it wasn't long before Brodax had been given a contract to start work on the project (subject to Epstein's approval of the screenplay). United Artists, however, were a little harder to persuade. The Beatles still owed the company a film, but since they wouldn't actually appear in this one, would it really be enough to fulfil their contractual obligations? Lennon was adamant that this "was the third film that we owed United Artists", and so was Epstein. Realising that another live-action Beatles feature wasn't likely to appear any time soon, the company agreed to the production and set a budget of one million dollars to make the film. It was, nonetheless, a gamble. Disney's last hit animated film, *101 Dalmatians*, was already six years old, while the British film industry hadn't produced an animated feature since *Animal Farm* over a decade earlier.

After getting the green light from United Artists, King Features signed a contract with NEMS Enterprises and Subafilms that gave the company the right to use 'Yellow Submarine' as the title song, as well as three new Beatles compositions. The contract also stipulated that King Features would "provide a writer to meet with Paul McCartney to fully discuss [the initial] treatment, and thereupon write a screen treatment based upon these discussions".[36]

All Al Brodax had to do therefore was find a writer who could come up with something that would please Epstein and McCartney. He first commissioned Lee Minoff to come up with a story, but Minoff's initial efforts were rejected as "candy floss" and needed multiple reworkings. Minoff was paid $15,000 for his first draft and $2,500 for a rewrite. Erich Segal, a professor of Greek and Latin literature, was brought in next on the strength of his having worked previously on a planned (but subsequently aborted) musical with Richard Rodgers. Segal was paid $16,000 for his Beatle screenplay, but it still needed further work. Performance poet Roger McGough (also a member of the comedy group The Scaffold) was called in to help with dialogue, while screenwriter Jack Mendelsohn was asked to rework several troublesome scenes.

The Beatles had little to do with the film, but, as McCartney's early involvement demonstrates, didn't want to put their name to any old thing. Nor did King Features. The company was keen to produce something special, and aimed to be as adventurous with the film as The Beatles were with their record-making. McCartney was pleasantly surprised by his meetings with Segal, particularly after discovering that King Features had taken "the psychedelic option".[37] (The film's mind-blowing visual style might not have been directly attributable to LSD, but the drug did have an indirect effect in that The Beatles had consumed rather a lot of it while making *Sgt Pepper's Lonely Hearts Club Band*, which director George Dunning was given an advance preview of before he started work on the film.)

Dunning was the co-founder of TV Cartoons, the company King Features hired to make *Yellow Submarine*. TV Cartoons employed 200 artists on the project, who between them worked on it from July 1967 to June 1968 – which was actually about a quarter of the time it usually took to produce a full-length animated feature. Because the film was being made in such a hurry, however, TV Cartoons overspent what was already a tight budget and ended up having to put £25,000 of its own money into the project in order to finish it on time.

"The film made money left and right," Dunning recalled, "but [not] for TV Cartoons."[38] Money was so tight that Dunning put some of the negatives in a bank vault as insurance against the production being taken over by King Features. "About three fourths of the way through the film, the money was getting short," claimed TV Cartoons accountant Ellen Hall. "[King Features] just wanted to put the receivers in, if you like, and take over."[39]

Despite these problems, TV Cartoons survived, the negatives were returned, and *Yellow Submarine* was completed on schedule. When The Beatles saw early rushes of the film their attitude to it changed. To their surprise it looked good – very good in fact. It was too late for them to have any real involvement with it: the script had been written, the actors hired, and production was well underway. What they did decide to do was to provide an additional song – Lennon's newly written 'Hey Bulldog' – for the soundtrack. (Ironically, the song was deleted from the US version of the film.) The Beatles also filmed a brief cameo, to be inserted into the end of the film, at Twickenham Film Studio on January 25th 1968, and turned up in force to the premiere, which was held at the London Pavilion on July 17th.

Yellow Submarine did well when it opened, taking £7,000 in its first week, but for some reason it was not given a full general release in Britain. The Rank Organisation, which distributed the film, claimed that the results of screening it in 12 theatres outside London were "rather disappointing", which led the company to cancel "a number of theatre bookings" on the grounds that the film was "obviously not appealing to some people whom one might expect it to".[40] There might be some truth in this, but it seems likely that Rank was more interested in promoting the three films of its own that had just been released – The Magnificent Two, The Long Duel, and The Jokers – than a rival company's production. Rank effectively destroyed any chance of Yellow Submarine succeeding in Britain, but the film performed much more strongly in America, leading to worldwide receipts of $8.2 million – a healthy (if not overly impressive) return on the original investment of one million dollars.

The Beatles once again issued a soundtrack to coincide with the film's release, but this time had only provided four songs for it, so it wasn't going to be much of an album. They originally planned to make it an EP instead, with 'Only A Northern Song', 'Hey Bulldog', and 'Across The Universe' on Side One, and 'All Together Now' and 'It's All Too Much' on Side Two. This would have been fine in Britain, where EPs still sold well (particularly if they were by The Beatles). In the USA, however, the EP format had never really caught on, so the decision was taken to put 'Across The Universe' back on the shelf and replace it with the film's title song and the group's recent hit 'All You Need Is Love'. Side Two of the album, as with previous Beatles soundtracks, consisted of instrumental recordings by George Martin.

The release of the Yellow Submarine soundtrack was delayed by several months so as not to upset the momentum of the double album The Beatles, which had only just come out. When Apple Records did eventually release it, the soundtrack did very well. It sold over a million copies and was only kept off the top spot on *Billboard* by *The Beatles*. (It reached Number 3 in the UK.)

Yellow Submarine completed The Beatles' three-picture deal with United Artists, but the relationship between the two parties continued. Within a year of recording their cameo appearances for the film, The Beatles were back at Twickenham Film Studios working on what ended up being their final feature-length film, *Let It Be*.

Towards the end of 1968 the group had come up with the idea of taping some low-key concerts to promote *The Beatles*. Having distanced themselves from the sophisticated multi-tracking of *Sgt Pepper*, The Beatles had returned to a sound that could more easily be reproduced in a live setting. In September 1968 *Melody Maker* quoted George Harrison as saying that the idea of returning to the stage "is appealing", and that he'd "like to be resident in a club, with the amps there all the time so you could just walk onstage and plug in".[41] All sorts of rumours appeared about what form a Beatles comeback gig might take. Some reports suggested that the group had booked London's Royal Albert Hall, but Tony Barrow denied it. "The Beatles want to do some sort of live show," he told *Disc & Music Echo*, "but it is almost certain to be before a special audience of perhaps 500. The show would be filmed for TV and would require a more intimate venue than the Albert Hall."[42]

In November it was suggested that The Beatles were planning to play at another London venue, the Roundhouse, from December 14th–21st. This time, however, it was Derek Taylor who was forced to come out and disappoint the fans with the announcement that both the Roundhouse gigs and another rumoured appearance in Liverpool were "unlikely" to go ahead.[43]

With *The Beatles* selling in its millions, the idea of a televised live show was put on hold, but the prospect of a concert remained. "The Beatles will appear live," Derek Taylor confirmed, "but not before the New Year. It will be on the lines of their 'Hey Jude' TV film, with a proper audience, but it will be a much longer performance."[44] Instead of performing songs from *The Beatles*, however, the group decided to start again in early 1969 and write and rehearse new material for the show. The idea, such as it was, came from McCartney. "It was another one like *Magical Mystery Tour*," Lennon later recalled. "Paul wanted us to go on the road or do something. He sort of set it up, and there were discussions about where to go and all that."[45]

The problem was deciding where to go. The possibilities were endless – the Roundhouse, a flourmill, a Roman amphitheatre – but none seemed quite right. McCartney aside, none of the other Beatles expressed much interest in the venture. At the suggestion of producer Denis O'Dell, however, they did at least start rehearsing. (They needed to get their act together by February 3rd, which was when Ringo Starr was due to start filming *The Magic Christian* with Peter Sellers.)

O'Dell booked The Beatles into Twickenham Film Studios, where they began rehearsals on January 2nd. He suggested that they film the rehearsals for use in a documentary to accompany the planned concert footage. "There's never been a film of The Beatles actually working," Derek Taylor announced. "It'll all be there, the works, the breaks, everything."[46] The director for the project was Michael Lindsay-Hogg, a veteran of *Ready Steady Go* who had also directed several Beatles promos as well as The Rolling Stones' as yet unreleased *Rock'n'Roll Circus*. He had originally planned to capture the events on videotape (an unusual choice of format at the time) but was encouraged by O'Dell to shoot on 16mm film instead, which proved fortuitous when it was decided to turn the resulting footage into a feature-length film rather than a television show.

Coming only 11 weeks after the conclusion of several months of fractious work on *The Beatles*, the Twickenham sessions didn't start well. As de facto leader, McCartney seemed to constantly annoy Harrison, who in turn was similarly irritated by Lennon. Yoko Ono's silent, brooding presence and Lennon's heroin addiction brought relations within the group to an all-time low. (Starr was no less affected by the situation, but seemed content to go with the flow as long as nothing interfered with his impending departure to work on *The Magic Christian*.)

Things came to a head on January 10th. After a blazing row with Lennon, Harrison quit The Beatles. Lennon, McCartney, and Starr carried on as if nothing had happened. Perhaps they were shocked; perhaps they didn't know what else to do. They went on as a three-piece after a lunch break, and even started jamming with Ono, but any hope of playing live or completing the film had come to a grinding halt. Harrison was given a few days to think things over before a band meeting was called. Although he was still minded to quit, he said he'd stay as long as some changes were made to the group's plans: there would be no playing live, but The Beatles should instead start work on a new album based on the songs they had rehearsed in Twickenham.

McCartney's concert film therefore became a document of The Beatles rehearsing and recording a new album. The next set of rehearsals began at Apple Studios on January 22nd, with Billy Preston invited along by Harrison to play keyboards (and ease the tension). Having Preston around made a big difference. While Lennon still called the sessions "six weeks of misery",[47] recording engineer Glyn Johns had a rather different view, claiming that he "didn't stop laughing for six weeks", partly because "John Lennon only had to walk in a room and I'd crack up".[48]

There was still the problem of turning all of this into a film. The whole thing needed to come to a more satisfying conclusion than just the completion of the album. During an Apple meeting on Sunday January 26th it was proposed that the group play on the roof of their headquarters at 3 Savile Row. Harrison grudgingly agreed; Starr wasn't keen. But four days later all four Beatles climbed the stairs to the roof and blasted central London for 40 minutes. Hidden from all but a handful of people, The Beatles gave their final public performance before eventually being stopped by the police.

The Beatles returned to Apple studios the following day to film three more songs: 'Let It Be', 'The Long And Winding Road', and 'Two Of Us' (none of which had been suitable for a rooftop performance).

Filming stopped after that, but the project was far from finished. What they needed now was a soundtrack album. Glyn Johns was given the job of putting an album together from the many hours of recordings The Beatles made at Apple. "We didn't want to know about it any more, so we just left it to Glyn," Lennon explained.[49] Johns started work on the project on March 4th. George Martin attempted to mix 'Get Back' on March 26th before giving the tapes back to him. When 'Get Back' was issued as a single, however, it didn't credit either producer, much to Johns's annoyance: "I sat them down and said, 'Look, I know you originally employed me [as an] engineer ... [but] as I was the only one there and actually put it together on my own, I'd really appreciate a producer's credit.'"[50]

Johns carried on mixing anyway, and by May 28th had completed work (or so he thought) on an album, provisionally entitled *Get Back*. The only problem was that nobody really liked it. Johns made a second attempt at piecing an album together, which he delivered to The Beatles on January 5th 1970 – a little over a year after the group had first started work on the project. Acetates were cut and mock-up jackets produced, but once again *Get Back* was put on hold. With the release of the film imminent, Phil Spector was called in to try to turn the tapes into something worthy of release. "He worked like a pig on it," Lennon later said. "He [had] always wanted to work with The Beatles, and he was given the shittiest load of badly recorded shit ... [but] he made something out of it."[51]

Spector started work on the album on March 23rd. Not only did he remix the tapes, he also overdubbed new orchestral parts onto 'The Long And Winding Road', 'Across The Universe', and 'I Me Mine', using 50 musicians at a cost of more than £1,000. Spector completed his work on the album on April 2nd, but McCartney hated it, and was even more incensed at the fact that Allen Klein had sanctioned the work without his approval.

"A few weeks ago, I was sent a remixed version of my song 'The Long And Winding Road', with harps, horns, an orchestra, and women's choir added," McCartney told London's *Evening Standard* newspaper. "No one had asked me what I thought. I couldn't believe it. I would never have female voices on a Beatles record." McCartney didn't blame Spector, he said, but felt that the episode proved that he was no longer in control of what went out on a Beatles record. "I've sent Klein a letter asking for some of the things to be altered, but I haven't received an answer yet."[52]

Eight days after work on the album was completed, McCartney announced that he'd left the group. With The Beatles now well and truly over, it came as no surprise that none of them attended the premieres of *Let It Be* in New York (on May 13th), Liverpool, or London (both May 20th). According to *Record*

Mirror, Allen Klein had negotiated for the film to be shown in 100 cities around the world on its release.

Although The Beatles had fulfilled the terms of their initial three-picture deal with United Artists, they still owed the company a soundtrack album, since the *Help!* and *Yellow Submarine* soundtracks had been distributed by Capitol. The upshot of this was that, while negotiating a distribution deal with United Artists for *Let It Be*, Allen Klein also gave the company the rights to distribute the soundtrack.

Bruce Markoe of MGM/UA confirmed that the deal had nothing to do with the original contract. He told the press that the *Let It Be* deal "was not connected to the original three-picture deal The Beatles made with United Artists," he told the press. "The business affairs person who actually made the deal confirmed with me that this was a completely separate deal."[53]

Ever the wheeler-dealer, Klein kept Capitol happy by having them manufacture the LP (which was issued by Apple) and thereby still make money from it. The United Artists distribution deal was for the USA only, so Capitol was able to work it in Canada and Mexico. According to *Billboard*, the album had shipped more than three million copies by June 6th. With a retail price of seven dollars per LP this represented a gross income of more than $22 million.

In Britain, *Let It Be* was issued by Apple and distributed by EMI. Because the British release was issued as a boxed set with a substantial book, it was sold at a higher price than usual: £2/19s/11d (a penny short of £3). Perhaps because of this, it took a few weeks to reach the top of the charts. It was also up against some fierce competition. In the week that *Let It Be* entered the British charts, Simon & Garfunkel's *Bridge Over Troubled Water* was at Number 1 and Paul's *McCartney* sat, perhaps fittingly, at Number 2.

Come And Get It
Expanding business and declining interest

"Apple was quite a nice little record company, if that had been what we wanted to do. But once the business hassles came in, we thought, 'Who needs a record company? I'd rather have my freedom.'"

PAUL McCARTNEY[1]

When John Lennon and Paul McCartney appeared on *The Johnny Carson Show* on May 15th 1968 to promote The Beatles' new company, Apple, they were keen to stress its business and creative aspirations. "We've got to run our own affairs now," Lennon explained, "so we've got this thing called Apple, which is going to be records, films, and electronics ... which all tie up."

Apple was intended, he said, to form "a sort of umbrella" so that "people who want to make films about ... grass ... don't have to go on their knees in an office, you know, begging for a break".[2] The Beatles had, in Lennon's words, decided to "play" businessmen.

He was being flippant to some extent: the group did after all employ experienced professionals to help manage their new company. But if they wanted to actually make money – rather than simply give it to the taxman, or to an endless cavalcade of freeloaders and freaks – they had to do more than just 'play' at being businessmen. They had to actually 'be' businessmen.

The Beatles had to take Apple seriously, or face the consequences. But the way that Lennon and McCartney described the company to Carson made it sound like a charity. Lennon and McCartney certainly were charitable – perhaps overly charitable at times – because they really felt that they could make a difference. If somebody came to them with a new or alternative idea, no matter how hair-brained, they were likely to be rewarded with some Beatles cash. "I think Apple must have given out a considerable amount of money, if you add it up," Apple's Press Officer, Derek Taylor, later admitted. "But it wouldn't get to six figures in all."[3]

Most of these handouts went to a select few, but there were a handful of other lucky recipients. One was 22-year-old David Peel (not the same David Peel who later signed to Apple), who came up with the idea of forming a troupe of 'strolling players' to perform for children. With the help of £100 of Apple money, The Apple Peel Players were able to give free performances on Brighton beach during the summer of 1968. "One of the reasons Apple was formed was to help young people to do things," Peel said. "With a name like mine I was made for them."[4]

Lennon and McCartney's explanations of what they wanted Apple to be sounded wonderful – and to people like Peel it was. McCartney's concept of "a controlled weirdness" or "a kind of western communism" probably sounded great to the other Beatles, too, albeit while they were stoned out of their heads. They knew what it was to go cap in hand to a faceless organisation only to get rejected or ripped off. Now the boot was on the other foot (not that The Beatles intended to rip anybody off).

As well as allowing them to give money to the likes of The Apple Peel Players, The Fool, and Magic Alex, The Beatles hoped that forming Apple would allow them to control their own destiny. Ultimately, however, Apple ended up controlling them. As with so many things to do with The Beatles' business empire, the idea of forming Apple didn't come from the group, but from one of their accountants. The Beatles were due to receive a huge royalty payment from EMI, but knew that if it was paid to them individually they would have to give most of it to the British government in tax. What became Apple Corps, therefore, was initially little more than a clever scheme devised to avoid paying 19s/6d of each pound they earned to the taxman.

Before putting the Apple plan into action, The Beatles had to restructure their business, which they did by forming a new company, Beatles & co, to replace their previous partnership, Beatles Ltd. Beatles & co was structured so that each of the four Beatles held five per cent, with the remaining 80 per cent being controlled by the newly formed Apple Corps, which was jointly owned by all four. All Beatles earnings (except for songwriting) would be paid directly to Beatles & co, and therefore taxed at a lower rate.

"Our accountant came up and said, 'We've got this amount of money. Do you want to give it to the government or do something with it?'" Lennon told Johnny Carson. The answer was obvious. The Beatles had £800,000 – almost $20 million today – to invest in their new company. The question was, if Apple was going to be more than just a revenue-collecting agency, what should they do with it? One suggestion was for the group to form a real-estate company, perhaps to invest in record shops, so that The Beatles could acquire a portfolio of properties while avoiding looking too much like greedy capitalists, but this came to nothing.

At the time, the public knew nothing of The Beatles plans to manage their own affairs. The first clue that something was happening in Beatleland was the cryptic reference to 'The Apple' on the back of the *Sgt Pepper* album. But given that the jacket was stuffed full of supposed clues about everything from drugs to Paul McCartney's apparent death, this 'apple' could have referred to anything. Three months later an article in *The Beatles Book* confirmed that 'The Apple' was a new Beatles venture but was unable to confirm exactly what it would do. "A brief and simple answer [to the question of 'What is Apple?'] is impossible because it may develop into many things," the magazine reported. "The Beatles DO have a direct interest in it … and very shortly it will start operating as The Apple Music Publishing House."[5]

The company had a name and a fancy new logo, but The Beatles still had no clear plans for it – at least not until fate intervened. The sad death of Brian Epstein on Sunday August 27th 1967 had a dramatic effect on the group and triggered a series of events that completely reshaped The Beatles' business empire. Dick James reasoned that Epstein's death signalled the end of the group and decided to sell his share of Northern Songs; The Beatles saw it as a way to terminate their contract with NEMS.

Epstein's death meant that both The Beatles and NEMS were without a manager. On August 31st *The Times* reported that The Beatles had decided to manage themselves. "There is no question of a replacement for Mr. Brian Epstein," a NEMS statement said. "However, the directors and staff of NEMS will continue to give [the group] every possible assistance in the conduct of their affairs."[6]

Speculation about the future of both NEMS and The Beatles persisted while the company waited to appoint a new chairman. There were several potential candidates for the position – including Clive Epstein, NEMS administration director Vic Lewis, and Robert Stigwood – but the decision could only be made after a meeting of the board of directors. "No board meeting has been scheduled," Tony Barrow told the September 2nd issue of *Disc & Music Echo*. "If there is one, it won't be until after the funeral."

A week later *Disc & Music Echo* reported that Clive Epstein had been elected to replace his brother. Stigwood would remain Managing Director, but nobody at NEMS would take over the personal management of The Beatles. The Beatles had always let Brian do everything for them but were now contemplating taking a more active role in NEMS. One idea was to use NEMS to develop new talent, but Clive Epstein wasn't convinced.

What the group didn't know at the time was that Epstein had made Stigwood co-managing director of NEMS in January 1967 with the intention of selling him everything but the company's two greatest assets (The Beatles and Cilla Black) at a later date. After Epstein's death Stigwood and his business partner, David Shaw, decided to exercise their option to buy a controlling interest in NEMS.

Stigwood's plan was to install himself as The Beatles' manager, but the group had other ideas. On October 31st it was reported in *The Times* that NEMS and The Robert Stigwood Organisation had parted – 'amicably', as ever – and that Stigwood had taken The Bee Gees and Cream with him. But The Beatles had already taken the first step towards self-management – regardless of what NEMS or Stigwood might have wanted – and within weeks of Epstein's death had begun to make plans for their next big project. *Magical Mystery Tour* was the first major Apple project, and the first sign therefore that The Beatles wanted to take control of their creative and business affairs.

"We've got to the point now where we've found out that if you rely on other people, things never work out," George Harrison told *Melody Maker* in September. "This may sound conceited, but it's not. It's just what happens … the moment you get involved with other people, it goes wrong."[7]

Unfortunately for The Beatles, things were about to go very wrong indeed. The only thing that the group had ever taken control of was their music. Now, in taking care of the business side of things as well, they were about to receive a rude awakening.

"The Beatles gave the impression that they were worldly and wise," recalled Apple PR man Tony Bramwell, "[but] in business terms they knew nothing. They were very much like Elvis Presley with Colonel Tom Parker in this respect." Like Presley, The Beatles had been used to letting somebody else 'take care of business'. As Bramwell put it, "I don't think they were capable of running their own lives, much less their careers, for some years."[8]

The Beatles needed Epstein now more than ever. All it would take is one bad decision and they'd have more than just bank balances to worry about. *Magical Mystery Tour* was a warning of things to come, and serves in hindsight as a metaphor for The Beatles' attempts at self-management. It was poorly planned, poorly executed, chaotic, amateurish, and generally over-ambitious – just as Apple Corps would be.

Since Apple didn't have its own offices yet, The Beatles took over part of NEMS's London headquarters. They didn't have a staff either, so decided to put their road managers in charge of organising the production of *Magical Mystery Tour*. Neil Aspinall and Mal Evens might have been experts at looking after guitars and drum kits, but knew very little about the logistics of filmmaking. (Needless to say, the production didn't run particularly smoothly.)

By the autumn of 1967 'The Apple' had started to take shape. New offices were set up at 94 Baker Street, and Neil Aspinall was appointed as Managing Director – not that he was entirely sure what that entailed. "I was running Apple, but I have no idea what my position was – possibly the lotus position," he recalled. "Running Apple at that time was hard work, in the sense that there were so many different ideas coming in, and people had different criteria for how Apple should be run, and what it should represent, and who should be on the label, and what colour the room should be decorated ..."[9]

The first division of the company to be set up was Apple Music Publishing. The Beatles had obviously learnt the value of publishing copyrights and were keen to get in on the action. But their choice of representative was, as ever, questionable to say the least. Tony Doran was a business associate of Epstein's and had previously managed a car dealership. How exactly this qualified him to manage a music-publishing company isn't clear, but he was a friend – and it was the summer of love, after all, so clarity of thought wasn't an issue. The fact that he could be trusted was more important than the level of business acumen he possessed.

Granting important roles to unqualified people had been one of Epstein's great failings, but on this occasion The Beatles were lucky. Doran's brief was to seek out and sign new talent. To this end Apple placed advertisements in several music papers soliciting submissions from struggling songwriters, but few (if any) new talents were discovered among the many tapes sent in. Those songwriters that were signed to Apple Publishing – among them Gallagher & Lyle and Jackie Lomax – came from contracts or via The Beatles themselves. Each was signed to a standard contract that gave the publisher 50 per cent of any income from copyrights, suggesting that, while they might have been dressed like hippies, The Beatles were 'bread heads' when it came to business. Despite having complained about the terms of their deal with Dick James and Northern Songs, they seemed to be more than happy to sign other writers to the same terms.

Doran's assistant was Mike Berry, a former DJ. Having been given the task of writing Apple's publishing contracts, he had a meeting with McCartney to discuss the standard terms. "I told him that in my opinion the 50 per cent the music publisher took for promoting the song and handling the business was far too much," Berry recalled. "But I also told him that Apple could legitimately take 50 per cent as the publisher and he was happy to run with it and sign writers to Apple on that basis."[10]

Apple Publishing began to acquire new songs at a remarkable rate. Writers were given the use of a small demo studio on the floor above Doran's office in which to record their latest compositions. Doran would listen through to these songs and pay the author £20 for each recording. The company had a handful of minor successes and a few big hits. Its greatest success was the team of Pete Ham and Tom Evans of Badfinger, who had hits with 'No Matter What', 'Day After Day', and 'Baby Blue'. Their song 'Without You' subsequently became an even bigger hit for both Harry Nilsson (in 1972) and Mariah Carey (in 1993). Publishing, as The Beatles had already discovered, was the music-business equivalent of the golden goose. A strong catalogue could make millions.

With Apple Publishing up and running, the next step with to try to unravel The Beatles' confused network of legal and financial contracts in order to give Apple a secure foundation on which to build. But, as ever, the group's attitude to the whole thing was little more than ambivalent. "We hadn't done the business planning," McCartney later admitted. "We were just goofing off and having a lot of fun."[11]

The Beatles gave the job of sorting out their accounts to their road manager, Neil Aspinall, but his job proved to be much easier in theory than in practice. "We didn't have a single piece of paper," he recalled. "Maybe The Beatles had been given copies of various contracts, I don't know. ... I didn't know what the contract was with EMI, or with the film people or the publishers or anything at all."[12]

While Aspinall attempted to bring order to the chaos, The Beatles carried on in their merry, befuddled state. Inspired by the hippie happenings taking place on the west coast of America, their vision for Apple grew more and more grandiose every day. "We were just tripping off, having a joint, and saying, 'Well, we could have films, and we could help young artists so they wouldn't have the trouble we had with all the tramping around and being undiscovered'," Lennon recalled.[13]

No longer content to restrict themselves to the music business, The Beatles decided that Apple should encompass every branch of popular culture, from literature to cinema, art to fashion, electronics to retail. According to an article in *The Beatles Book*, the group saw Apple as "a vast concept ... capable of making and selling all kinds of assorted goods and services". There was no logical reason, the magazine argued, why Apple couldn't go into producing anything from "electric shavers" to "motorbikes".[14]

With Doran and Aspinall working away in the background, Apple slowly began to develop a public profile. Christmas 1967 saw the release of The Beatles' *Magical Mystery Tour* film and soundtrack, both of which featured the Apple logo, while the group's fan club record for that year featured the message "another little bite of The Apple". The festive season also marked the opening, one day before the release of the *Magical Mystery Tour* EP, of the Apple Boutique, which was celebrated with a party attended by the great and good of London town.

The Apple Boutique occupied the ground floor of 94 Baker Street, and was initially planned to be the first in a series of retail outlets (the rest never appeared). No expense was spared when it came to stocking and decorating the shop, on which a reported £100,000 was spent. The Dutch art collective The Fool were commissioned to paint a psychedelic mural on the outside of the building and design posters and clothes to be sold inside, while one of Lennon's old school friends, Pete Shotton, was installed as the shop's manager. Shotton had previously run a successful supermarket, owned in part by The Beatles, on Hayling Island, but his stewardship of the Apple Boutique was doomed from the start.

This wasn't so much Shotton's fault as that of The Fool, who certainly lived up to their name. The hippie collective had once owned a boutique of their own in Amsterdam, but the business collapsed amid spiralling overheads. After that they ended up in London and found themselves commissioned to paint Lennon and Harrison's homes in a fabulous hippie style. They were then invited to sell their wares in the boutique, but their attitude to money – particularly anybody else's – prevented The Beatles from making a profit.

"When they used to open shops it was just after the bread of the people, not after turning them on," The Fool's Simon Posthuma told *The Sunday Times*. "We want to turn people on."[15] So did The Beatles, who had already sung about wanting to "turn you on" on record and were keen to help 'struggling artists'. But they also wanted to make a profit – something that wouldn't be easy with The Fool to contend with.

With no thought given to profit margins and other budgetary concerns, The Fool insisted on making their clothes using authentic Moroccan fabrics. Pete Shotton duly arranged for them to go on a shopping expedition to Morocco to buy fabrics and antiques for the boutique, but nothing ever made it back to London. After that, The Fool insisted on using labels woven from pure silk. It didn't matter to them that these labels would cost more than the clothes they were sewn into, because somebody else was paying the bill. But Shotton was powerless to stop it. When he told Lennon that this wasn't good business practice he met with further resistance. "Remember, Pete," Lennon told him, "we're not business freaks, we're artists. That's what Apple's all about – artists ... if we don't make any money, what does it fucking matter?"[16]

Lennon had spent much of 1967 taking copious amounts of LSD in an attempt to destroy his ego. Now he seemed intent on destroying his bank balance as well. "It could never make sense to me to have money and yet think the way I thought," he later explained. "I had to give it away or lose it. I gave a lot of money away, which is one way of losing it; and the other way is disregarding it and not paying attention to it; not taking responsibility for what I really was, which is a guy with a lot of money."[17]

Apple's accountants had a rather different perspective. In January 1968 The Fool were told by the head of the company's wholesale division that there could be "no expenditure of any kind" without written authority. In February Apple's head of retail claimed that The Fool had "a considerable amount of items as yet unpaid". By March the Dutch artists were told that they would be barred if they continued to take items from the boutique without paying for them. Apple had grown tired of this troupe of hippies and wanted rid of them. The feeling was mutual. The Fool were bored of Apple and its penny-pinching, and saw a better future in the form of a rashly offered recording contract from Irving Green, the president of Mercury Records.

Without The Fool, the Apple Boutique began, according to George Harrison, to make "a good profit" – the kind that "the average owner would have been satisfied with". The Beatles, however, had become tired of what Harrison called "the whole thing", so "decided to give it away".[18] However, less conservative estimates suggest that, by the time it closed its doors in July 1968, the Apple Boutique had cost The Beatles something in the region of £160,000.

Whether the shop was making money or not, The Beatles had had enough of playing shopkeepers and decided to give away all of the remaining stock, thereby turning the whole sorry fiasco into a photo opportunity. "It was a big event and all the kids came and just took everything," Lennon recalled. "That was the best thing about the whole shop, when we gave it all away."[19] (The night before, Lennon admitted, The Beatles had themselves been in and "took what we wanted".)

Five months after opening its Baker Street boutique, Apple unveiled another, less well-known retail outlet. On May 23rd 1968 Apple Tailoring (Civil & Theatric) opened its doors at 161 King's Road, London. The King's Road was – and is – full of fashionable clothes shops. It was even hipper, in fact, than Carnaby Street. The famous Granny Takes A Trip catered for many a pop star on the lookout for something special, while Hung On You and Emmerton & Lambert catered for the beautiful people's every fashion whim.

A few years later, it was along the King's Road that Malcolm McLaren and Vivienne Westwood opened the shop that kick-started punk rock. Apple Tailoring wasn't anywhere near as influential, however, nor did it last as long. The same location had been home, since 1966, to Dandie Fashions, which was owned by Neil Winterbottom and Guinness heir Tara Browne (of 'A Day In The Life' fame) and sold designs by John Crittle, whose clients included Brian Jones, Jimi Hendrix, and The Beatles. Neil Aspinall and Apple accountant Stephen Maltz were such fans of Dandie Fashions that they became directors of the shop, which subsequently mutated into Apple Tailoring. Despite a lavish opening event attended by Lennon and Harrison, however, Apple Tailoring failed to turn a profit and closed within months.

Not content with losing large amounts of money to hippie collectives and hip tailors, The Beatles squandered yet more cash on an electronics division. This time their 'Fool' was Yanni 'John' Alexis Mardas, born in Athens, Greece, and better known as Magic Alex. Mardas called himself an electronics wizard but was actually a television repairman. Having been introduced by Brian Jones, Mardas and Lennon began hanging out together, with Lennon even claiming that Mardas helped to write 'What's The New Mary Jane'.

The technophobic Lennon was impressed by Mardas's knowledge of electronics (which was actually fairly basic) and assertions that he could build The Beatles a much better recording facility than EMI Studios. With the words 'anything is possible' still ringing in their ears, the group invited Mardas to invent some new gadgets to sell in their boutique. The Beatles were committed, according to McCartney, to the idea of making "the little gadgets of tomorrow", such as "wallpaper speakers" and "the phone that would respond to voice commands".[20]

On August 24th 1967, Lennon and McCartney attended an Apple board meeting and agreed to put Mardas on a wage of £40 per week, plus 10 per cent of any profit made on his inventions with a guaranteed minimum of £3,000 per year. Before he could start inventing, however, Mardas needed somewhere to work, so was duly given a 'laboratory' in Boston Place and a budget of £300,000. Like The Fool, Mardas was no slouch when it came to spending The

Beatles' money, as demonstrated by a memo from Apple, reproduced in *The Beatles Anthology*, that wondered what had become of the "200 light machines" he once ordered.[21]

The best thing the hapless Mardas came up with was the Electric Apple: a rectangular 'sound-to-light' box that could be hooked up to a sound system. It was used during the Apple Boutique's opening night party and remained as the shop's sound and lighting system, but never made it past the prototype stage. In fact, nothing Mardas 'invented' ever went into production. But that's not to say that he didn't have some grand designs. A memo dated January 19th 1968 suggested that he was looking into the possibility of buying a factory – presumably in order to give him somewhere to manufacture his Electric Apples and Nothing Boxes – and working on designs for a "distortion machine" for EMI, as well as preparing to build recording studios for George Harrison, The Rolling Stones, and The Beatles.

Although he never got round to building a studio for the Stones, Mardas did at least make a start on one for The Beatles. In July 1968 Apple had moved to a new five-storey building at 3 Savile Row, London, at a cost of £500,000. The building had a substantial basement, which the group planned to convert into a recording studio. The July 1968 issue of *The Beatles Book* reported that the basement had been "converted into a magnificent recording studio" – which might well have been true, but the recording facilities themselves were nothing short of a shambles.

Geoff Emerick, who engineered many of The Beatles' recording sessions, was given the job of evaluating Mardas's work, and was shocked at what he found. Among his many complaints were that were "no wiring conduits between the control room and the studio"; the speakers "sounded atrocious"; and that the mixing console "barely worked at all" – unsurprisingly, given that it consisted of "a sheet of plywood with 16 faders and an oscilloscope stuck in the middle, which acted as an inefficient level meter".[22] There is no record of exactly what Mardas spent building the console, but Emerick claims he later sold it on a second-hand shop on the Edgware Road for five pounds.

The Beatles didn't attempt to use the studio until January 20th 1969, having moved there from Twickenham Film Studios (where they'd been working on what became *Let It Be*). It appears that nobody bothered to check on what Mardas was doing – or whether his 'inventions' might work – during the intervening six-month period. It soon became clear that his console was unusable, so George Martin had to borrow one from EMI.

Mardas's botched attempts at creating a state-of-the-art studio cost The Beatles more than just the bother of having to refit it with working equipment. While the studio was being revamped it was discovered that Mardas had removed important structural supports from the basement of 3 Savile Row, which cost several thousand pounds to rectify.

Although Mardas was long gone by the time Allen Klein arrived on the scene in 1969, he didn't officially 'resign' from Apple Electronics until May 1971. His laboratory at Boston Place was cleared out and used first to house a library of tape and film and later as a temporary home for a rather more profitable Apple enterprise: mastering.

Mastering is a highly skilled craft. A good mastering engineer can make or break a record. Well aware of this, The Beatles had already hired one of the best in the business, Malcolm Davies, to work exclusively for Apple artists. One of the first records to be mastered at Apple was 'Hey Jude', which was followed by numerous other Beatles discs and solo Beatle projects.

Once George Peckham, formerly of The Foremost, joined the mastering team in September 1968 it quickly became clear that Apple's facilities could become rather valuable. As somebody who "used to go out clubbing every night", Peckham knew a number of other musicians on the scene. "When they found out that I worked at Apple," he later recalled, "they used to ask me to cut their records." He mentioned this to Harrison, who agreed to the idea of opening Apple up to outside clients.

The success of Apple Studios was ensured not just by Peckham's skills but also by the fact that it was one of only a handful of independent mastering suites in London. It wasn't long before everybody from The Rolling Stones (*Get Yer Ya-Ya's Out* album) to The Who ('Won't Get Fooled Again' single) were having their records mastered at Apple, followed by Eric Clapton, Led Zeppelin, and Genesis – all of whom were happy to pay handsomely for Peckham's (and Apple's) services.

With the mastering room up and running, it was time for somebody to put right Mardas's ham-fisted attempt at building a recording studio. If people were queuing up to have their records mastered at Apple, the company reasoned, they would surely pay handsomely to record there as well. Geoff Emerick was installed as studio manager and given the task of transforming the studio.

As with so many Apple schemes, this proved to be a bigger and more expensive job than was initially assumed. Before work on restoring the studio could begin, the mastering room had to be moved to Boston Place. The basement studio was then gutted and completely redesigned for better use of space. Because of the studio's central London location, special soundproofing had to be put in to deaden the sound of the nearby underground trains, while Emerick insisted on bringing in only the most technically advanced equipment available. (His plan to install a custom-made Neumann mixing console was vetoed.)

Under Emerick's management, Apple Studios became one of the best in London – and one of the most expensive. The cost of designing, planning, and rebuilding it ran to more than £600,000. George Harrison might have liked the oak beams and open fireplace of the original basement, but this new studio was modern and comfortable. "Having learned from the mistakes at Abbey Road," Emerick recalled, "I was determined to make Apple studios a pleasant place to work; a space that would encourage rather than discourage the creative flow."[23] At 30 by 45 feet, with an 11-foot-high ceiling, Apple Studios was quite a bit smaller than Abbey Road but its equal in all other respects.

The refit took 18 months to complete. George Harrison attended the opening party in August 1971 and later recorded some of his *Living In The Material World* album there. The studio was soon running at capacity, as was the mastering room (which returned to Savile Row once the restoration was complete). While the first act to use the new facilities was an Apple signing, Lon & Derrek Van Eaton, the studio was soon being used by a wide range of artists including Harry Nilsson, Roger Daltrey, Marc Bolan, and Ian Dury, who recorded there with his band Kilburn & The High-Roads.

No sooner had the studio opened for business, however, than it was faced with massive disruption. Ringo Starr, who was immersed in the film business at the time, decided that he wanted to build a film-scoring studio on the ground floor of 3 Savile Row, which meant that the entire building would need to be gutted from the ground floor up – thereby disrupting the busy and profitable basement studio. Emerick thought it was a crazy idea, but as it was Starr's it got the go ahead. But while Apple was prepared to spend a small fortune on Starr's pet project, the company wasn't keen, according to George Peckham, to modernise the equipment in the basement studio or the mastering room.

In the end, Starr's film-scoring scheme came to nothing. Emerick was so unhappy with all that been going on that he decided to quit and went to work instead at George Martin's AIR Studios. It wasn't long before Peckham too had left for pastures new, which included mastering the Monty Python comedy outfit's 'three-sided' *Matching Tie And Handkerchief* set.

By 1973 Apple Studios had passed its peak. None of The Beatles were using it. Harrison might have recorded part of *Living In The Material World* there, but he soon decided to set up his own FPSHOT studio. Meanwhile McCartney was happy at EMI, and Lennon was living and working in America. Apple Studios limped on until late 1974. Badfinger – who had left Apple Records by this time – returned for one last session, but after that no further records of note were recorded there.

It should be remembered, however, that Apple Studios was one of the few areas of its parent company to make any money. It had a superb reputation and good facilities, and was always busy. Despite this, Apple decided to cancel all of its existing bookings and forget about it. Like so many other things associated with the company, it was left to decay with no firm decision made about its future.

Even before Apple Studios opened, The Beatles had decided that, if they were to manage a multimedia entertainment organisation, the one thing they needed above all others was a record label. It's a dream that many rock stars over the years have shared. Often – as with The Beatles – the driving impulse stems from the idea of greater artistic freedom, and of building a company focused on creativity rather than slavishly following the charts.

"I wouldn't mind if we turned out something like Sue Records," George Harrison told the *Disc & Music Echo* paper in 1968, while the label was still in its infancy. "They don't often reach the hit parade with their records, but all the stuff they issued was great. We don't want to be associated with anything we don't like ..."

Sue Records was a British independent label that specialised in rhythm & blues and soul. It was launched by Chris Blackwell (better known as the founder of Island Records) with the release of 'Mockingbird' by Inez & Charlie Foxx, but its subsequent identity was shaped more strongly by Guy Stevens, who went on to produce The Clash. Stevens insisted on issuing the records he believed in, regardless of whether they were likely to be hits or not. Apple was run with the same passion (albeit with a slightly better hit rate).

The Beatles weren't alone in seeking independence from the major labels. After receiving little support from MGM, Frank Zappa broke away to form Bizarre Inc, which like Apple had plans beyond simply issuing records. Bizarre Inc offered management services, too, but managed to steer clear of hangers-on with wild ideas about wallpaper speakers and Electric Apples. It wasn't as successful as Apple but did help launch Captain Beefheart and Alice Cooper.

Elsewhere, The Beach Boys formed Brother Records, which like Apple was distributed by Capitol in America; Jefferson Airplane started Grunt; and The Who's management company founded Track Records as a means of independently releasing the group's music. And Frank Sinatra, of course, had started his Reprise label long before The Beatles came up with the idea.

The common thread between all of these deals was that they only offered limited independence. Each of the acts in question was still tied to a parent company. The Beatles might have put out records with an Apple label but they remained well and truly tied to EMI/Capitol. Deals such as these were a way for major record companies to keep their acts sweet while also maintaining control of them. Go ahead and form a record label, they might have said, but don't forget you're still ours until your contract expires.

By February 1968 there were five divisions of Apple – Merchandising (Retail and Wholesale), Electronics, Films, Publicity, and Music (Publishing and Records) – but no communication between them. The left hand really didn't know what the right was doing. Apple already had offices in Baker Street and Wigmore Street, and was about to open a third in Savile Row. It fell to McCartney to sort out the mess after a frank exchange with Apple Publishing man Mike Berry. Asked by the Beatle why and how "this chaos has been created", Berry replied that "no one in the organisation knew what anyone else was doing". Worst of all, Berry said, was the fact that no agreements could be made "without the signature of a Beatle", each of whom was often hard to track down.

McCartney was furious. "He immediately arranged a meeting of all staff at Wigmore Street," Berry recalled, "where during a three-hour meeting everyone was introduced to everyone else and made aware of their duties."[24] It was also agreed that an overall coordinator should be appointed. Derek Taylor was given the job, but while communications between the various departments improved, it was far from perfect. (On one occasion, needing a Beatle's signature on an important contract, Berry discovered that Taylor had flown out to Los Angeles without telling anybody.)

It was from this chaos that Apple Records emerged. The Beatles wasted no time in recruiting people to run their record division, notably Ron Kass, formerly the head of Liberty Records in Britain, whom they installed as the label's president. Ken Mansfield was appointed as the label's American manager on the grounds that he was the only young Capitol executive that The Beatles knew. Despite running the US division, however, Mansfield remained an employee of Capitol Records, and later noted that, far from getting a new office or "a special logo or sign", the only thing that changed was his stationery.[25]

Next to be recruited was the man who almost became McCartney's brother-in-law, Peter Asher, who was given the job of A&R manager. Asher had previously had a Lennon/McCartney-assisted hit as half of the pop duo Peter & Gordon. He wasn't all that experienced but had produced a few records and, like Kass, knew his way around the record industry. Head Of Promotions Tony Bramwell got his job by default. He had been working for Apple Films while the record division was preparing to launch, so simply moved sideways when the time came.

The most influential member of the Apple Records staff was the last to join. Derek Taylor was a charismatic, charming man who had been lured away from his job as a journalist by Brian Epstein to become The Beatles' Press Officer (and to ghost-write Epstein's autobiography, *A Cellarful Of Noise*). He had moved to America in 1965 and worked as a freelance publicist for The Byrds and The Beach Boys. He also played an important role in organising the 1967 Monterey Pop Festival, but returned to Britain at The Beatles' insistence in 1968 to become Apple Records' Press Officer.

With the key players in place, The Beatles went off to India, leaving the job of signing new acts, booking studios, and planning release schedules to Apple's management team. One of the label's first signings was James Taylor, who as luck would have it had arrived in Britain in 1968 in search of a recording contract. Having just won a British talent show called *Opportunity Knocks*, Mary Hopkin was then recommended to McCartney by Cilla Black. Harrison meanwhile signed and produced Jackie Lomax, formerly the lead vocalist in Merseyside group The Undertakers.

In February 1968 Neil Aspinall was sent to New York to begin negotiations with five major record companies each seeking to manufacture and distribute Apple records in the USA. According to Ken Mansfield, many in the industry had assumed that Capitol Records would get the job by default, despite having "no more rights to distribute the label than anyone else".[26] But while this was true of any new act signed to Apple, Capitol had one very strong advantage over their major-label rivals: The Beatles. If The Beatles wanted to put records out on their own label, they could only do so by signing a manufacturing and distribution deal with Capitol.

Having agreed a deal with Capitol, Apple needed a nice label to put on its records. Until it started releasing records, the company had used a variety of logos. Now that the record label was about to go global, however, it was time to reinforce the Apple brand. Gene Mahon, a graphic designer working at the Geer Dubois agency was given the job of designing the new logo. He wanted to produce "a pure symbol" unimpeded by any other "stuff".

"The apple with the information on it should be sliced," he said later, "to give it a light surface on which to put type."[27] Unfortunately for Mahon, British law at the time required both sides of a record to detail its contents. He was unlucky, too, in that although he was working for Apple, NEMS wrote the cheques. "They were very loath to pay," he later recalled. "I'd be standing outside the office, talking to a secretary through the speakerphone from the street, trying to get payment for an invoice that was months old."[28]

On June 20th 1968 Capitol announced to the world its new partnership with Apple. "The Beatles themselves will in the future be released on their Apple label," the company said. A subsequent statement confirmed that Apple would be a "fully functional record company" and that future releases would include a "successor to *Magical Mystery Tour*" and an LP "featuring the voice, guitar, and songs" of James Taylor.[29]

Taylor might have been Apple's first signing, but he didn't have the distinction of featuring on the label's first release. The Beatles enjoyed that privilege. Apple planned to launch its new label with the simultaneous release of five records – four singles and one album. News that Apple was about to issue its first records appeared in the press in early August 1968. On August 6th Ron Kass issued a statement to the press to the effect that "Apple has no intention of becoming another Music Corporation Of America, a giant of talent and booking", and that "The Beatles don't want to build an empire".[30]

Profits, according to Kass, were "abstract" to The Beatles. And the group was true to its word: like Sue Records, Apple was more interested in originality than commercial gain. It constantly issued records that sold to a minority audience. The biggest sellers were always by The Beatles, although the label did achieve a few sizeable hits with its other acts, such as Badfinger and Mary Hopkin.

To promote the label's first batch of records, Apple hired the Wolfe & Ollins advertising agency to prepare a special presentation pack for 'Our First Four'. The press kit included the label's first four singles – 'Hey Jude', Mary Hopkin's 'Those Were The Days', 'Sour Milk Sea' by Jackie Lomax, and The Black Dyke Mills Band's 'Thingumybob' – alongside short biographies and photographs of the four acts.

Ken Mansfield meanwhile gave a lot of thought to how to position Apple Records in the American marketplace – "*the* market", as Mansfield put it. "It was always clear what the first four records were going to be," he later claimed, "except for 'Hey Jude'."[31] McCartney was worried that the song was too long for radio. But on his way back to Los Angeles, Mansfield played it to representatives of several major radio stations, all of whom were keen to support it. On his return to Los Angeles, Mansfield took his "six best men" out of 50 promotional people at Capitol and created a team to promote Apple. The label's first four singles were promoted with a presentation package similar to that produced by Wolfe & Ollins in the UK, put together at a cost of $8,000 (over $46,000 today) for 1,300 press kits.

Apple Records got off to a fantastic start. Two of its first four singles were smash hits. 'Hey Jude' topped the charts almost everywhere and sold by the bucketload. Having sold almost six million copies by the end of November, it was confirmed as the bestselling debut release of any record label ever. It remains the Beatles' most commercially successful single. Mary Hopkin's 'Those Were The Days' did well too, reaching Number 1 in the UK and Number 2 in the USA on its way to selling a million copies. But neither Jackie Lomax nor The Black Dyke Mills Band charted on either side of the Atlantic.

Apple's first album release had a similarly inauspicious start. George Harrison's *Wonderwall* failed to chart in Britain and stalled at Number 49 on *Billboard*. (*Cash Box* and *Record World* placed it somewhat higher, at Numbers 39 and 33 respectively.) James Taylor's debut, the first non-Beatle LP released by Apple, also failed to chart in Britain and America, but the label wasn't unduly concerned. It didn't matter too much if 50 per cent of its releases weren't hits. In the spirit of Sue Records, Apple was releasing records that its founders believed in. And the company always had an ace up its sleeve: The Beatles, who had spent most of the summer recording an album that would prove beyond doubt that they were just as popular as they had ever been.

On November 22nd 1968 Apple issued *The Beatles* (or *The White Album*, as it is more commonly known), a double album of 30 songs. Everything about the record was impressive, from the scope and variety of the songs to the immense sales it achieved. The album was so successful that even a month before its release it had advance orders of 150,000. On October 6th, *The Times* reported that it would "push EMI's share of the overall market from [its] current 28 per cent to around 40 per cent". The Beatles were so good for business, *The Times* claimed, that EMI was expecting total pre-Christmas sales of ten million pounds; so good, in fact, that EMI was struggling to meet demand for *The Beatles*. Having pressed an initial 250,000 copies, the label was forced to introduce "some form of rationing between record dealers" to ensure an even spread.[32] *The Beatles* sold equally well in America, leading Capitol to announce first-week dealer orders of 1.9 million copies.

If only every Apple release had been as successful as *The Beatles*. But while the group continued to score hit after hit, the label's other releases weren't nearly as successful. This was partly due to the eclectic roster it gathered. There was no way that The Modern Jazz Quartet or Yoko Ono were going to have hit records. But when Apple did have hits with other artists, the label struggled to maintain their commercial momentum. By the time they came out, follow-up records tended to flop.

Having The Beatles as your boss could be a double-edged sword. If The Beatles weren't completely behind you, your chances of success were severely limited. "We had to put a lot of effort into non-Beatle acts," Apple employee Jack Oliver recalled, "because The Beatles themselves would sit on us." One group that The Beatles apparently weren't fond of was White Trash. "If they didn't like it and they didn't bring pressure to bear on everybody," Oliver continued, "then people would push their efforts into other directions."[33]

One direction The Beatles were keen to push in was away from the commercial mainstream. In early 1969 Apple launched a shortlived subsidiary called Zapple, intended for spoken word and avant-garde albums by Lenny Bruce, Richard Brautigan, Allen Ginsberg, Charles Bukowski, and others. Zapple was supposed to be a 'budget' label, putting out records that would likely be listened to once and then disposed of – an inadvertent precursor to the audio book. By the time Zapple was up and running, however, Allen Klein had arrived and slashed its funding. Only two of the intended albums were issued, and both were self-indulgent solo projects by Beatles: *Electronic Sound* by George Harrison and *Unfinished Music No. 2: Life With The Lions* by John Lennon & Yoko Ono. (Both were sold at full price, rather than at the intended budget discount.)

Klein's arrival came in part as a result of the fact that, while Apple Records was doing well, the rest of the company continued to lose money. On February 4th 1969 *The Times* reported that Harrison felt that The Beatles had given too much money to "the wrong people", while Lennon claimed that, should Apple continue to lose money at the rate that it was, "all of us will be broke in the next six months".

Lennon's claims were exaggerated. Despite reports in the *New York Times* that the company had lost $100,000 in its first year, there was actually a lot more money coming in than flowing out. In fact, Apple made a profit of somewhere between £175,000 and £2.2 million every year until 1985.

Nonetheless, at Lennon's insistence, Allen Klein took over the management of Apple. Lennon wanted somebody to sort out the financial mess The Beatles had created, and Klein seemed like the best man for the job. He was after all, according to the *New York Times*, "the toughest wheeler-dealer in the pop jungle".[34]

The Apple mess certainly needed untangling, but Paul McCartney wanted nothing to do with the company's new chief. Klein's appearance signalled the beginning of the end. McCartney headed off for the Scottish Highlands and virtually stopped going in to Apple's Savile Row office. Klein might have sorted out The Beatles' financial problems, but he drove a wedge between the bandmembers that ultimately led to their break-up.

Apple Records carried on amidst the growing unease. While neither of the Zapple albums set the charts of fire, the company did well with Mary Hopkin's *Postcard*. Produced by McCartney, it reached Number 3 in Britain and, after climbing to Number 28 on *Billboard*, was Apple's first non-Beatles album to enter the US Top 30. Jackie Lomax's *Is This What You Want* sold poorly, however, as did albums by The Modern Jazz Quartet and Billy Preston. Better things were expected of 'Maybe Tomorrow' by The Iveys but that too made little impression on the charts, leading to plans for an album release to be scrapped. In time, however, The Iveys would become the most successful non-Beatles act on the label.

Brought to Apple Records by Mal Evans, The Iveys received little support from A&R manager Peter Asher but did draw the attention of McCartney and

Harrison. After changing their name to one derived from the original title of 'With A Little Help From My Friends' ('Bad Finger Boogie') and recording a new McCartney composition, 'Come And Get It', the group's fortunes were transformed. With a Beatles-esque sound, the full force of Apple's marketing department behind them, and production from McCartney or Harrison, Badfinger simply couldn't fail. They issued a string of hit singles and albums from 1969–73.

By the end of that period, however, the group's relationship with Apple had begun to deteriorate. Although Apple treated them fairly, they suffered as a result of Allen Klein's cutbacks and the closure of Apple's British headquarters, and often complained of living in the shadow of The Beatles. The group's final Apple album had a particularly telling title: *Ass.* When Badfinger moved to Warner Bros, however, the hits all but dried up. The group ended in extremely sad circumstances. Pete Ham committed suicide in 1975, while his partner, Tom Evans, followed suit in 1983.

Although Apple Records did well with Badfinger, its resources were stretched by other less commercial acts. Yoko Ono released four solo albums on Apple from 1970–73. Two of them were expensive two-record sets. She also issued six singles. Because Ono was Mrs Lennon the label was under considerable pressure to be seen promoting her records even if they didn't stand a snowball's chance in hell of becoming hits.

Even the more commercial records Ono issued after abandoning the avant-garde needed promotion, and because her husband was a company director there could be no skimping. While some acts with more obvious commercial potential struggled to get their records promoted, Apple placed full-page advertisements in the music press for Ono singles that were destined for the bargain bin. Everyone at Apple – except Lennon – knew they were flogging a dead horse. But while Allen Klein abhorred the amount of money being squandered on promoting Ono's records, even he felt unable to do anything about it because of his relationship with Lennon. Apple PR man Al Steckler later recalled an incident in which Klein asked, "How do I tell a man that his wife is fucking away millions of his dollars?"[35] Neither man appeared to have the answer.

While others were appearing to spend as much of Apple's cash as they could, George Harrison was keen to put the label's money to better use. Having had his attention drawn by friend and labelmate Ravi Shankar to the humanitarian disaster taking place in East Pakistan, he wrote, recorded, and released what was perhaps the word's first charity single, 'Bangla-Desh', with which he intended to raise both money and awareness of the situation. Harrison pressed Apple to release Shankar's 'Joi Bangla' as a single alongside his own. He also organised a special star-studded concert featuring some of his famous friends – including Bob Dylan, Eric Clapton, and Ringo Starr – to raise funds to help the starving of East Pakistan. Apple met the concert's production and transportation costs, which were estimated at $30,000, and filmed and recorded the event. The label also covered the costs of the record's expensive packaging, which included a 64-page colour book.

Complications arose when it came to obtaining performing rights for the various featured artists, most of whom were signed to different labels. Most labels gave full permission without question, but Columbia Records took on the role of the corporate villain when it demanded compensation for the five Bob Dylan songs featured – even though the album was for charity and nobody else was being paid. Now was the time for Klein to step in and earn his keep. He brokered a deal that gave Capitol distribution of the vinyl album in North America but allowed Columbia to distribute the tape format there and both formats in the rest of the world.

Next it was Capitol's turn to sully its reputation by requesting that it kept its distribution fees. That the money would be better spent helping starving people didn't seem to matter. It wasn't until Harrison criticised Capitol President Bhaskar Menon on *The Dick Cavett Show* that the label gave in and waived its distribution fees.

The *Concert For Bangla-Desh* film and triple album were intended to provide even more much needed cash to help the starving people of East Pakistan. Three days before the album hit the record shops, Capitol paid Apple an advance of $3.75 million, but because the concert had not been registered in advance as a charity, up to $15 million sat in an Inland Revenue escrow account for years before it could be released.

The Concert For Bangla-Desh (and its spin-offs) revealed just how far Apple was willing to go in order to uphold its 'countercultural' approach to business. Everyone else – including some retailers – seemed keen to make a fast buck from the project, but Apple ensured that every penny made from album and film went to those who needed it most.

With Badfinger and Yoko Ono counterbalancing the books, however, the label did still need to find ways to turn a profit. Apple had a huge roster of talent, but as good as John Tavener, Ravi Shankar, and Elephant's Memory might have been they were never likely to set the charts on fire. The only records that could guarantee strong sales were those by the ex-Fab Four.

Having lost Badfinger, whose last Apple album was issued in November 1973, the label released all non-Beatles from their contracts. By 1974 only Lennon, McCartney, Harrison, and Starr remained, and they were all really signed to EMI/Capitol. Apple Records was wound down at the same time as The Beatles began to reach an agreement to dissolve the business partnership they had formed in 1967. Lennon, Harrison, and Starr terminated their management contract with Klein in 1973, and in November of the same year took Klein and ABKCO to court, claiming damages for alleged misrepresentation. (Klein responded with a counter claim for lost fees, commissions, and expenses.)

With Klein out of the picture, lawyers for Apple and Paul McCartney began negotiations to bring an end to McCartney's long-standing efforts to dissolve the group's partnership. A deal was brokered that meant that The Beatles would no longer have to put their individual earnings into one communal pot (to be shared out equally), but all four remained as co-owners of Apple.

By late 1974 it looked as though the four of them were ready to dissolve their partnership. Lennon, McCartney, and Harrison were due to meet in New York and sign the papers; Starr arranged to sign in London because he wanted to avoid the possibility of being served with court papers by Klein. But with everything in place, Lennon refused to sign. Had he done so he would have been liable to pay the Inland Revenue Service one million dollars in tax, and was justifiably put off by the prospect. The Beatles' partnership remained intact, but the end was in sight.

Lennon eventually signed the papers in January 1975. But while this brought an end to Beatles & co, both Apple and Apple Records carried on. The label continued to issue albums by Lennon, Harrison, and Starr until their contracts with EMI expired in 1976. (McCartney had ditched Apple for Capitol in 1975.) Even though The Beatles had split up some time earlier, the four ex-members continued to sell millions of records. It wasn't unusual for all of them to be in the charts simultaneously.

Between them, the ex-Beatles scored a number of big hits. Lennon's 'Imagine' (and its parent album); McCartney's *Band On The Run* (and its title track); Harrison's *All Things Must Pass* and 'My Sweet Lord'; and Starr's *Ringo* and 'Photograph' were all certified gold records. But the music scene was changing, and when the end came, Apple Records went out with a whimper. The last two records it issued in early 1976 – Harrison's 'This Guitar (Can't Keep From Crying)' and Starr's 'Oh My My' – both failed to chart. After that Apple Records went silent for the best part of 15 years.

When Apple Records reappeared it was as a reissue label rather than as an outlet for new talent. In the summer of 1991 the label announced its intention to begin reissuing long-deleted old records, having signed new licensing agreements with Capitol and EMI. But while it was nice to see Apple albums back on the shelves, speculation was rife that the label's sudden return had more to do with a court case brought against Apple Computer Inc than any desire by The Beatles to see albums by The Modern Jazz Quartet and John Tavener back on sale. The fact that Apple's relaunch was delayed twice – and only went ahead after the label had won its case against Apple Computer Inc – would appear to confirm these suggestions.

Part of the battle with Apple Computer Inc (discussed in more detail in the following chapter) had been over the right of each company to distribute music on physical media such as CDs, records, and tapes. By reissuing its back catalogue, Apple Records could prove that it was still actively using its trademarks and logos worldwide.

Although none of the albums Apple reissued would sell in vast quantities there was still a demand for groups such as Badfinger, whose albums had been out of print for more than a decade. Better still, these reissued albums were becoming available on CD for the first time, and often included bonus tracks. The first phase of the reissue campaign began on November 11th 1991 with *James Taylor* (which at Taylor's insistence did not include any bonus material), *Postcard* by Mary Hopkin, *Is This What You Want* by Jackie Lomax, *That's The Way God Planned It* by Billy Preston, and *Magic Christian Music* by Badfinger. (The Modern Jazz Quartet's *Under The Jasmin Tree* had been scheduled for release in the first phase of the campaign but was postponed because of licensing problems.)

Apple's reissue campaign rumbled on into 1996 with the re-release of such lost classics as Harrison's *Electronic Sound* and *Space* by The Modern Jazz Quartet. Despite there being one or two albums conspicuous by their absence, such as Lennon-produced works by Elephant's Memory and David Peel, Apple had little left in its archive to reissue. It had however established itself as one of the world's most successful reissue labels – particularly after releasing several albums worth of previously unheard Beatles material in the form of *Live At The BBC* and the *Anthology* series.

Apple's release schedule has slowed considerably since, but it continues to issue 'new' Beatles albums, among them the *Yellow Submarine Songtrack, Let It Be … Naked*, and *Love*. *Love* did particularly well, peaking at Number 3 in the UK and debuting at Number 4 on the *Billboard* 200. Within four weeks of its initial release it was confirmed as the 15th bestselling album of 2006, having sold 2.8 million copies.

While Apple Records continued to release its mixed bag of hits and misses during the late 1960s and early 1970s, The Beatles busied themselves with the formation of yet another division of the company: Apple Films. On March 19th 1964 *The Times* had reported that The Beatles and Brian Epstein had bought shares in Woodfall Films, one of five business groups associated with the acquisition of British Lion Films. Epstein became a member of the board of the newly formed Lion-Woodfall, on which he represented both his own and The Beatles' interests.

The Beatles subsequently formed Subafilms, which in 1966 joined forces with King Features to produce a film based on the Beatles song 'Yellow

Submarine'. Within a year the group had begun making plans to turn *Sgt Pepper* into a film as well. A production budget was drawn up and Tony Bramwell (who would later take over the day-to-day running of Apple Films) was given the task of filming The Beatles as they recorded the orchestral overdub for 'A Day In The Life' at EMI Studios, Abbey Road.

Plans for the *Sgt Pepper* film came to nothing, but the group's next film project ended up being much more successful. *Magical Mystery Tour* was conceived, written, and directed by The Beatles. The first major project undertaken by the group after Epstein's death, it was a critical failure but a financial success. As expected the soundtrack album – a double EP in Britain and an LP in the USA – raced up the charts.

The film itself cost £40,000 to make but quickly recouped its costs. The BBC paid £10,000 to screen the film; NBC-TV was intending to pay considerably more for the US broadcast rights but pulled out of the deal because of the lukewarm response to the film in Britain. In the end that worked out to The Beatles' advantage. Instead of offering the film to another American broadcaster, Apple decided to give *Magical Mystery Tour* a limited theatrical release (mostly on university and college campuses), from which it grossed two million dollars.

The Beatles hired Denis O'Dell, whom they had known for several years, to produce *Magical Mystery Tour*. O'Dell was an associate producer of *A Hard Day's Night* and *How I Won The War*, in which Lennon starred as Private Gripweed. Lennon went on to mention O'Dell (or "O'Bell") in the song 'You Know My Name (Look Up The Number)'.

As The Beatles had surrounded themselves with people they knew and trusted in so many other areas, it came as no surprise when O'Dell was appointed as a director of Apple Films. Unlike the Apple Boutique or Electronics division, which were given hundreds of thousands of pounds to play with, Apple Films was to operate under a strict annual budget of £40,000. It quickly put several ideas into pre-production, among them *Walkabout*, a coming-of-age tale set in the Australian outback; and *Traffic Jam*, a film about gridlock in Britain. In its first year, however, Apple Films was mostly focused on Beatles projects, co-producing *Yellow Submarine* and distributing *Magical*

Mystery Tour and John and Yoko's *Film No. Five (Smile).* Apple Films was also approached to finance another Ono project, *One Thousand Ways*, which was about birthing methods, and for which Ono wanted £10,000 – 25 per cent of the company's annual budget. O'Dell rejected the idea on the grounds that there was already plenty of existing footage in hospitals and other medical institutions. Ono didn't have to look far for funding after that, however. Lennon willingly produced her next film, *Rape*, and several others after that.

Apple Films' first major project was originally set to be *Get Back*, but tensions within the band and an inability to find a suitable live venue led it to become something rather different – *Let It Be*, as discussed in the previous chapter. O'Dell is seen in outtakes from the film, but his days at Apple were numbered. In February 1969 he left with Ringo Starr to work on *The Magic Christian* and never returned.

The arrival of Allen Klein seemed initially to have had much the same effect on Apple Films as it did on many of the company's other divisions. The staff were dismissed and all current projects quickly forgotten about. But in 1971 Apple's film division was reinstated to document George Harrison's *Concert For Bangla-Desh*. The film's release, in 1972, coincided with a major launch of Apple Films, with Ringo Starr appointed as the company's director.

Starr quickly started work on a number of film projects involving his rockstar buddies. One of his ideas was to make a series of documentaries about contemporary stars. While his proposed films about Richard Burton and Elizabeth Taylor and the footballer George Best never materialised, he did make one alongside Marc Bolan, the elfin king of glam, whose band T. Rex had developed the kind of hysterical following previously reserved only for The Beatles. After hearing that Bolan wanted to film a series of concerts at London's Wembley Empire Pool, Starr arranged a deal for Apple Films to co-produce in collaboration with Bolan's Wizard Artists.

In the years since pop had morphed into rock, the Empire Pool had become a popular venue among groups who had outgrown the theatre circuit. Led Zeppelin played two legendary shows there in November 1971. Bolan planned to do the same and capture it all on film for posterity. *Born To Boogie* would be, in Bolan's words, "audio-visual space age rock'n'roll".[36] Instead of a conventional narrative, the film juxtaposed concert footage with other surreal scenes, among them an episode in which Starr, dressed as a mouse, drives a Cadillac, and a kind of Mad Hatter's Tea Party shot on the grounds of Lennon's Tittenhurst Park estate.

Starr shot 50 hours of footage, which were later whittled down to a more palatable 64 minutes. *Born To Boogie* had its British premiere on December 14th 1972 at Oscar's cinema in London's Soho district before being released around the UK in the New Year. The film itself, released at the height of T.Rextasy, was modelled on the exploitation films of old. Like *A Hard Day's Night* it was made quickly and cheaply to yield big returns – which it did. (The only difference was that Apple didn't get a soundtrack album out of the deal.)

Born To Boogie was infinitely more enjoyable than Starr's next project: 1974's *Son Of Dracula*, a musical comedy in which he co-starred alongside Harry Nilsson. The two men had been drinking buddies for some time, which perhaps explains why they thought a spoof horror movie might work. (Nilsson had already toyed with the idea on his *Son Of Schmilsson* album, on which Starr played drums.)

Starr had originally wanted David Bowie to play Dracula. But while the Thin White Duke had the good sense to turn down the role, Nilsson didn't. The result was a critical and – one assumes – financial disaster. Starr himself has since virtually disowned it. "In America, the movie only played in towns that had one cinema," he told Q magazine in 1998, "because if it had two, no matter what was on down the road, they'd all go there!" Starr later returned to the studio with writer and comedian Graham Chapman to rework a lot of the film, but admitted to Q that it "makes even less sense now".

The final Apple Films production was *Little Malcolm And His Struggle Against The Eunuchs*, playwright David Halliwell's satire about the 1960s protest movement. Produced by Harrison rather than Starr, it fared much better than *Son Of Dracula*, even winning the Silver Bear award at the Berlin Film Festival in 1974. It featured the group Splinter performing 'Lonely Man', which was originally planned to be issued as a single by Apple Records. Since the label had effectively closed, however, Splinter signed to – and recorded an album for – Harrison's newly formed Dark Horse Records instead.

In the end Apple Films went the same way as Apple Records, the Apple Boutique, Apple Electronics, and all the rest. It had its successes, but like so many Apple initiatives it was driven by individual whims rather than collective business acumen. By 1976, Apple had become exactly what the accountants had originally envisioned: a litigious, revenue-collecting tax shelter. The Beatles' dreams of "controlled weirdness" and "western communism" were well and truly over.

Apple Bonkers
Waging a war against Apple Computer Inc

"Under this new agreement, Apple Inc will own all of the trademarks related to 'Apple' and will license certain of those trademarks back to Apple Corps for their continued use."

JOINT STATEMENT ISSUED BY APPLE INC AND APPLE CORPS, APRIL 5th 2007[1]

There wasn't a computer in sight when The Beatles entered EMI Studios on Wednesday June 6th 1962 to record their first session for the company. Computers back then were the size of a large room, huge cabinets filled with massive reels of magnetic tape and flashing lights. The only place they were likely to be seen was in films such *The Italian Job* or *The Billion Dollar Brain*, in which they were operated by mad scientists in white coats; they simply weren't something you encountered in everyday life. Anybody who did talk about computers in those days probably sounded like Professor Frink, the nutty professor in *The Simpsons*: "I predict that within 100 years, computers will be twice as powerful, 10,000 times larger, and so expensive that only the five richest kings of Europe will own them."

No one could have foreseen the massive explosion in home computing that took place in the 1980s – or that it would subsequently be possible to download music onto a hard drive, an MP3 player, or a mobile phone. Recording and music-reproduction technologies back then were entirely analogue. Music was recorded onto tapes using machines with valves (tubes), while records were cut using lathes, manufactured on industrial presses, and packed by hand by middle-aged housewives.

The Beatles might have had, in Magic Alex, a resident nutty professor of their own, but their interest in computing and electronics was fleeting at best. By the time the group's contract with EMI expired in 1976, however, a small revolution had begun. A growing number of people were beginning to build their own computers, among them a young American man by the name of Steve Jobs who started selling basic home computers through small retailers. Few took his Apple I seriously when it first appeared in April 1976, and even fewer could afford the $666.66 price tag. But by the time the Apple III went on sale in 1980, Jobs's machines were selling for as much as $7,800.

Later that year, in response to an ITV documentary called *The Mighty Micro* in which Dr Christopher Evans from the National Physical Laboratory predicted an imminent computer revolution, the BBC initiated its Computer Literacy Project. This, coupled with a growth in arcade gaming, helped fuel interest in home computing. By the mid 1980s it was even possible to play games online. Downloading music might still have been a long way off, but computers were slowly becoming integrated into people's lives.

Steve Jobs is a Beatles fan, and must surely have been well aware, when naming his company Apple Computer Inc, of the similarity to the name of The Beatles' business empire. Apple Computer's official line was always that it had chosen the name simply as a means of positioning itself ahead of Atari in the phone book. But when Apple Corps took Apple Computer Inc to court in 2006, Neil Aspinall claimed that Steve Jobs had once admitted to him that the company had been named after Apple Corps.[1]

Had Jobs bothered to think of an original name for his company, he might have spared himself decades of legal battles. The trouble began in 1978, when George Harrison spotted an advert for an Apple computer in a magazine. The 'quiet one' knew a copyright infringement when he saw one and tipped off Apple Corps, which sued Apple Computer for trademark infringement. The lawsuit was settled in 1981 when Apple Computer paid Apple Corps $80,000 and agreed to stay clear of the music business. But this was only the first round of a 25-year dispute.

As the years passed, Apple Computer began to incorporate new features into its computers. One of these was a sampled 'alert' sound called Chimes, which was later renamed Sosumi – or perhaps "so sue me". While that in itself wasn't enough to justify a lawsuit, the introduction of the Sound Manager program was deemed by Apple Corps to be a violation of the 1981 agreement and led to another court battle, the result of which was that Apple Computer was forced to pay a $26 million settlement. Round two to Apple Corps.

In 1991 an agreement was made that sought to outline each company's rights to the name Apple. Apple Corps maintained the right to sue Apple Computer for any creative works whose principal content is music. Apple Computer was allowed to manufacture goods to reproduce, run, play, or otherwise deliver such content, but not the physical media – CDs, tapes, records – on which said content could be distributed. Crucially, the agreement did not cover digital files, as hardly anybody would have been aware of such things at the time. (The German company Fraunhofer-Gesellschaft was granted a German patent for the MP3 in April 1989 but didn't receive an American patent until 1996.)

Apple Corps struck again in September 2003 after Apple Computer introduced first its iPod music player and then the iTunes Music Store – both clear violations, Apple Corps felt, of its rival's agreement not to distribute music. Like The Beatles before them, Apple Computer had turned music into big business. By the start of 2008 the company had sold over four billion songs on iTunes and over 120 million iPods to play them on, having announced record earnings of more than seven billion dollars for 2007 – 48 per cent of which came from the sale of iPods.

It's no wonder, then, that Apple Corps wanted a slice of the pie. But surely it would have been easier to do so by licensing The Beatles' music to iTunes, rather than undertaking another expensive lawsuit? Selling Beatles songs on iTunes would have reintroduced the group to a new, youthful audience and generated a vast amount of money from online sales.

The digital revolution that Dr Christopher Evans predicted in the late 1970s had changed the way people bought and listened to music. Today, fewer and fewer albums are being sold in physical formats. Digital downloads overtook sales of CD singles for the first time in 2006, and rose by 54 per cent the following year. One might have expected Apple Corps to take notice and indeed take advantage of this trend. But where The Beatles once led the way, they now seemed to be years – if not decades – behind the times, and decided once again to go to court.

The latest Apple vs Apple trial opened at London's High Courts on March 29th 2006 and closed just over a month later, on May 8th. This time the judge, Mr Justice Mann, ruled in favour of Apple Computer Inc, concluding that it had used the Apple logo in association with its iTunes store but not the music it sold, so was not in breach of the 1991 agreement. Round three to the Mac nerds.

Unfortunately for Apple Corps, that wasn't the end of it. As part of a deal with Apple Computer, the company was forced to relinquish all of its 'Apple' trademarks. Documents logged on April 5th 2007 at the US Patent And Trademark Office reveal that as of that date the newly renamed Apple Inc could now use The Beatles' iconic Apple logo as it saw fit. Apple Inc was at least willing to "license certain of those trademarks back to Apple Corps", but once again The Beatles appeared to have lost control of something that was once theirs.

The deal effectively put an end to the long-running dispute between the two companies and paved the way for iTunes to sell music by Apple Records artists. "We love The Beatles, and it has been painful being at odds with them over these trademarks," Steve Jobs said after the hearing. "It feels great to resolve this in a positive manner, and in a way that should remove the potential of further disagreements in the future."[2] Within hours of the end of the trial the internet was ablaze with rumours that The Beatles were about to sign a deal with Apple Inc. But there was still one more obstacle to overcome before The Beatles would agree to license their music for downloading.

The current model for digital sales is that record companies license their recordings to download companies, who pay an agreed fee for each download. But because most recording contracts were drawn up before the advent of the MP3, the AAC, and so on, record companies have continued to pay their artists as though downloads are physical sales, thereby taking a 'packaging allowance' – which of course is not applicable to a digital file. Downloads also cause problems with music publishing. Because digital sales are still relatively new, the percentage of publishing money that artists should be paid for music sold in this way is still in dispute. As a result many artists have sought to renegotiate their contracts – The Beatles naturally being among them.

Since The Beatles were suing EMI for unpaid royalties at the same they were suing Apple Computer, the prospect of any of the group's songs being available online looked remote. But on April 13th 2007, two days after Neil Aspinall resigned as chief executive of Apple Corps, EMI settled its royalty dispute with the company. "I can confirm that we have reached a mutually acceptable settlement and that we are not going to say anything more than that," an EMI spokesperson said, although it was also suggested that the company was working towards a way to get The Beatles on iTunes.[3]

While all of this was going on, Paul McCartney took the first major step towards making The Beatles' music available online. Having already left EMI in favour of a more lucrative deal with Starbucks' Hear Music label, McCartney announced a deal to sell his entire solo back catalogue through iTunes in May 2007. Within a few months Ringo Starr's solo albums were also available on iTunes. Many assumed that it wouldn't be long now before The Beatles joined them. But in August 2007 it was announced that the scheme had been delayed again, this time reportedly by Yoko Ono – despite the fact that she had already signed an agreement with iTunes to make John Lennon's solo recordings available online. (She wasn't the only Beatles widow to do so: Olivia Harrison followed suit in October.)

By the end of 2007 it was possible to download virtually every solo recording by The Beatles from iTunes, but none of the music they made together. But it can only be a matter of time. "It's all happening soon," McCartney told *Billboard* in November 2007. "Most of us are sort of ready. The whole thing is primed, ready to go – there's just maybe one little sticking point left, and I think it's being cleared up as we speak, so it shouldn't be too long. It's down to fine-tuning, but I'm pretty sure it'll be happening next year."[4]

By the time you read this it might already be possible to download 'Hey Jude' and 'Strawberry Fields Forever' from iTunes. On the other hand, we might still be waiting for the two Apples to sort out the small print. One thing's for sure: when it does happen it will be one of the biggest news stories of the year. Beatles songs will once again flood the charts and many more millions of dollars will pour into their already bulging coffers.

Endnotes

Introduction (pp16–21)
1 *Time* (February 21st 1964)
2 http://www.contactmusic.com
3 *Time* (October 2nd 1964)

Chapter 1 (pp22–61)
1 Roy Carr *Beatles At The Movies*
2 Hans Olaf Gottfridsson *From Cavern To Star-Club*
3 The Big Three *The Cavern Stomp* liner notes
4 The Big Three *The Cavern Stomp* liner notes
5 Keith Badman *The Beatles Off The Record*
6 Gareth L. Pawlowski *How They Became The Beatles*
7 The Beatles *Anthology*
8 The Beatles *Anthology*
9 Hans Olaf Gottfridsson *From Cavern To Star-Club*
10 Gareth L. Pawlowski *How They Became The Beatles*
11 The Beatles *Anthology*
12 Hans Olaf Gottfridsson *From Cavern To Star-Club*
13 Mark Lewisohn *The Complete Beatles Chronicle*
14 Spencer Leigh *Let's Go Down The Cavern*
15 Johnny Black *The Beatles, The Band Of The Century*
16 W. Fraser Sandercombe *The Beatles: Press Reports*
17 Ray Coleman *John Winston Lennon*
18 The Beatles *Anthology*
19 The Beatles *Anthology*
20 The Beatles *Anthology*
21 The Big Three *The Cavern Stomp* liner notes
22 Mark Lewisohn *Beatles Chronicle*
23 Ken Garner *In Session Tonight*
24 Debbie Geller *The Brian Epstein Story*
25 *New Record Mirror* (February 16th 1963)
26 *Mersey Beat* (June 14th–28th 1962)
27 Debbie Geller *The Brian Epstein Story*
28 Debbie Geller *The Brian Epstein Story*
29 *Mersey Beat* (August 23rd 1962)
30 *The Beatles Book* (October 1963)
31 *The Beatles Book* (January 1964)
32 Gerry Marsden *I'll Never Walk Alone*
33 http://www.beatlesstory.com
34 Arthur Marwick *The Sixties*
35 Spencer Leigh *Let's Go Down The Cavern*
36 *The Beatles Book* (January 1984)
37 *The Beatles Book* (January 1984)
38 Debbie Geller *The Brian Epstein Story*
39 The Big Three *The Cavern Stomp* liner notes
40 *New Musical Express* (October 12th 1963)
41 The Beatles *Anthology*
42 *The Beatles Book* (March 1983)
43 *Melody Maker* (February 9th 1963)
44 *The Beatles Book* (March 1983)
45 *Melody Maker* (March 23rd 1963)
46 *The Beatles Book* (August 1983)
47 *New Musical Express* (October 12th 1963)
48 Keith Badman *The Beatles Off The Record*
49 *Play And Player* (January 1965)
50 Spencer Leigh *Let's Go Down The Cavern*

Chapter 2 (pp62–91)
1 The Beatles *Anthology*
2 Hans Olaf Gottfridsson *From Cavern To Star-Club*
3 Hans Olaf Gottfridsson *Beatles Bop*
4 Hans Olaf Gottfridsson *Beatles Bop*
5 Hans Olaf Gottfridsson *Beatles Bop*
6 Hans Olaf Gottfridsson *Beatles Bop*
7 John Repsch *The Legendary Joe Meek*
8 Paul Trynka *The Beatles: 10 Years That Shock The World*
9 Hans Olaf Gottfridsson *From Cavern To Star-Club*
10 Paul Trynka *The Beatles: 10 Years That Shock The World*
11 Hans Olaf Gottfridsson *From Cavern To Star-Club*
12 Paul Trynka *The Beatles: 10 Years That Shock The World*
13 Mark Lewisohn *The Complete Beatles Chronicle*
14 *Mojo* (March 2007)
15 Debbie Geller *The Brian Epstein Story*
16 Debbie Geller *The Brian Epstein Story*
17 Brian Southall *Northern Songs*
18 Author's interview (August 30th 2007)
19 Bruce Spizer *The Beatles On Vee-Jay*
20 *Goldmine* (May 1981)
21 Bruce Spizer *The Beatles On Vee-Jay*
22 Craig Cross *Beatles-Discography.com*
23 Bruce Spizer *The Beatles On Vee-Jay*
24 Bruce Spizer *The Beatles On Vee-Jay*
25 Bruce Spizer *The Beatles On Vee-Jay*
26 Mark Lewisohn *The Beatles Live*
27 Debbie Geller *The Brian Epstein Story*
28 *Time* (October 2nd 1964)
29 Debbie Geller *The Brian Epstein Story*
30 Debbie Geller *The Brian Epstein Story*

31 Geoffrey Ellis *I Should Have Known Better*
32 Author's interview (August 30th 2007)
33 Mark Lewisohn *The Complete Beatles Recording Sessions*
34 Bruce Spizer *The Beatles Are Coming*
35 Debbie Geller *The Brian Epstein Story*
36 Keith Badman *The Beatles Off The Record*
37 Peter McCabe, Robert D. Schonfeld *John Lennon: For The Record*
38 Keith Badman *The Beatles Off The Record*
39 Keith Badman *The Beatles Off The Record*
40 Keith Badman *The Beatles Off The Record*
41 Paul Trynka *The Beatles: 10 Years That Shock The World*
42 The Beatles *Anthology*
43 http://www.rockmine.com/Klein.html
44 Peter McCabe *Apple To The Core*
45 Peter McCabe *Apple To The Core*
46 Peter McCabe *Apple To The Core*
47 Peter McCabe *Apple To The Core*
48 http://www.rockmine.com/Klein.html
49 *The Beatles Book* (December 1989)
50 *The Beatles Book* (November 1994)
51 BBC News (December 16th 2005)

Chapter 3 (pp100–129)

1 *Playboy* (February 1965)
2 Barry Miles *Paul McCartney: Many Years From Now*
3 The Beatles *Anthology*
4 Author's interview (August 30th 2007)
5 The Beatles *Anthology*
6 Debbie Geller *The Brian Epstein Story*
7 Keith Badman *The Beatles Off The Record*
8 Keith Badman *The Beatles Off The Record*
9 Author's interview (August 30th 2007)
10 Author's interview (August 30th 2007)
11 Debbie Geller *The Brian Epstein Story*
12 Keith Badman *The Beatles Off The Record*
13 Barry Miles *Paul McCartney: Many Years From Now*
14 Barry Miles *Paul McCartney: Many Years From Now*
15 *The Beatles Book* (March 1983)
16 *The Observer* (September 17th 2006)
17 Debbie Geller *The Brian Epstein Story*
18 *The Beatles Book* (April 1965)
19 *The Beatles Book* (April 1965)
20 Brian Southall *Northern Songs*
21 *Time* (October 2nd 1964)

22 Brian Southall *Northern Songs*
23 Brian Southall *Northern Songs*
24 Barry Miles *Paul McCartney: Many Years From Now*
25 Geoff Emerick *Here, There, And Everywhere*
26 The Beatles *Anthology*
27 *Only A Northern Song*, BBC Radio 2 (July 24th 2007)
28 *Only A Northern Song*, BBC Radio 2 (July 24th 2007)
29 *The Times* Business News (March 29th 1969)
30 Geoffrey Ellis *I Should Have Known Better*
31 Keith Badman *The Beatles Off The Record*
32 Brian Southall *Northern Songs*
33 *The Times* (April 20th 1969)
34 *The Times* (April 30th 1969)
35 Keith Badman *The Beatles Off The Record*
36 Brian Southall *Northern Songs*
37 *The Independent* (December 21st 2005)
38 *The Times* (April 14th 2006)
39 *The Times* (April 14th 2006)
40 Court TV (2000)
41 Q (December 1996)
42 Q (December 1996)
43 Q (December 1996)
44 http://www.primarywavemusic.com

Chapter 4 (pp130–159)

1 *Playboy* (February 1965)
2 Arthur Marwick *The Sixties*
3 http://triumphpc.com/mersey-beat/birth/
4 http://triumphpc.com/mersey-beat/birth/
5 http://triumphpc.com/mersey-beat/birth/
6 Bill Harry *Mersey Beat: The Beginnings Of The Beatles*
7 http://triumphpc.com/mersey-beat/birth/
8 *Mersey Beat* (January 4th 1962)
9 Paul Trynka *The Beatles: 10 Years that shook The World*
10 *The Beatles Book* (November 1982)
11 Johnny Dean *The Best of The Beatles Book*
12 *Disc* (October 6th 1962)
13 *New Musical Express* (February 1st 1963)
14 *Mersey Beat* (November 29th 1962)
15 *Mersey Beat* (January 3rd 1963)
16 *Melody Maker* (February 9th 1963)
17 *Pop Weekly* (February 2nd 1963)
18 *Pop Weekly* (March 3rd 1963)
19 *Melody Maker* (February 23rd 1963)
20 *Melody Maker* (March 23rd 1963)

21 *New Record Mirror* (January 12th 1963)
22 *New Record Mirror* (January 12th 1963)
23 *Cash Box* (February 23rd 1963)
24 *Cash Box* (June 1st 1963)
25 *Pop Weekly* (March 23rd 1963)
26 *New Record Mirror* (February 2nd 1963)
27 *New Musical Express* (February 15th 1963)
28 *New Musical Express* (February 15th 1963)
29 *The Beatles Book* (May 1983)
30 *New Musical Express* (June 5th 1963)
31 *Melody Maker* (July 27th 1963)
32 *Melody Maker* (June 29th 1963)
33 *Melody Maker* (August 24th 1963)
34 *Melody Maker* (July 27th 1963)
35 *Melody Maker* (August 3rd 1963)
36 *Billboard* (November 2nd 1963)
37 *Cash Box* (November 9th 1963)
38 *Billboard* (November 2nd 1963)
39 *Billboard* (November 2nd 1963)
40 *The Times* (February 11th 1964)
41 *Billboard* (February 1st 1964)
42 *Billboard* (February 15th 1964)
43 *Billboard* (February 15th 1964)
44 *The Believer* (June/July 2007)
45 *Mersey Beat* (October 1st–8th 1964)
46 Ray Coleman *John Winston Lennon*
47 *Time* (May 1st 1964)

Chapter 5 (pp160–173)
1 *The Beatles Book* (May 1964)
2 Jonathon Green *Days In The Life*
3 Mark Abrams *The Teenage Consumer*
4 *The Beatles Book* (October 1980)
5 *The Beatles Book* (May 1964)
6 *The Beatles Book* (May 1964)
7 Gareth L. Pawlowski *How They Became The Beatles*
8 Gareth L. Pawlowski *How They Became The Beatles*
9 Gareth L. Pawlowski *How They Became The Beatles*
10 Johnny Dean *The Best Of The Beatles Book*
11 *The Beatles Book* (January 1964)
12 *The Beatles Book* (May 1964)
13 Beatles Fan Club Newsletter (October 1964)
14 *The Beatles Book* (April 1965)

Chapter 6 (pp174–189)
1 Geoffrey Stokes *The Beatles*
2 Bruce Spizer *The Beatles Are Coming*

3 Bruce Spizer *The Beatles Swan Song*
4 Michael R. Frontani *The Beatles: Image And The Media*
5 Bruce Spizer *The Beatles Are Coming*
6 Keith Badman *The Beatles Off The Record*
7 The Beatles *Anthology*
8 *New York Times* Magazine (December 1st 1963)
9 *Time* (February 21st 1964)
10 *Billboard* (February 29th 1964)
11 Barry Miles *Paul McCartney: Many Years From Now*
12 Michael R. Frontani *The Beatles: Image And The Media*
13 Geoffrey Stokes *The Beatles*
14 Craig Cross *Beatles-Discography.com*
15 Bruce Spizer *The Beatles Are Coming*
16 Bruce Spizer *The Beatles Are Coming*
17 Bruce Spizer *The Beatles Are Coming*

Chapter 7 (pp190–207)
1 *Playboy* (February 1965)
2 Debbie Geller *The Brian Epstein Story*
3 *The Beatles Book* (January 1964)
4 Philip Norman *Shout*
5 Ray Coleman *The Man Who Made The Beatles*
6 Ray Coleman *The Man Who Made The Beatles*
7 Debbie Geller *The Brian Epstein Story*
8 Philip Norman *Shout*
9 *New York Times* (February 17th 1964)
10 Debbie Geller *The Brian Epstein Story*
11 Philip Norman *Shout*
12 Debbie Geller *The Brian Epstein Story*
13 Geoffrey Ellis *I Should Have Know Better*
14 Ray Coleman *The Man Who Made The Beatles*
15 Debbie Geller *The Brian Epstein Story*
16 Paul Trynka *The Beatles: 10 Years That Shook The World*
17 Author's interview (August 30th 2007)

Chapter 8 (pp208–233)
1 *Late Night Line-up*, BBC2 (December 10th 1969)
2 The Beatles *Anthology*
3 Roy Carr *Beatles At The Movies*
4 Roy Carr *Beatles At The Movies*
5 The Beatles *Anthology*
6 *Melody Maker* (November 7th 1964)
7 The Beatles *A Hard Day's Night* DVD
8 Bruce Spizer *The Beatles Swan Song*
9 Lorraine Rolston *A Hard Day's Night*
10 The Beatles *A Hard Day's Night* DVD

11 The Beatles *A Hard Day's Night* DVD
12 The Beatles *A Hard Day's Night* DVD
13 The Editors Of *Goldmine* Magazine *The Beatles Digest*
14 *Disc Weekly* (July 11th 1964)
15 Paul Trynka *The Beatles: 10 Years That Shook The World*
16 *New York Times* (January 5th 1965)
17 Paul Trynka *The Beatles: 10 Years That Shook The World*
18 *Mojo* (December 2007)
19 *British Calendar News* (December 6th 1965)
20 The Beatles *Anthology*
21 *Mojo* (December 2007)
22 The Beatles *Anthology*
23 *Melody Maker* (October 31st 1964)
24 *Mojo* (December 2007)
25 *Melody Maker* (February 27th 1965)
26 *Melody Maker* (February 27th 1965)
27 *New York Times* (August 24th 1965)
28 *The Beatles Book* (August 1985)
29 *Disc Weekly* (July 31st 1965)
30 Roland Reiter *Screening The Beatles Myth*
31 Al Brodax *Up Periscope Yellow*
32 *New York Times* (June 1st 1965)
33 Roy Carr *Beatles At The Movies*
34 Roland Reiter *Screening The Beatles Myth*
35 *Melody Maker* (May 7th 1966)
36 The Beatles *Anthology*
37 The Beatles *Anthology*
38 Robert R. Hieronimus *Inside The Yellow Submarine*
39 Robert R. Hieronimus *Inside The Yellow Submarine*
40 Roy Carr *Beatles At The Movies*
41 *Melody Maker* (September 26th 1968)
42 *Disc & Music Echo* (October 12th 1968)
43 *Melody Maker* (December 7th 1968)
44 *Disc & Music Echo* October 12th 1968
45 Barry Miles *The Beatles In Their Own Words*
46 *Melody Maker* (January 18th 1969)
47 Barry Miles *The Beatles In Their Own Words*
48 Roy Carr *Beatles At The Movies*
49 Barry Miles *The Beatles In Their Own Words*
50 Roy Carr *Beatles At The Movies*
51 Barry Miles *The Beatles In Their Own Words*
52 Barry Miles *The Beatles Diary Volume 1: The Beatles Years*
53 Robert R. Hieronimus *Inside The Yellow Submarine*

Chapter 9 (pp234–265)

1 The Beatles *Anthology*
2 *The Tonight Show*, NBC-TV (May 14th 1968)
3 Jonathon Green *Days In The Life*
4 *The Times* (June 24th 1968)
5 *The Beatles Book* (September 1967)
6 *The Times* (August 31st 1967)
7 W. Fraser Sandercombe *The Beatles: Press Reports*
8 Tony Bramwell, Rosemary Kingsland *Magical Mystery Tours*
9 The Beatles *Anthology*
10 Brian Southall *Northern Songs*
11 The Beatles *Anthology*
12 Stefan Granados *Those Were The Days*
13 The Beatles *Anthology*
14 *The Beatles Book* (April 1968)
15 Barry Miles *Paul McCartney: Many Years From Now*
16 Barry Miles *Paul McCartney: Many Years From Now*
17 The Beatles *Anthology*
18 *Disc & Music Echo* (August 3rd 1968)
19 The Beatles *Anthology*
20 Barry Miles *Paul McCartney: Many Years From Now*
21 The Beatles *Anthology*
22 Geoff Emerick *Here, There, And Everywhere*
23 Geoff Emerick *Here, There, And Everywhere*
24 http://www.mersey-beat.net
25 Stefan Granados *Those Were The Days*
26 Ken Mansfield *The White Book*
27 Jonathon Green *Days In The Life*
28 Jonathon Green *Days In The Life*
29 Bruce Spizer *The Beatles On Apple Records*
30 *New York Times* (August 7th 1968)
31 Stefan Granados *Those Were The Days*
32 *The Times* (November 21st 1968)
33 Stefan Granados *Those Were The Days*
34 *New York Times* (May 21st 1969)
35 Stefan Granados *Those Were The Days*
36 *Beat Instrumental* (October 1972)

Chapter 10 (pp266–272)

1 *Financial Times* (Apr 3rd 2006)
2 BBC News (February 5th 2007)
3 ABC Online (April 13th 2007)
4 *Billboard* (November 14th 2007)

Timeline

July 6th 1957: Paul McCartney meets John Lennon at the Woolton Parish Church fete after a performance by Lennon's group, The Quarry Men, and soon joins them.

February 1st 1958: George Harrison joins The Quarry Men.

May 10th 1960: Now known as The Silver Beetles, the group auditions for Larry Parnes.

May 20th 1960: The Silver Beetles back Johnny Gentle on a tour of Scotland.

August 17th 1960: First visit to Hamburg, Germany, with Stuart Sutcliffe on bass and Pete Best on drums. They perform at the Indra Club before transferring to the larger Kaiserkeller.

February 21st 1961: First appearance at the Cavern Club, Liverpool.

March 27th 1961: Start of 14-week residency at the Top Ten Club, Hamburg.

June 22nd–23rd 1961: Recording session with Tony Sheridan and German producer / orchestra-leader Bert Kaempfert.

November 9th 1961: Brian Epstein sees The Beatles at the Cavern Club.

January 1st 1962: Decca Records audition.

January 5th 1962: 'My Bonnie' / 'The Saints' by Tony Sheridan & The Beatles (Polydor NH 66833) released in the UK.

January 24th 1962: The Beatles sign a management contract with Brian Epstein, as witnessed by his assistant Alistair Taylor. (Epstein does not sign the contract.)

March 7th 1962: Radio debut on the BBC Light Programme show *Teenagers' Turn – Here We Go*.

April 10th 1962: Stuart Sutcliffe dies.

April 13th 1962: Start of 48-night residency at the Star-Club, Hamburg.

May 9th 1962: Brian Epstein meets George Martin.

June 6th 1962: Parlophone Records audition at EMI Studios, Abbey Road.

June 26th 1962: Brain Epstein and his brother Clive form NEMS Enterprises Limited.

August 16th 1962: Pete Best is sacked from The Beatles.

August 18th 1962: Ringo Starr makes his first appearance with the group.

August 22nd 1962: Granada Television films The Beatles at the Cavern.

September 4th 1962: First session with George Martin.

October 1st 1962: The Beatles sign a revised management contract with Epstein – which he signs too, this time.

October 5th 1962: 'Love Me Do' / 'PS I Love You' (Parlophone 45-R 4949) released in the UK.

October 17th 1962: Television debut on Granada's *People And Places*, broadcast live from Manchester.

November 1st 1962: Start of fourth residency at the Star-Club.

December 18th 1962: Start of fifth and final residency at the Star-Club.

January 11th 1963: 'Please Please Me' / 'Ask Me Why' (Parlophone 45-R 4983) released in the UK.

February 2nd 1963: Opening night of first nationwide tour, with Helen Shapiro, at the Gaumont Cinema, Bradford.

February 20th 1963: 'Please Please Me' / 'Ask Me Why' (Vee-Jay 498) released in the USA.

February 22nd 1963: Brian Epstein becomes co-director, with Dick James, of Northern Songs, which is established to publish compositions by Lennon and McCartney.

March 22nd 1963: *Please Please Me* LP (Parlophone PMC 1202) released in the UK. Side One: 'I Saw Her Standing There', 'Misery', 'Anna (Go To Him)', 'Chains', 'Boys', 'Ask Me Why', 'Please Please Me'; Side Two: 'Love Me Do', 'PS I Love You', 'Baby It's You', 'Do You Want To Know A Secret', 'A Taste Of Honey', 'There's A Place', 'Twist And Shout'.

April 11th 1963: 'From Me To You' / 'Thank You Girl' (Parlophone R 5015) released in the UK.

May 6th 1963: 'From Me To You' / 'Thank You Girl' (Vee-Jay 522) released in the USA.

June 20th 1963: The Beatles Ltd is formed, with Epstein as a director.

July 12th 1963: *Twist And Shout* EP (Parlophone GEP 8882) released in the UK: Side One: 'Twist And Shout', 'A Taste Of Honey'; Side Two: 'Do You Want To Know A Secret', 'There's A Place'.

August 1st 1963: Sean O'Mahony publishes the first issue of *The Beatles Book*.

August 23rd 1963: 'She Loves You' / 'I'll Get You' (Parlophone R 5055) released in the UK.

September 6th 1963: *The Beatles' Hits* EP (Parlophone GEP 8880) released in the UK. Side One: 'From Me To You', 'Thank You Girl'; Side Two: 'Please Please Me', 'Love Me Do'.

October 13th 1963: The Beatles top the bill for *Val Parnell's Sunday Night At The London Palladium*.

October 29th 1963: Epstein meets with Walter Shenson and agrees a deal for The Beatles' first feature-length film.

November 4th 1963: Perform at the Prince Of Wales Theatre, London, as part of the Royal Command Performance. The Queen Mother, Princess Margaret, and Lord Snowdon are in the audience.

November 11th 1963: Epstein meets with Ed Sullivan in New York City to arrange for The Beatles to appear on *The Ed Sullivan Show*.

November 22nd 1963: *With The Beatles* (Parlophone PMC 1206) released in the UK. Side One: 'It Won't Be Long', 'All I've Got To Do', 'All My Loving', 'Don't Bother Me', 'Little Child', 'Till There Was You', 'Please Mister Postman'; Side Two: 'Roll Over Beethoven', 'You Really Got A Hold On Me', 'I Wanna Be Your Man', '(There's A) Devil In Her Heart', 'Not A Second Time', 'Money (That's What I Want)'.

November 29th 1963: 'I Want To Hold Your Hand' / 'This Boy' (Parlophone R 5084) released in the UK after record-breaking advance orders of over one million copies.

December 24th 1963: The Beatles Christmas Show begins at the Astoria Cinema, Finsbury Park, London, and will be attended by almost 100,000 people.

December 26th 1963: 'I Want To Hold Your Hand' / 'I Saw Her Standing There' (Capitol 5112) released in the USA.

January 10th 1964: *Introducing The Beatles* (Vee-Jay VJLP 1062) released in the USA. Side One: 'I Saw Her Standing There', 'Misery', 'Anna (Go To Him)', 'Chains', 'Boys', 'Love Me Do'; Side Two: 'PS I Love You', 'Baby It's You', 'Do You Want To Know A Secret', 'A Taste Of Honey', 'There's A Place', 'Twist And Shout'.

January 17th 1964: 'I Want To Hold Your Hand' tops US chart as Beatles perform at Olympia Theatre, Paris.

January 20th 1964: *Meet The Beatles* (Capitol T 2047) released in the USA. Side One: 'I Want To Hold Your Hand', 'I Saw Her Standing There', 'This Boy', 'It Won't Be Long', 'All I've Got To Do', 'All My Loving'; Side Two: 'Don't Bother Me', 'Little Child', 'Till There Was You', 'Hold Me Tight', 'I Wanna Be Your Man', 'Not A Second Time'.

February 7th 1964: *All My Loving* EP (Parlophone GEP 8891) released in the UK, on the same day that The Beatles arrive in America. Side One: 'All My Loving', 'Ask Me Why'; Side Two: 'Money (That's What I Want)', 'PS I Love You'.

February 9th 1964: First appearance on *The Ed Sullivan Show*.

February 11th 1964: First US concert, at the Washington Coliseum.

March 2nd 1964: Shooting of *A Hard Day's Night* begins.

April 4th 1964: The Beatles have 12 entries on the *Billboard* singles chart.

April 10th 1964: *The Beatles' Second Album* (Capitol T 2080) released in the USA. Side One: 'Roll Over Beethoven', 'Thank You Girl', 'You Really Got A Hold On Me', 'Devil In Her Heart', 'Money (That's What I Want)', 'You Can't Do That'; Side Two: 'Long Tall Sally', 'I Call Your Name', 'Please Mister Postman', 'I'll Get You', 'She Loves You'.

May 11th 1964: *Four By The Beatles* EP (Capitol EAP 1-1-2121) released in the USA. Side 1: 'Roll Over

Beethoven', 'All My Loving'; Side Two: 'This Boy', 'Please Mister Postman'.

May 12th 1964: Lenmac Enterprises Ltd is formed.

June 11th 1964: Arrive in Sydney, Australia, ready for performance at the Centennial Hall, Adelaide, a day later.

June 26th 1964: *A Hard Day's Night* (United Artists 3366) released in the USA. Side One: 'A Hard Day's Night', 'Tell Me Why', 'I'll Cry Instead', 'I Should Have Known Better' (instrumental), 'I'm Happy Just To Dance With You', 'And I Love Her' (instrumental); Side Two: 'I Should Have Known Better', 'If I Fell', 'And I Love Her', 'Ringo's Theme (This Boy)' (instrumental), 'Can't Buy Me Love', 'A Hard Day's Night' (instrumental).

July 6th 1964: *A Hard Day's Night* receives its premiere in Piccadilly Circus, London.

July 10th 1964: 'A Hard Day's Night' / 'Things We Said Today' (Parlophone R 5160) and *A Hard Day's Night* (Parlophone PMC 1230) released in the UK. LP Side One: 'A Hard Day's Night', 'I Should Have Known Better', 'If I Fell', 'I'm Happy Just To Dance With You', 'And I Love Her', 'Tell Me Why', 'Can't Buy Me Love'; Side Two: 'Any Time At All', 'I'll Cry Instead', 'Things We Said Today', 'When I Get Home', 'You Can't Do That', 'I'll Be Back'.

July 13th 1964: 'A Hard Day's Night' / 'I Should Have Known Better' (Capitol 5222) released in the USA.

July 20th 1964: 'I'll Cry Instead' / 'I'm Happy Just To Dance With You' (Capitol 5234), 'And I Love Her' / 'If I Fell' (Capitol 5235), and *Something New* (Capitol T 2108) released in the USA. LP Side One: 'I'll Cry Instead', 'Things We Said Today', 'Anytime At All', 'When I Get Home', 'Slow Down', 'Matchbox'; Side Two: 'Tell Me Why', 'And I Love Her', 'I'm Happy Just To Dance With You', 'If I Fell', 'Komm, Gib Mir Deine Hand'.

August 12th 1964: *A Hard Day's Night* opens in 500 theatres across America.

August 19th 1964: Second US tour begins at the Cow Palace, San Francisco, California.

October 9th 1964: Four-week tour of the UK begins at the Gaumont Cinema, Bradford.

October 12th 1964: *Songs, Pictures And Stories Of The Fabulous Beatles* (Vee-Jay VJLP 1092) released in the USA. Side One: 'I Saw Her Standing There', 'Misery', 'Anna (Go To Him)', 'Chains', 'Boys', 'Ask Me Why'; Side Two: 'Please Please Me', 'Baby, It's You', 'Do You Want To Know A Secret', 'A Taste Of Honey', 'There's A Place', 'Twist And Shout'.

November 4th 1964: *Extracts From The Film A Hard Day's Night* EP (Parlophone GEP 8920) released in the UK. Side One: 'I Should Have Known Better', 'If I Fell'; Side Two: 'Tell Me Why', 'And I Love Her'.

November 6th 1964: *Extracts From The Album A Hard Day's Night* (Parlophone GEP 8924) released in the UK. Side One: 'Anytime At All', 'I'll Cry Instead'; Side Two: 'Things We Said Today', 'When I Get Home'.

November 23rd 1964: 'I Feel Fine' / 'She's A Woman' (Capitol 5327) released in the USA.

November 27th 1964: 'I Feel Fine' / 'She's A Woman' (Parlophone R 5200) released in the UK.

December 4th 1964: *Beatles For Sale* (Parlophone PCS 3062) released in the UK. Side One: 'No Reply', 'I'm A Loser', 'Baby's In Black', 'Rock And Roll Music', 'I'll Follow The Sun', 'Mr Moonlight', 'Kansas City'/'Hey, Hey, Hey, Hey'; Side Two: 'Eight Days A Week', 'Words Of Love', 'Honey Don't', 'Every Little Thing', 'I Don't Want To Spoil The Party', 'What You're Doing', 'Everybody's Trying To Be My Baby.

December 15th 1964: *Beatles '65* (Capitol ST 2228) released in the USA. Side One: 'No Reply', 'I'm A Loser', 'Baby's In Black', 'Rock And Roll Music', 'I'll Follow The Sun', 'Mr. Moonlight'; Side Two: 'Honey Don't', 'I'll Be Back', 'She's A Woman', 'I Feel Fine', 'Everybody's Trying To Be My Baby'.

December 24th 1964: *Another Beatles' Christmas Show* opens at the Hammersmith Odeon, London.

February 1st 1965: *4 By The Beatles* (Capitol R-5365) released in the USA. Side One: 'Honey Don't', 'I'm A Loser'; Side Two: 'Mr. Moonlight', 'Everybody's Trying To Be My Baby'.

February 4th 1965: Maclen (Music) Ltd is formed, with Lennon, McCartney, and Epstein as directors.

February 18th 1965: Northern Songs is floated on the London Stock Exchange.

February 15th 1965: 'Eight Days A Week' / 'I Don't Want To Spoil The Party' (Capitol 5371) released in the USA.

February 23, 1965: Shooting of the second Beatles film begins on New Providence Island, Bahamas.

March 22nd 1965: *The Early Beatles* (Capitol T-2309) released in the USA. Side One: 'Love Me Do', 'Twist And Shout', 'Anna (Go To Him)', 'Chains', 'Boys', 'Ask Me Why'; Side Two: 'Please Please Me', 'PS I Love You', 'Baby, It's You', 'A Taste Of Honey', 'Do You Want To Know A Secret'.

April 6th 1965: *Beatles For Sale* EP (Parlophone GEP 8931) released in the UK: Side One: 'No Reply', 'I'm A Loser'; Side Two: 'Rock And Roll Music', 'Eight Days A Week'.

April 9th 1965: 'Ticket To Ride' / 'Yes It Is' (Parlophone R 5265) released in the UK.

April 19th 1965: 'Ticket to Ride' / 'Yes It Is' (Capitol 5407) released in the USA.

June 4th 1965: *Beatles For Sale 2* EP (Parlophone GEP 8938) released in the UK. Side One: 'I'll Follow The Sun', 'Baby's In Black'; Side Two: 'Words Of Love', 'I Don't Want To Spoil The Party'.

June 14, 1965: *Beatles VI* (Capitol T-2358) released in the USA. Side One: 'Kansas City'/'Hey, Hey, Hey, Hey', 'Eight Days A Week', 'You Like Me Too Much', 'Bad Boy', 'I Don't Want To Spoil The Party', 'Words Of Love'; Side Two: 'What You're Doing', 'Yes It Is', 'Dizzy Miss Lizzy', 'Tell Me What You See', 'Every Little Thing'.

June 20th 1965: European tour begins in Paris.

July 19th 1965: 'Help!' / 'I'm Down' (Capitol 5476) released in the USA.

July 23rd 1965: 'Help!' / 'I'm Down' (Parlophone R 5305) released in the UK.

July 29th 1965: *Help!* premieres in London.

August 6th 1965: *Help!* (Parlophone PMC 1255) released in the UK. Side One: 'Help!', 'The Night Before', 'You've Got To Hide Your Love Away', 'I Need You', 'Another Girl', 'You're Going To Lose That Girl', 'Ticket To Ride'; Side Two: 'Act Naturally', 'It's Only Love', 'You Like Me Too Much', 'Tell Me What You See', 'I've Just Seen A Face', 'Yesterday', 'Dizzy Miss Lizzy'.

August 11th 1965: *Help!* premieres in New York.

August 13th 1965: *Help!* (Capitol MAS-2386) released in the USA. Side One: 'The James Bond Theme' (The George Martin Orchestra), 'Help!', 'The Night Before', 'From Me To You Fantasy' (The George Martin Orchestra), 'You've Got To Hide Your Love Away', 'I Need You', 'In The Tyrol' (The George Martin Orchestra); Side Two: 'Another Girl', 'Another Hard Day's Night' (The George Martin Orchestra), 'Ticket To Ride', 'The Bitter End'/'You Can't Do That' (The George Martin Orchestra), 'You're Going To Lose That Girl', 'The Chase' (The George Martin Orchestra).

August 15th 1965: The Beatles perform at Shea Stadium.

September 13th 1965: 'Yesterday '/ 'Act Naturally' (Capitol 5498) released in the USA.

September 25th 1965: The first episode of the Beatles cartoon series, *The Beatles*, is broadcast in the USA.

October 26th 1965: The Beatles receive their MBEs from the Queen.

December 3rd 1965: 'Day Tripper' / 'We Can Work It Out' (Parlophone R 5389) and *Rubber Soul* (Parlophone PMC 1267) released in the UK. LP Side One: 'Drive My Car', 'Norwegian Wood (This Bird Has Flown)', 'You Won't See Me', 'Nowhere Man', 'Think For Yourself', 'The Word', 'Michelle'; Side Two: 'What Goes On', 'Girl', 'I'm Looking Through You', 'In My Life', 'Wait', 'If I Needed Someone', 'Run For Your Life'. The Beatles began their final UK tour with two sets at the Odeon Cinema, Glasgow.

December 6th 1965: 'Day Tripper' / 'We Can Work It Out' (Capitol 5555) and *Rubber Soul* (Capitol T-2442) released in the USA. LP Side One: 'I've Just Seen A Face', 'Norwegian Wood (This Bird Has Flown)', 'You Won't See Me', 'Think For Yourself', 'The Word', 'Michelle'; Side Two: 'It's Only Love', 'Girl', 'I'm Looking Through You', 'In My Life', 'Wait', 'Run For Your Life'.

December 6th 1965: *The Beatles' Million Sellers* EP (Parlophone GEP 8946) released in the UK. Side One: 'She Loves You', 'I Want To Hold Your Hand'; Side Two: 'Can't Buy Me Love', 'I Feel Fine'.

February 21st 1966: 'Nowhere Man' / 'What Goes On' (Capitol 5587) released in the USA.

March 1st 1966: *The Beatles At Shea Stadium* airs on BBC1 in the UK.

May 30th 1966: 'Paperback Writer' / 'Rain' (Capitol 5651) released in the USA.

June 10th 1966: 'Paperback Writer' / 'Rain' (Parlophone R 5452) released in the UK.

June 15th 1966: *Yesterday . . . And Today* (Capitol T-2553) released in the USA. Side One: 'Drive My Car', 'I'm Only Sleeping', 'Nowhere Man', 'Doctor Robert', 'Yesterday', 'Act Naturally'. Side Two: 'And Your Bird Can Sing', 'If I Needed Someone', 'We Can Work It Out', 'What Goes On', 'Day Tripper'.

July 1st 1966: Two concerts at the Nippon Budokan Hall, Japan, both of which are filmed for television.

July 4th 1966: Not quite realising the potential consequences, The Beatles decline an invitation to breakfast with Imelda Marcos.

July 29th 1966: *Datebook* publishes Maureen Cleave's infamous interview with John Lennon, in which he claims: "We're bigger than Jesus now."

August 5th 1966: 'Yellow Submarine' / 'Eleanor Rigby' (Parlophone R 5493) and *Revolver* (Parlophone PMC 7009) released in the UK. LP Side One: 'Taxman', 'Eleanor Rigby', 'I'm Only Sleeping', 'Love You To', 'Here, There And Everywhere', 'Yellow Submarine', 'She Said She Said'; Side Two: 'Good Day Sunshine', 'And Your Bird Can Sing', 'For No One', 'Doctor Robert', 'I Want To Tell You', 'Got To Get You Into My Life', 'Tomorrow Never Knows'.

August 8th 1966: *Revolver* (Capitol T 2576) released in the USA. Side One: 'Taxman', 'Eleanor Rigby', 'Love You To', 'Here, There And Everywhere', 'Yellow Submarine', 'She Said She Said'; Side Two: 'Good Day Sunshine', 'For No One', 'I Want To Tell You', 'Got To Get You Into My Life', 'Tomorrow Never Knows'.

August 29th 1966: Final public concert, in San Francisco's Candlestick Park.

November 9th 1966: John Lennon meets Yoko Ono at the Indica Gallery in Mason's Yard, London.

December 10th 1966: *A Collection of Beatles Oldies* (Parlophone PMC 7016) released in the UK. Side One: 'She Loves You', 'From Me To You', 'We Can Work It Out', 'Help!', 'Michelle', 'Yesterday', 'I Feel Fine', 'Yellow Submarine'; Side Two: 'Can't Buy Me Love', 'Bad Boy', 'Day Tripper', 'A Hard Day's Night', 'Ticket To Ride', 'Paperback Writer', 'Eleanor Rigby', 'I Want To Hold Your Hand'.

February 13th 1967: 'Penny Lane' / 'Strawberry Fields Forever' (Capitol 5810) released in the USA.

February 17th 1967: 'Penny Lane' / 'Strawberry Fields Forever' (Parlophone R 5570) released in the UK.

April 19th 1967: The Beatles are advised to form an umbrella company to control their subsidiary interests. This company eventually becomes Apple Corps with The Beatles sharing income from group and solo work (except songwriting).

June 1st 1967: *Sgt Pepper's Lonely Hearts Club Band* (Parlophone PMC 7027) released in the UK. Side One: 'Sgt. Pepper's Lonely Hearts Club Band', 'With A Little Help From My Friends', 'Lucy In The Sky With Diamonds', 'Getting Better', 'Fixing A Hole', 'She's Leaving Home', 'Being For The Benefit Of Mr. Kite'; Side Two: 'Within You Without You', 'When I'm Sixty Four', 'Lovely Rita', 'Good Morning Good Morning', 'Sgt. Pepper's Lonely Hearts Club Band (reprise)', 'A Day In The Life'.

June 2nd 1967: *Sgt Pepper's Lonely Hearts Club Band* (Capitol MAS 2653) in the USA (tracklisting as above).

July 7th 1967: 'All You Need Is Love' / 'Baby You're A Rich Man' (Parlophone R 5620) released in the UK.

July 17th 1967: 'All You Need Is Love' / 'Baby You're A Rich Man' (Capitol 5964) released in the USA.

August 25th 1967: Beatles, wives, and girlfriends spend the weekend with the Maharishi in Bangor, Wales.

August 27th 1967: Brian Epstein dies.

November 24th 1967: 'Hello Goodbye' / 'I Am The Walrus' (Parlophone R 5655) released in the UK.

November 27, 1967: 'Hello Goodbye' / 'I Am The Walrus' (Capitol 2056) and *Magical Mystery Tour* (Capitol SMAL 2835) released in the USA. LP Side One: 'Magical Mystery Tour', 'The Fool On The Hill', 'Flying', 'Blue Jay Way' Your Mother Should Know', 'I Am The Walrus'; Side Two; 'Hello Goodbye', 'Strawberry Fields Forever', 'Penny lane', 'Baby You're A Rich Man', 'All You Need Is Love'.

December 8th 1967: *Magical Mystery Tour* EP (Parlophone MMT I) released in the UK. Side One: 'Magical Mystery Tour', 'Your Mother Should Know'; Side Two: 'I Am The Walrus'; Side Three: 'The Fool On The Hill', 'Flying'; Side Four: 'Blue Jay Way'.

December 26th 1967: The *Magical Mystery Tour* film is given its world premiere on BBC Television.

January 22nd 1968: Apple Corps opens its offices at 95 Wigmore St, London.

February 20th 1968: Arrive in India to study at the Academy of Transcendental Meditation.

March 15th 1968: 'Lady Madonna' / 'The Inner Light' (Parlophone R 5675) released in the UK.

March 18th 1968: 'Lady Madonna' / 'The Inner Light' (Capitol 2138) released in the USA.

July 17th 1968: *Yellow Submarine* receives its premiere at the London Pavilion on Piccadilly Circus.

August 11th 1968: The Beatles publicise the launch of Apple Records with 'National Apple Week'. The label announces plans to issue four singles: 'Hey Jude' by The Beatles, 'Sour Milk Sea' by Jackie Lomax, 'Thingumybob' by The Black Dyke Mills Band, and 'Those Were The Days' by Mary Hopkin.

August 22nd 1968: Ringo Starr leaves the group.

August 26th 1968: 'Hey Jude' / 'Revolution' (Apple 2276) released in the USA.

August 30, 1968: 'Hey Jude' / 'Revolution' (Apple R 5722) released in the UK.

September 3rd 1968: Ringo Starr returns to the fold.

November 1st 1968: *Wonderwall Music (Original Soundtrack Album)* by George Harrison (Apple APCOR 1) released in the UK. Side One: 'Microbes', 'Red Lady', 'Medley', 'Tabia and Pakavaj', 'In The Park', 'Medley', 'Greasy Legs', 'Ski-ing and Gat Kirwani', 'Dream Scene'; Side Two: 'Party Seacombe', 'Medley', 'Love Scene', 'Crying', 'Cowboy Museum', 'Fantasy Sequins', 'Glass Box', 'On The Bed', 'Wonderwall To Be Here', 'Singing Ohm'.

November 22nd 1968: *The Beatles* (Apple PMC 7067-7068) released in the UK. Side One: 'Back In The USSR', 'Dear Prudence', 'Glass Onion', 'Ob-La-Di, Ob-La-Da', 'Wild Honey Pie', 'The Continuing Story Of Bungalow Bill', 'While My Guitar Gently Weeps', 'Happiness Is A Warm Gun'; Side Two: 'Martha My Dear', 'I'm So Tired', 'Blackbird', 'Piggies', 'Rocky Raccoon', 'Don't Pass Me By', 'Why Don't We Do It In The Road', 'I Will', 'Julia'; Side Three: 'Birthday', 'Yer Blues', 'Mother Nature's Son', 'Everybody's Got Something To

Hide Except Me And My Monkey', 'Sexy Sadie', 'Helter Skelter', 'Long Long Long'; Side Four: 'Revolution 1', 'Honey Pie', 'Savoy Truffle', 'Cry Baby Cry', 'Revolution 9', 'Good Night'.

November 25th 1968: *The Beatles* (Apple SWBO 101) released in the USA (tracklisting as above).

November 29th 1968: *Unfinished Music No. 1: Two Virgins* by John Lennon & Yoko Ono (Apple APCOR2) released in the UK. Side One: 'Two Virgins No. 1', 'Together', 'Two Virgins Nos. 2–6'. Side Two: 'Two Virgins', 'Hushabye Hushabye', 'Two Virgins Nos. 7–10'.

January 2nd 1969: Shooting of *Get Back* begins at Twickenham Studios.

January 10th 1969: George Harrison quits.

January 13th 1969: *Yellow Submarine* (Apple SW 385) released in the USA. Side One: 'Yellow Submarine', 'Only A Northern Song', 'All Together Now', 'Hey Bulldog', 'It's All Too Much', 'All You Need Is Love'; Side Two (by The George Martin Orchestra): 'Pepperland', 'Sea Of Time', 'Sea Of Holes', 'Sea Of Monsters', 'March Of The Meanies', 'Pepperland Laid Waste', 'Yellow Submarine In Pepperland'.

January 15th 1969: George Harrison rejoins The Beatles.

January 17th 1969: *Yellow Submarine* (Apple PMC 7070) released in the UK (tracklisting as above).

January 30th 1969: Final public appearance given from the rooftop of the group's Savile Row HQ.

February 8th 1969: Allen Klein appointed as financial adviser to Apple.

February 12th 1969: Paul McCartney forms a new company, Adagrose Ltd (later renamed McCartney Productions Ltd).

February 24th 1969: Triumph Investment group gains control of NEMS Enterprises.

March 21st 1969: Allen Klein appointed business manager of Apple.

March 25th 1969: Lennon and Ono fly to Amsterdam to begin a seven-day 'bed-in' at the Hilton Hotel.

April 11th 1969: 'Get Back' / 'Don't Let Me Down' (Apple R 5777) released in the UK.

May 2nd 1969: *Unfinished Music No.2: Life With The Lions* by John Lennon & Yoko Ono (Zapple 01) and *Electronic Sound* by George Harrison (Zapple 02) released in the UK.

May 19th 1969: Lew Grade's ATV gains control of Northern Songs Limited.

May 26th 1969: *Unfinished Music No.2: Life With The Lions* (Zapple ST 3357) and *Electronic Sound* (Zapple ST 3358) released in the USA.

May 30th 1969: 'The Ballad Of John And Yoko' / 'Old Brown Shoe' (Apple R 5786) released in the UK.

June 4th 1969: 'The Ballad Of John And Yoko' / 'Old Brown Shoe' (Apple 2531) released in the USA.

July 4th 1969: 'Give Peace A Chance' / 'Remember Love' by The Plastic Ono Band (Apple 13) released in the UK.

July 7th 1969: 'Give Peace A Chance' / 'Remember Love' (Apple 1809) released in the USA.

September 20th 1969: Allen Klein negotiates a new contract for The Beatles with EMI/Capitol that gives them an increased royalty rate.

September 26th 1969: *Abbey Road* (Apple PCS 7088) released in the UK. Side One: 'Come Together', 'Something', 'Maxwell's Silver Hammer', 'Oh! Darling', 'Octopus's Garden', 'I Want You (She's So Heavy)'; Side Two: 'Here Comes The Sun', 'Because', 'You Never Give Me Your Money', 'Sun King'/'Mean Mr. Mustard', 'Polythene Pam'/'She Came In Through The Bathroom Window', 'Golden Slumbers'/'Carry That Weight', 'The End', 'Her Majesty'.

October 1st 1969: *Abbey Road* (Apple SO 383) released in the USA (tracklisting as above).

October 6th 1969: 'Something' / 'Come Together' (Apple 2654) released in the USA.

October 20th 1969: 'Cold Turkey' / 'Mummy's Only Looking For A Hand In The Snow' by The Plastic Ono Band (Apple 1813) and *Wedding Album* by John Lennon & Yoko Ono (Apple SMAX 3361) released in the USA. Side One: 'John And Yoko'; Side Two: 'Amsterdam'.October 31st 1969: 'Something' / 'Come Together' (Apple R 5814) released in the UK.

December 12th 1969: *The Plastic Ono Band – Live Peace In Toronto* (Apple CORE 2001) released in the UK and the USA. Side One: 'Introduction Of The Band', 'Blue Suede Shoes', 'Money (That's What I Want)', 'Dizzy Miss Lizzy', 'Yer Blues', 'Cold Turkey', 'Give Peace A Chance'; Side Two: 'Don't Worry Kyoko (Mummy's Only Looking For Her Hand In The Snow)', 'John, John (Let's Hope For Peace)'.

February 6th 1970: 'Instant Karma! (We All Shine On)' / 'Who Has Seen The Wind?' by The Plastic Ono Band (Apple 1003) released in the UK.

February 26th 1970: *Hey Jude* (Apple SW 385) released in the USA. Side One: 'Can't Buy Me Love', 'I Should Have Known Better', 'Paperback Writer', 'Rain', 'Lady Madonna', 'Revolution'; Side Two: 'Hey Jude', 'Old Brown Shoe', 'Don't Let Me Down', 'The Ballad Of John And Yoko'.

March 6th 1970: 'Let It Be' / 'You Know My Name (Look Up The Number)' (Apple R 5833) released in the UK.

April 10th 1970: McCartney announces that he has left The Beatles.

May 8th 1970: *Let It Be* (Apple PCS 7096) released in the UK. Side One: 'Two Of Us', 'Dig A Pony', 'Across The Universe', 'I Me Mine', 'Dig It', 'Let It Be', 'Maggie May'; Side Two: 'I've Got A Feeling', 'The One After 909', 'The Long And Winding Road', 'For You Blue', 'Get Back'.

May 11th 1970: 'The Long And Winding Road' / 'For You Blue' (Apple 2832) released in the USA.

May 13th 1970: The *Let It Be* film premieres in New York.

May 18th 1970: *Let It Be* (Apple AR 34001) released in the USA (tracklisting as above).

May 20th 1970: *Let It Be* premieres in Liverpool and London; no Beatles attend.

December 31st 1970: McCartney begins proceedings in London's High Court Of Justice in London to dissolve The Beatles.

Bibliography

Keith Badman *The Beatles Off The Record* (Omnibus 2001)
Tony Barrow, Julian Newby *Inside The Music Business* (Routledge 1995)
The Beatles *Anthology* (Chronicle 1995)
Pete Best, Patrick Doncaster *Beatle!* (Plexus 1985)
Tony Bramwell, Rosemary Kingsland *Magical Mystery Tours* (Thomas Dunne 2005)
Al Brodax *Up Periscope Yellow* (Limelight Editions 2004)
Roy Carr *Beatles At The Movies* (UFO Music 1996)
Ray Coleman *John Winston Lennon* (Sidgwick & Jackson 1984)
Ray Coleman *The Man Who Made The Beatles* (Penguin 1989)
Fredric Dannen *Hitmen* (Helter Skelter 2003)
Johnny Dean *The Best Of The Beatles Book* (Beat Publications 2005)
Geoffrey Ellis *I Should Have Known Better* (Thorogood 2004)
Geoff Emerick *Here, There, And Everywhere* (Gotham 2006)
Brian Epstein *A Cellarful Of Noise* (New English Library 1981)
Simon Frith, Howard Horne *Art Into Pop* (Routledge 1987)
Michael R. Frontani *The Beatles: Image And The Media* (University Of Mississippi 2007)
Ken Garner *In Session Tonight* (BBC 1993)
Debbie Geller *The Brian Epstein Story* (Faber 1999)
Goldmine magazine *The Beatles Digest* (Krause 2000)
Hans Olaf Gottfridsson *Beatles Bop* (Bear Family 2003)
Hans Olaf Gottfridsson *From Cavern To Star-Club* (Premium Forlag 1997)
Stefan Granados *Those Were The Days* (Cherry Red 2002)
Jonathon Green *Days In The Life* (Pimlico 1988)
Ann Harrison *Music: The Business* (Virgin 2005)
Robert R. Hieronimus *Inside The Yellow Submarine* (Krause Publications 2002)
Spencer Leigh *Let's Go Down The Cavern* (Vermilion 1984)
Jeffery Levy *Apple Log Fifth Edition* (Apple Log 2007)
Mark Lewisohn *The Beatles Live* (Henry Holt 1986)

Mark Lewisohn *The Complete Beatles Chronicle* (Random House 1992)
Mark Lewisohn *The Complete Beatles Recording Sessions* (Hamlyn 1988)
Ian MacDonald *Revolution In The Head* (Fourth Estate 1994)
Gerry Marsden *I'll Never Walk Alone* (Bloomsbury 1993)
Ken Mansfield *The White Book* (Nelson Current 2007)
Arthur Marwick *The Sixties* (Oxford University Press 1998)
Peter McCabe *Apple To The Core* (Martin Brian & O'Keeffe 1972)
Peter McCabe, Robert D. Schonfeld *John Lennon: For The Record* (Bantam 1984)
Barry Miles *The Beatles In Their Own Words* (Omnibus 1978)
Barry Miles *Paul McCartney: Many Years From Now* (Secker & Warburg 1997)
Philip Norman *Shout* (Elm Tree 1981)
Denis O'Dell *At The Apple's Core* (Peter Owen 2002)
Gareth L. Pawlowski *How They Became The Beatles* (E. P. Dutton 1989)
Roland Reiter *Screening The Beatles Myth* (Dissertation.com 2005)
John Repsch *The Legendary Joe Meek* (Woodford House 1989)
Lorraine Rolston *A Hard Day's Night: The Beatles Digest* (York 2001)
W. Fraser Sandercombe *The Beatles: Press Reports* (Collector's Guide 2007)
Stuart Shea, Robert Rodriguez *Fab Four FAQ* (Hal Leonard 2007)
David E. Shi *For The Record* (W. W. Norton 1999)
Brian Southall *Abbey Road* (Patrick Stephens 1982)
Brian Southall *Northern Songs* (Omnibus 2006)
Bruce Spizer *The Beatles Are Coming!* (Four Ninety-Eight 2003)
Bruce Spizer *The Beatles On Apple Records* (Four Ninety-Eight 2003)
Bruce Spizer *The Beatles On Vee-Jay* (Four Ninety-Eight 1998)
Bruce Spizer *The Beatles Swan Song* (Four Ninety-Eight 2007)
Geoffrey Stokes *The Beatles* (W. H. Allen 1981)
Paul Trynka *The Beatles: 10 Years That Shock The World* (DK 2004)

Periodicals

Beat Instrumental, The Beatles Book, Beatles Fan Club Newsletter, The Believer, Billboard, Cash Box, Disc, Disc & Music Echo, Disc Weekly, Financial Times, Goldmine, The Independent, Mersey Beat, Melody Maker, Mojo, New Musical Express, New Record Mirror, New York Times, New York Times Magazine, The Observer, Play And Player, Playboy, Pop Weekly, Q, Q: The Beatles, The Band Of The Century, Time, The Times.

Index

Picture Credits

Jacket John Launois/Eyevine. 2 Stroud/Express/Getty. 6–7 John Lennon/Keystone /Getty. 7 Terrence Spencer/Time Life/Getty; Evening Standard/Getty. 8 Pace/Getty. 9 Rex; Keystone/Getty; David Magnus/Rex. 10 Harry Myers/Rex. 10–11 Keystone/Getty. 11 Fiona Adams/Redfern's. 12 Cummings Archive/Redfern's; Keystone/Getty. 13 David Magnus/Rex. 14 Frederick R. Bunt/Evening Standard/Getty; Bob Aylott/Keystone/Getty. 15 Tom Hanley/Redfern's; Wesley/Keystone/Getty. 16–17 Express/Getty.

Acknowledgements

My sincere thanks go to Tony Bacon, Mr Larry Page, Brian Southall, Alan Clayson, Ian Mundwyler, Rachel Claveau, Jane Langtree, Catherine Blackmore, Paul McColm, Justine Green, Jill Rose, Graham Goodyear, Clive Hacker, Jason Knight, Neil McPherson, Colin Newton, Steve Rolf, Peter Strange, Gary Jones, Nicole and Phil, Jackie and Paul, the good people at Jawbone, the New York Library of Performing Arts, Chicago Public Library, British Library Newspapers, and the BBC Written Archive. An extra special thank you to my parents. No thanx to EMI Archives. As John Lennon said, "A conspiracy of silence speaks louder than words." Right on, John!

Trademarks

"It was like you'd been in the presence of Midas, and somehow you were glorified, but you'd also been infected in some strange way. Very much reflected light, I must say."
ELEANOR BRON, co-star of *Help!*